LOOK GOOD IN 3D

Andrew Reese

VENTANA

MW01520555

Looking Good in 3D
Copyright © 1997 by Andrew Reese

All rights reserved. This book may not be duplicated in any way without the expressed written consent of the publisher, except in the form of brief excerpts or quotations for the purposes of review. The information contained herein is for the personal use of the reader and may not be incorporated in any commercial programs, other books, databases, or any kind of software without written consent of the publisher or author. Making copies of this book or any portion for any purpose other than your own is a violation of United States copyright laws.

Library of Congress Cataloging-in-Publication Data
Reese, Andrew.
    Looking Good in 3D / Andrew Reese.
       p. cm.
    Includes index.
    ISBN 1-56604-494-4
    1. Computer graphics. 2. Three-dimensional display systems.
3. Desktop publishing. I. Title.
T385.R438 1996
006.6—dc20   96-33313
                                     CIP

First Edition 9 8 7 6 5 4 3 2 1

Printed in the United States of America

Ventana Communications Group, Inc.
P.O. Box 13964
Research Triangle Park, NC 27709-3964
919.544.9404
FAX 919.544.9472
http://www.vmedia.com

Limits of Liability & Disclaimer of Warranty
The author and publisher of this book have used their best efforts in preparing the book and the programs contained in it. These efforts include the development, research, and testing of the theories and programs to determine their effectiveness. The author and publisher make no warranty of any kind, expressed or implied, with regard to these programs or the documentation contained in this book.

The author and publisher shall not be liable in the event of incidental or consequential damages in connection with, or arising out of, the furnishing, performance or use of the programs, associated instructions and/or claims of productivity gains.

Trademarks
Trademarked names appear throughout this book, and on the accompanying compact disk. Rather than list the names and entities that own the trademarks or insert a trademark symbol with each mention of the trademarked name, the publisher states that it is using the names only for editorial purposes and to the benefit of the trademark owner with no intention of infringing upon that trademark.

Chief Executive Officer
Josef Woodman

**Vice President of
Content Development**
Karen A. Bluestein

Managing Editor
Lois J. Principe

Production Manager
John Cotterman

**Technology Operations
Manager**
Kerry L. B. Foster

**Product Marketing
Manager**
Jamie Jaeger Fiocco

**Creative Services
Manager**
Diane Lennox

Art Director
Marcia Webb

Acquisitions Editor
Neweleen A. Trebnik

Project Editor
Amy E. Moyers

Developmental Editor
Michelle Corbin Nichols

Copy Editor
Judy Flynn

CD-ROM Specialist
Patrick Bragg

Technical Director
Dan Brown

Technical Reviewer
Brian Little

Desktop Publisher
Patrick Berry

Proofreader
Kortney Trebnik

Indexer
Dick Evans

Cover Illustrator
Alice Whicker Heitchue

About the Author

Andrew Reese is a freelance writer specializing in 3D, gaming, and other computer topics. He has written books, manuals, newsletters, marketing materials, and magazine articles. His recent books include *Apache Strategies and Secrets* (Sybex) and *Doom Battlebook* (Prima). Reese was also the developmental and technical editor for Ventana's *3D Studio Max f/x* book.

Acknowledgments

If writing is a solitary occupation, then publishing is a collegial one, and that's something that few readers ever understand. My name may be on the cover of this book, but it's there only because a team of talented professionals conspired to get it there.

In the beginning, there was Neweleen. A book is naught until an acquisitions editor brings writer, idea, and contract together. The talented seer on this book was Neweleen Trebnik, an incredibly hard-working and talented woman, to me: the soul of Ventana.

And then there was Amy. Amy Moyers is the project editor who kept this book on track, put the pieces together, kept everyone on the same page, and generally helped me out in any way she could.

Okay, I'll skip the begats—they probably have no place in an acknowledgments section anyway.

But there are so many others to thank:

- Karen Bluestein, publisher at Ventana, who first said "Yes."

- Michelle Nichols, my developmental editor, who made this a much better book with her tireless work.

- Patrick Berry, my desktop publisher, who helped put it all together.

- Judy Flynn, my stalwart and patient copy editor (Okay, I *think* I get it this time!)

- Brian Little, my wonderful, knowledgeable, and funny technical editor, Macophile that he is (ROFL).

- Becky Steele, whose title is Traffic Coordinator, but whom I know as the woman who cleared the way for my purple prose to flow to North Carolina.

- Melanie Stepp, Acquisitions coordinator extraordinaire, lightning rod for author's gripes, and expediter of funds.

- And a big thanks goes to Patrick Bragg, Jeanne Taylor, and Dan Brown for putting the CD-ROM components together.

- And to all those at Ventana who had a hand in making this book better than I thought it could be, THANK YOU!

I also want to thank others who helped out with hardware, software, images, and support. Without all of you, this book would be a "non-starter!"

- "Max" Maxfield and Intergraph for the loan of a dream PC. You never really know how good a computer can be until you have the chance to work with a really good one. And the Intergraph TDZ is a *great* computer.

- Melanie Swanson, Burt Holmes, and Wacom Technologies for the loan of an ArtZ II tablet; if you're interested in computer art, this is the tablet to try.

- Sean Hammon and Viewpoint DataLabs International, Inc. for the use of some of their wide selection of 3D models.

- Mara Pratt at McLean Public Relations and Fractal Design Corp. for Fractal Painter and Poser, two excellent programs for artists.

- CompuServe Information Service for access and for keeping it running all these years.

- All the folks at Waggener & Edstrom and Microsoft for use of some really fine products.

- David Schryver and William Vablais at Softimage for powering up my system with Softimage | 3D.

- Gary Yost and the folks at Yost Group and Kinetix for 3D Studio MAX; what a program!

- Michael Girard and Kinetix for Character Studio.

- For the use of images and for their assistance: R/Greenburg & Associates and Shell Oil Company; Metrolight Studios; Silicon Graphics, Inc.; Manuel Nguema and MetaReyes, S.A.; Tim Stiles and MetaTools, Inc.; ChromaKey, Inc.; Jim Foster and Science.D.Visions; Jean-Yves Sgro; the Geneva University Hospital, the University of Geneva, Switzerland; Dr. Manuel C. Peitsch of the Glaxo Institute of Molecular Biology; Mike De La Flor of the University of Houston Medical School–Houston; AEGIS, Inc.; Artewisdom, Ltd.; and Amy Woodward-Parrish and Greg Swayne of A.D.A.M. Software.

- Finally, for all the fine people who helped, supported, or prodded me in this quest for a different and better 3D book: Dennis and Nancy Hein; Sylvia Kondikas, Jon Bell and Joan Gale Frank; my grown kids—Chris, Steve, and Lis; my first granddaughter, Brittney Louise McCoin (yes, you can sit on Grampa's lap and watch the kangaroo jump on the 'puter); and always my patient and talented daughter, Caytlin—a pretty darned good writer herself!

Danville, California
November 1996

Dedication

This book is dedicated to that pillar of support, that believer beyond belief, my wife and partner, Stephanie Reese.

Contents

Introduction

You hold in your hands a different kind of 3D book. This book won't tell you which icons to click to render an image or how to configure your virtual memory. It's not product-specific or platform-dependent. It doesn't rely on your having *ever* used a 3D program. For that matter, you don't even have to be a computer junkie to read it! So . . . what is it?

Looking Good in 3D is a guidebook to the world of computer-generated 3D imagery: how to create it, how to apply it, and how to understand its burgeoning place in our complex technological world. Like Leonardo da Vinci, 3D is incredibly versatile. It both permits and demands the same versatility from its practitioners.

I've tried in this book to integrate 3D into the larger world, to show how it borrows from other media, the science it relies upon for realistic action, and its many applications in science, entertainment, advertising, law, and so on. You'll also learn the diverse methods available today to create 3D models, images, and animations and learn how high-end 3D software differs from low-end. You won't be burdened with feature-by-feature reviews, but you will gain a good sense of the questions to ask before choosing your first or next 3D program.

With the broad background you'll gain from reading this book, you'll be well on the way to becoming a 21st century Leonardo yourself!

Who Should Read This Book

Looking Good in 3D is written primarily for 2D graphic artists for whom the 3D world is still a mystery. But it's also for artists of all types who want to delve deeper into the 3D world and find answers to their most troublesome 3D questions. In short, anyone who is:

- a 2D computer artist looking for ways to incorporate 3D into his/her work.

- a 3D neophyte looking for a clear, concise, and understandable explanation of 3D and its components.

- an advanced 3D artist seeking a fresh approach to his/her work.

- an art student wanting to put 3D in perspective.

- anyone wondering "how'd they do that" when he or she sees 3D effects or characters in the movies or on television.

I assume that you have a basic understanding of computers before you begin this book. But since *Looking Good in 3D* is most emphatically not a "button-pushing" book, you won't need highly technical knowledge, just the basics.

How to Use This Book

For 2D artists, students, or others who are neophytes to 3D, I recommend that you read *Looking Good in 3D* from start to finish; it will give you a clear, concise, and integrated picture of 3D concepts, tools, uses, and sources. More advanced 3D artists may feel that they can skip chapters, but you'll find great hints, tips, and inspiration in every chapter. And if you bought this book because it looked like fun, well, just pick it up and read it however you want!

Looking Good in 3D is divided into three parts. The first part (Chapters 1 through 3) is intended to give you basic concepts from science, art, and the media that you should understand to work effectively in 3D. It begins with the concept of reality and moves on to physics, and human anatomy and motion. It concludes with a discussion of what 3D borrows from other media, such as film, video, and fine art.

Even if you feel you have a solid grasp of all of these subjects, please at least skim this part. After all, "the test at the end of the semester will cover all of the material from the first day of class." For a 3D artist the test comes every day, and you might have missed something that will turn your next project into a stone cold winner!

The second part of *Looking Good in 3D* (Chapters 4 through 6) looks at the 3D creation process. How do you create a 3D universe? How do you make it look the way you envision? What tools are used to create 3D models and just what is a NURB, anyway? And, finally, how do you incorporate 3D output into other forms of media? This is the meat of the book. It teaches the hard stuff: how 3D is made and used.

The third part of *Looking Good in 3D* (Chapters 7 through 9) is about putting 3D to work. What does a 3D artist really *do* with the 3D imagery he or she creates? How are the media using 3D today? How do you create 3D that works well with video? This section is loaded with hints and tips for creating more dramatic and useful 3D art.

Finally, two appendices explain the contents of the CD-ROM and how to use it and provide a resource guide that covers everything from animation and 3D schools to World Wide Web sites of interest to all you 3D junkies to books on everything from animation to art to anatomy.

How This Book Is Organized

Chapter 1, "Mirroring & Creating Reality." In this chapter, you are confronted with the question of "What is reality?" Through an analysis of how we view our world, you will begin to see how you must be acutely aware of the world around you in order to create your *own* world in 3D. This chapter also gives you a better idea about what makes a 3D scene good or bad.

Chapter 2, "Understanding Your World," gives you a better understanding of things like gravity, inertia, matter, and how light is transmitted. All of these subjects seemingly dredged up from your high school physics class will probably seem newly important in the context of creating a 3D scene!

Chapter 3, "Human Anatomy & Movement," is a very important chapter for those of you wanting to create characters to people your 3D scenes. Even if your objects aren't human, this chapter will help you make them more believable.

Chapter 4, "Learning From Other Media," scans the immense panorama of art and media and shows how 3D borrows techniques and concepts from film, video, photography, the stage, sculpture, and fine art painting. This chapter is full of great information that is easily translated to creating better 3D art.

Chapter 5, "The Practical Side of 3D," tells you everything you ever wanted to know about 3D production, what the differences are in creating reality versus fantasy and what hardware will work for you.

Chapter 6, "Creating 3D Imagery," really shows you how to create *great* 3D imagery. It shows you how to choose the correct viewpoints for your scenes, how to model effectively, the tools and techniques available to 3D artists to create persuasive surfaces, and how to animate objects in your scenes.

Chapter 7, "Integrating 3D With Other Media," shows how 3D is integrated into 2D imagery, whether it's in advertising, movies, or games.

Chapter 8, "Applications," surveys the myriad applications of 3D, explaining how it can be used (and abused) to inform, persuade, and entertain.

Chapter 9, "Tips & Tricks," gives you many tricks and concepts that you can use to enhance your 3D creations. You'll learn what colors work best in video, how to create an image of the right size, quick ways to simulate the features your software doesn't have, and many others.

Online Updates

As we all know, the Internet is constantly changing. As hard as we've tried to make our information current, the truth is that new sites will come online as soon as this book goes to press (and continually thereafter). Ventana provides an excellent way to tackle this problem and to keep the information in the book up-to-date: the Looking Good in 3D Online Updates. You can access this valuable resource via Ventana's World Wide Web site at http://www.vmedia.com/updates.html. Once there, you'll find updated material relevant to Looking Good in 3D as well as various programs the author has made available on the CD-ROM.

Above all else, I've tried to make this book *readable* as well as informative. It's not your average computer book—enjoy!

Andrew Reese
Danville, CA
November, 1996

Mirroring or Creating Reality?

Philosophers, scientists, madmen, clerics, and artists have argued since recorded history began about what reality *is* without reaching any real agreement. Depending upon your philosophical starting point, reality can be what we perceive with our senses, what we can measure with our instruments, or it can be something intangible. But generally, we all have to deal with reality every day. It's a fact of life...or is it?

The desktop computer age has brought with it amazing possibilities. You can now sit down at a desktop computer in your own home or office and, using today's powerful 3D software, wander around in a world that you created. This synthetic world can either reflect the reality you see around you in the real world or create an entirely new version of reality. And it's all in your hands.

Reality

This may seem to be an unduly philosophical way to begin a computer book, sort of *Zen & the Art of 3D Imagery*, but I believe that to become a good 3D artist, you must first understand the real world around you, how it looks, how it works, *and* how it fools us. When you have a reasonably firm grasp on reality (and how firm is any of our grasps?), you can then turn to mirroring that reality in your 3D scenes or creating your own special brand of reality.

Reality can be defined in a number of ways, and that, in part, is the cause of the centuries of squabbling about its definition. To a scientist working at the macro level (I'm not even going to try to discuss the reality of quarks and other bizarre subatomic phenomena), reality is what can be observed by the senses and measured by instruments. It's a fairly safe way to define reality; one that—barring observer interference with whatever's being observed—can provide a consistent description of events that can generally be agreed upon by other observers.

Let's take the example of a scientist observing the behavior of an airplane model in a wind tunnel. To create an accurate account of the events, she records data generated by measuring instruments in the tunnel, videotapes the action through an observation port, and records her own observations verbally. In this way, she creates a record that others can examine, test, and attempt to re-create. This scientific data reflects one type of reality, and as 3D artists and animators, we can take the reality recorded by this data and reproduce the action in a 3D scene which, presumably, would accurately reflect the events in the wind tunnel.

But what if our scientist is nearly blind and a schizophrenic to boot? Can we trust her observations? By definition, a schizophrenic is a person who is not in touch with reality, so can we really trust her measurements? Did she record them manually? You see the problems.

The answer, then, must be to have more than one observer. Surely *then* the observations will be accurate, you say. Hardly. If anything, the observations will be *more* varied and *less* reliable than before. At least when you start with a single visually impaired, schizophrenic scientist, you start from a known, definable quantity. Multiple observers just multiply the unknowns.

Every police investigator understands this problem: The more people that witness a crime, the more versions of that crime and descriptions of the crook you'll have. People differ in so many ways. Some may have more experience and training in observation (like police investigators), others may have had superior vantage points, but all bring to the observing experience their own set of physical handicaps and acuities, experiences, and biases. To a short person, a crook may look tall; to a tall person a crook may seem short. To an agoraphobe, even a kindly priest may seem frightening in a public place. And we have all heard the culturally illiterate bias that's spouted as "they all look alike to me."

Many years ago (*too* many years ago), I was a criminal defense lawyer who tried hundreds and hundreds of cases to juries. With the prosecution bearing the burden of proving a single set of facts to be the *truth*, there was nothing I liked better when representing a defendant than to have a dozen witnesses to a bar fight. I was sure to be able to elicit at least a dozen versions of want happened. Most juries just threw up their hands and decided that they couldn't determine "the truth of the matter"—the reality—and acquitted my clients, guilt or innocence undecided.

The point I want to make here is that a 3D creator must be concerned with at least two kinds of reality: the reality that scientists understand and the reality that cops and lawyers understand. One is "hard" and repeatable and the other varies according to the person defining it. You may not like this statement, but you certainly must recognize it to be true.

3D work also may involve the creation of *artistic* works. Putting aside the larger question of *What is art?*, working in 3D will almost surely require an artisan to meet another's expectations, another's version of artistic reality. The designer of a detergent bottle must please the design firm's client, who may be a group of soap company executives with absolutely no understanding of anything artistic.

A video game designer must please the ultimate players of the game (mostly adolescent boys) and create a reality within the game that doesn't at all reflect the reality of the thirty-five-year-old, married designer with three kids, two cars, and a mortgage.

Working in 3D will almost surely require an artisan to meet another's expectations, another's version of artistic reality.

Always think about what reality is, how it's reflected in your work, and whose reality it is anyhow.

As you go through this book, then, and as you proceed with your work in 3D, I want you always to think about what reality is, how it's reflected in your work, and whose reality it is anyhow. If you are conscious of these questions, your work will be much easier and you will be able to assume the proper role for the job.

Viewing the World

We each view the world through our own set of experiences, our own more or less imperfect senses. But I think that we should all be able to agree ("Can't we all just get along?") to divide the world of digital images into two classes: *unaltered photographs* and *digitally created or modified images*.

This second class includes several types of images. It includes photographs that have been digitally retouched or otherwise altered to change the original reality and drawings. Also included (for convenience as much as anything) are inaccurate depictions that are imported into the computer and viewed without changing them. Typical of this second group are pencil sketches scanned into the computer for use as animation tests. The dividing line here is between "raw," unaltered photographs and everything else.

Photography—The "Perfect" Image Recorder

When we look at a photograph of a picnic, murder scene, or the flowers shown in Figure 1-1, we are looking at what seems to be a faithful re-creation of the original subject. We even have coined a term, *photorealistic*, to mean that the image looks like a photograph. We'll see later, however, that this term is something of a misnomer.

If we think a bit about the photographic *process*, however, we realize that every photograph is the result of many conscious and unconscious choices made by the photographer. He chose the subject, pose, angle, viewing point, camera, film, lens, filter, lighting, and shutter speed to produce a particular effect. We have probably all seen a professional photographer at work at a wedding or in a studio and been awed by the artistic dance of lenses, poses, viewpoints, and lights to get the "perfect" shot.

Figure 1-1: A photograph may seem to accurately reflect the reality captured by the lens and film, but first this reality was filtered by the photographer who selected the viewing point, angle, lens, lighting, shutter speed, and film combination that produced the image, not to mention the processing in the lab that produced the final print or slide.

Every photograph has an implicit viewpoint, or in other words, every photo reflects a *manipulation of reality* by the photographer.

Of course, the fewer the choices offered by a camera, the fewer the opportunities for conscious manipulation of the image by the photographer. But even a simple, fixed-lens, single-speed, throwaway camera lets the photographer manipulate how each picture looks by choosing the subject, pose, angle, and lighting. Flip through your last set of beach snapshots and you'll see what I mean.

The bottom line is, then, that every photograph has an implicit viewpoint, or in other words, every photo reflects a *manipulation of reality* by the photographer.

Now, what about digitally created images?

Digital Imagery Means Never Having to Say You're Sorry

When we move into the digital realm, where images are either intentionally manipulated or created out of whole cloth by the artist, we can have even less faith in the accuracy of the reality. The digital realm allows us so much freedom, so much power to control the appearance of images, that we can no longer completely believe our senses.

Digital Cameras & Reality

The digital revolution in photography may seem to have blurred the distinction between photographic and digitally created images. But the current crop of digital cameras still tries faithfully to record the light passing through the lens.

There will certainly come a time when automatic image processing within the digital camera will produce results that are far from faithful. For example, directors of B movies today often use a dark blue lens filter to make a daylight sequence look like it occurred at night. This "day for night" sleight-of-hand could also be done easily in a digital camera, just by pressing a button.

Similarly, I can also envision image processing systems that reproduce the "warm" or "cool" tones of certain types of color slide film. For example, Kodak's Kodachrome slide film always seemed to produce warm flesh tones, while their Ektachrome film produced bluer, cooler tones. Why couldn't a digital camera do this for you?

If—no, not if, *when*—this is available, I will have to draw the line between raw film and unprocessed digital photographs on the one hand and processed digital or unreal images on the other.

A digital artist can manipulate objects and patterns of pixels to make cars dance with gas pumps, as shown in Figure 1-2, or extinct dinosaurs walk the earth again. In this realm, *anything* is possible, although the impossible may take just a little longer to finish under budget.

Figure 1-2: R/Greenburg & Associates created this famous commercial for Shell Oil in which a car demonstrated its love for a gas pump. Reality? Well, someone's!

Looking back through history, we find that this manipulation of reality is really nothing new. The history of art can be viewed in part as a series of attempts to convey different aspects of the artists' realities. Depending upon which "ism" you study— romanticism, impressionism, abstract expressionism, surrealism, realism, cubism, regionalism, neoexpressionism, or new realism—you find more or less faithful reproduction of the scientific reality of a scene and less or more depiction of the underlying emotional reality expressed by the artist.

Some artists strive to present their feelings on canvas and evoke the same in the viewer. In Figure 1-3, what's important in the painting is not the ships and sky, but the placidity evoked by the work.

Figure 1-3: A peaceful scene of a harbor at sunset. The low horizon and expansive sky, coupled with the soft, suggestive treatment of the ships, de-emphasizes the factual reality in favor of the emotional reality.

Other artists paint more realistically, striving to include every detail of the original. Some, like the example in Figure 1-4, are so detailed and accurate, that they look like a photograph.

Figure 1-4: The detail in this painting makes it look like a photograph. Note the texture of the skin and the water dripping from the trunk and mouth. Is this reality? Compare it to the reality of the previous figure.

Whether you use a camera, a paintbrush, or a computer to create an image, your final result will reflect as much of *you* as it does of your subject.

The Final Truth

The final truth, then, is that no matter whether you use a camera, a paintbrush, or a computer to create an image, your final result will reflect as much of *you* as it does of your subject.

Down From the Mountain: Basics of Computer-generated Imagery

Okay, we've sat on the mountaintop and pretty well summarized a world of philosophy and art in a few short pages. Now let's come back down the mountain and turn our attention to some basic information about computer imagery.

First, for the sake of getting a handle on this topic, let's divide the world of computer-generated imagery (CGI) into two basic classes: *still images* and *moving images*, that is, animation. (Remember, I'm including in the term *computer-generated* all images that originated outside the computer and have been modified digitally or that were not photographs originally.)

Creating Still Images

To create still computer-generated imagery, you can use one of several tools. They're generally grouped into three types, although most of today's more sophisticated programs cross over into other types. The three general types are paint, drawing, and 3D programs.

Paint Programs

First, you can engage in what is sometimes called "pixel bashing." This means using a *paint* program such as Microsoft Paint, the simple pixel-based program familiar to Windows users. Programs like these let you change the color of each pixel in the image, one-by-one or by using tools designed after familiar nondigital painting tools. The quality and recognizability of the resultant image depends almost wholly on your artistic abilities (combined with your ability to translate those abilities into the digital realm). Paint programs are powerful, but in these days of 3D and image processing, their use is usually limited to the artistically talented, particularly those with the patience to nurture each pixel.

The output of a paint program is typically a *bitmap file*, an organized data file that describes the color and placement of each pixel. When a bitmap file is loaded into a program that can display it, each pixel is replaced in its proper place and the image is restored to its original glory.

Note that unlike a photograph, a pixel-defined image is composed of discrete rectangular or square blocks of color. (Pixel is a New Age contraction of *picture* —or *pix* —and *element*.) As you get closer and closer to the image, the blocks become more and more obvious, as shown in Figure 1-5.

Pixel-based images rely on our brains' ability to integrate discrete data into recognizable shapes.

Figure 1-5: Compare the smooth-looking picture of Frosty in the top image with the close-up of his face below. Thanks to our brains' ability to integrate incomplete data, we could recognize him even with his jagged appearance.

Pixel-based images rely on our brains' ability to integrate discrete data into recognizable shapes. Without this ability, we'd never be able to pick out our friends' faces in a crowd or from shadows.

If you have enough pixels to work with in an image, a palette of enough colors, and enough talent, you could create an image that might rival a work by Pissarro in its subtlety and beauty. Reduce any of the three components sufficiently, however, and your result is more likely to resemble a child's crayon work.

Drawing Programs

Drawing programs take a different tack. Rather than make (or let) you work at the pixel level, drawing programs are shape oriented. Programs like CorelDRAW! or FreeHand (see Figure 1-6) direct your energies into creating lines and shapes. If you can combine these lines and shapes into a recognizable form, well, so much the better—you have artistic ability and could probably succeed using whatever form of art program you chose.

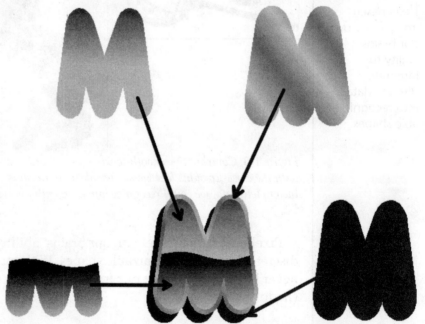

Figure 1-6: A drawing program like CorelDRAW! or FreeHand assembles a picture not from pixels, but from discrete shapes and fills. The fancy letter M in the middle was assembled from the four filled shapes around it.

A drawing program can typically produce two kinds of output: a bitmap file like those from paint programs and a drawing file. The latter stores separate descriptions of all of the lines, shapes, and colors that make up a drawing. For example, where a bitmap file describes a horizontal line as a series of pixels of the same color in the same row, a drawing file might describe it as a line of a certain width drawn from point A to point B.

Drawing programs have many uses, such as business graphics, charts, and so forth, but clearly, it would be extremely difficult if not impossible to emulate Pissarro using one. In fact, with the exception of the subtlety of the splash, it would be easier to emulate the realistic and straight-forward shapes in David Hockney's painting shown in Figure 1-4.

3D Programs

Finally, you can use a 3D program to create a still image. In a 3D program, you don't work at a pixel level as in paint programs, and you don't ultimately work in two-dimensional shapes as in a drawing program. In a 3D program, you use mathematical and visual representations of objects set in a universe of your design. By adding the programmatic equivalents of lights and a camera, you can organize a scene to contain what you want viewed as you want it. Figure 1-7 was created and rendered in a 3D modeling and animation program called Trispectives Professional.

The key to 3D is that the program is smart (or at least well-informed); it incorporates mathematical descriptions of reality in its code. The software understands the effect of blue light on a red ball; it understands perspective and telephoto lenses; it understands how fog reduces visibility.

The program applies its version of reality to the scene as you defined it and, pixel-by-pixel, line-by-line, it produces a bitmapped image output that depicts the objects as if they were lit by your lights, viewed by your camera, and obscured by your fog. You don't need to understand perspective—the program does. You don't necessarily need to understand how light works—just try different lights in different ways.

In a 3D program, you use mathematical and visual representations of objects set in a universe of your design.

Figure 1-7: This 3D image was created and rendered in an architectural CADD program called ArchiTECH.PC. You can try this powerful 2D and 3D program yourself; it's included on the CD-ROM.

The question arises here of how much artistic ability you need to create 3D images. The short answer is that artistic ability always helps, but you need less artistic ability to create a workmanlike, usable, even *attractive* image using a decent 3D program than with any paint or drawing program. It might not be *art*, of course, but the 3D program replaces much of the artistic talent with its intrinsic mathematical simulation of natural events, such as light and shadow.

Making Images Move

A still image is one thing, you say, but creating moving computer-generated imagery? Well, it can be a problem, especially if you are limited to 2D programs. But first, let's review the principles that enable us to create any images that appear to move.

From Reality to CGI

Let's talk about how to make something move, first in the real world, and then by translating it into computer screen movement. For someone to accept computer animation as a re-creation of reality or even as a new synthetic reality, objects in the world must behave predictably and acceptably. Objects must either follow the physical laws of the real world or obey a synthetic set of laws consistently and predictably. In other words, it's OK for citizens of your synthetic world to have antigravity boots, but they should work "properly." Otherwise, no one will accept the effect.

In the real world, everything has mass and can be moved from its resting place by application of a force. We'll get a bit more into the physics of this in Chapter 2, but for now, accept that:

For someone to accept computer animation as reality, objects in the world must behave predictably and acceptably.

- *A body at rest tends to remain at rest.* (If a baseball is sitting on the outfield grass, it will stay there until a player comes over and picks it up.)

- *A body in motion tends to remain in motion.* (When the pitcher throws the ball toward the plate, it continues in the direction it's thrown and doesn't suddenly take off for the hotdog stand.)

- *To change the status quo requires the application of a force.* (To change the direction of a pitched ball and send it over the outfield fence, the batter must apply force to the ball with a bat.)

As we grow from infancy, one critical area of learning is the judgment of distance and speed. Without it, we can't feed ourselves, walk, or avoid a thrown cream pie—or a driven automobile. Most adults can judge distances and speeds that are within their common experience fairly well. We know the difference between an inch and a foot, and between twenty and fifty miles per hour. We probably can't distinguish between 1,500 and 2,500 miles per hour, because that's not in our common experience, but we can usually tell whether a car is going 20 or 50 miles per hour.

Example: Animating a Baseball Throw

Because of our experiences, we may also know that a hot major league third baseman can throw a baseball across the diamond from third base to first base at a speed approaching 90 miles per hour. If we do the math:

$$\frac{90 \; \frac{miles}{hour} \; \times \; 5280 \; \frac{feet}{mile}}{60 \; \frac{seconds}{minute} \; \times \; 60 \; \frac{minutes}{hour}} \; = \; \frac{475,000 \; feet}{3,600 \; second}$$

or 132 feet per second.

A major league baseball diamond is a square 90 feet on a side. The diagonal of a square is 1.414 times the length of a side, so the distance from third base to first base is 1.414 X 90, or roughly 127 feet.

Now, we can determine that at 90 miles per hour, the throw will only take:

$$\frac{127 \; feet}{132 \; \frac{feet}{second}}$$

or .96 seconds to travel the distance from the time it leaves the third baseman's hand until it arrives over first base. If your task as an animator was to animate a baseball game realistically, you would have to move your synthetic baseball from third base to first base in the same time it would take in the real game, just a bit less than a second.

Let's say that you decided to cheat and do this animation the easiest way by showing the ball at third base and then again at first base. You'd only need to draw two frames, but the animation would not be realistic—or believable—because the ball would not appear to travel across the intervening distance and would take much less than that one predetermined second to arrive.

Grumblingly, you now decide that you will have to animate the ball moving across the diamond in order to "sell" the idea that your computerized third baseman threw it to your computerized first baseman. You decide to round the actual time the ball will take to an even second and then check with the programmers doing the game to see how many frames per second (fps) they are going to show. In other words, you want to know the *frame rate*. They tell you that they're shooting for a minimum of fifteen frames per second on the target computer system.

You're almost ready now. You have the frame rate and now all you need is the distance in pixels between the two bases. For the sake of this example, let's assume that your game will be displayed at a resolution of 640 pixels across by 480 pixels down, and that the diamond when viewed from overhead will take up a horizontal distance of three-fourths of the screen.

$$\tfrac{3}{4} \text{ screen} \quad \times \quad 640 \, \tfrac{\text{pixels}}{\text{screen}} \quad = \quad 480 \text{ pixels}$$

Thus, the ball must travel 480 pixels in one second. To determine how many pixels the ball must move each frame, we divide the distance the ball must travel across the screen (480 pixels) by the number of images to be displayed while the ball travels that distance (one second, or 15 frames):

$$\frac{480 \text{ pixels}}{15 \text{ frames}} \quad = \quad 32 \, \tfrac{\text{pixels}}{\text{frame}}$$

Thus, the ball must move 32 pixels every frame. Easy, right?

Now you can see just a bit of what is required to reproduce real-world action on a computer. Just so you can move that little white ball realistically across the screen, you need to have an understanding of the real world both in terms of physics and the physical dimensions of the playing field, plus an understanding of how a synthetic world is created in the computer.

Effects of Delivery Systems

In our baseball example in the last section, we went through an exercise that illustrated how to move from the real world to the synthetic, computer-generated world. We posited two alternative displays in that example, a 2-frame animation and a 15-frame animation. The first was clearly ineffective, and the second was "real-world" accurate. The question arises, then: How many frames do I need? There are several answers to this question.

The effectiveness of animation in creating the illusion of movement is dependent upon the physical human characteristic called *persistence of vision*. We'll explore that phenomenon in the next section. But there are necessary answers to the question posed above.

In a perfect world, every target device on which we intended to play computer graphics would have the same excellent display capability. Animators then would need to concern themselves only with how to create the desired effect and not the limitations of the delivery devices. In the real world of computer graphics, however, the display is very much limited by the available technology.

Computer animation is used in many different ways. It's used in film production, video production, and computer and video games, and for architectural walk-throughs, courtroom simulations, and business graphics. And each use typically requires a different image size and frame rate. Table 1-1 shows the frame rate for the various applications that use computer animation.

Application	Frame Rate (fps)
Film	24
Video (US, SECAM)	30
Video (PAL)	25
Cartoon	14 or 28
Video or computer game	Varies according to target platform

Table 1-1: Frame rate for various applications using computer animation.

To determine the proper animation frame rate for a particular project, you must first determine where it's going to be shown, using what delivery system. For example, film requires very high resolutions to approach the visual quality of fine-grain movie film, but the display rate is only 24 frames per second.

Video display quality is much lower than film, but the display rate can be higher—for example, up to 30 frames per second (25 per second in the European PAL system).

Animation created for computer or video games varies in resolution and display rate, depending upon the target system. A state-of-the-art, Pentium Pro or Power PC computer system with a top-of-the-line display card, high-speed CD-ROM, and fast bus and memory probably will be able to display a 640 X 480 pixel animation at 30 frames per second. But an older-generation 16-bit video game system like the Super Nintendo Game System may only be able to display a resolution of 320 X 200 at a rate of 20 frames per second. You *must* know the delivery platform before you can specify the appropriate size and speed of the animation. We'll come back to this in Part 3, "Applying Your Knowledge."

One last consideration when determining a resolution and frame rate is whether the animation is intended to reflect real-time or to compress or expand time. One of the advantages of animation is that you can re-create events that occur either too slow or too fast for the human eye to detect. By changing the frame rate at which an event occurs, we can either speed up or slow down the appearance of the event when it is played back.

For example, if we had created 30 frames to record the travel of our synthetic baseball rather than 15 and played them back at the same 15 fps rate, the result would be slow motion; the ball would take twice as long to reach first base.

In film, this process is called *slow motion* photography. The shutter is typically triggered at least three or four times as often to capture events that occur too quickly for the eye to detect. Computer simulations of such events can also use the same technique to make a high-speed engine failure understandable to the jury in a courtroom or to allow coaches to study the mechanics of a high-diver's triple somersault.

> To determine the proper animation frame rate for a particular project, you must first determine where it's going to be shown, using what delivery system.

Change the display or capture rate in the other direction and processes that take longer than we can detect can seem to occur in a few seconds. Erosion, blooming flowers, or groundwater pollution can all be compressed to appear to occur in a few seconds. Disney's nature photographers used *time lapse photography* many times to show us a flower blooming from a bud in seconds.

Computer animation can simulate both of these phenomena either for scientific, artistic, or even legal purposes. *Forensic animation*, computer animation created for use in court, has become quite commonplace in the second half of the '90s, but the restrictions imposed by the limited nature of the proceedings make its creation quite demanding on the artist. It's "realism" taken to the extreme.

The artist, then, must know the capabilities of the delivery platform and the intended use for the work in order to design it properly.

Persistence of Vision

Persistence of vision makes motion pictures possible.

Animation, video, and motion pictures are all based on one thing: a design limitation of the human visual system. You see, the human visual system just can't separate two events that occur in less than about 0.25 seconds. It takes that long for the eye to receive an image and transmit along the optic nerve and for the brain to register and interpret it. If an event occurs in less than that time, it persists in the visual system, and if another event occurs, the two overlap and seem to blend together.

This phenomenon was first noted by Peter Mark Roget, an English scholar, who in 1824 published *The Persistence of Vision With Regard to Moving Objects*. The phrase coined by Roget, *persistence of vision*, is still used to describe this phenomenon. (I'm telling you this bit of trivia only so that you can nod knowingly whenever another animation junkie mentions Roget.)

Persistence of vision makes motion pictures possible. Successive images, or frames, are projected onto the screen at a rate of 24 frames per second. Since this is much faster that we can separate them, we see continuous motion on the movie screen.

Television also relies upon persistence of vision, but in two ways. Complete images are displayed on the screen at a rate of 30 fps; because of persistence of vision, they too seem to blend into continuous motion. But because of the way television was developed in the U.S., persistence of vision is also important to integrate each frame.

A television picture is made up of 525 separate lines. Trust me; you don't have to count them, they're there. But the odd thing (odd to laypeople, that is) is that an image is not just scanned onto the television screen from top to bottom, line 1 to line 525. Instead, it's painted on every *other* line first, then filled in. This is called *interlaced scanning*; each half of the picture is called a *field* and the two fields together are again called a frame. See Figure 1-8 for a helpful illustration of this technique.

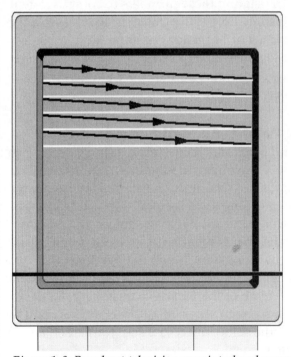

Figure 1-8: Broadcast television uses interlaced scanning to achieve its display rate of 30 frames per second. The first half of the image—or field—is scanned in line-by-line (black lines); the beam retraces after each scan line (white lines). Then the other field is scanned onto the screen in between each pair of the first set of scan lines.

You can imagine how tricky it is to paint a picture on a television screen 30 times a second by scanning a beam across it. It's even trickier if you have to skip every other line and then fill it in. Thanks to persistence of vision, however, we never notice that we never really see a complete image on the screen. It all just looks like moving video.

Now, to animation: the same principles apply. Show images at a rate that exceeds the persistence of human vision and you'll create the illusion of motion. For film animation, this is typically 28 fps, but cartoons usually show each frame twice so that the actual number of different images displayed per second is 14. In the grand days of the Disney studio, they actually animated their cartoons at the full 28 fps rate. In part, this was what produced the beautiful quality of movement for which they're known.

Translating these numbers to computer-generated imagery, we find some horrifying statistics: Even if we adopt the lowest standard of 14 fps for our animation, we still must create 14 X 60 or *840 different images for each minute of animation!* And if we must draw each frame by hand, we have an enormous burden. But luckily there are some solutions.

2D Paint & Animation Programs

Paint programs let us create a single image pixel by pixel. This power is wonderful when we want to tweak an individual pixel, but it's not wonderful when you are tasked with filling a Saturday morning kids' cartoon show with animation. You need more power—and special tools that let you animate with less drudgery.

And that is what much of animation is: drudgery. See the sidebar for a description of who does what in a cartoon factory. It takes an army of talented people to create an animated feature, and much of the work is painstaking detail work, ensuring that, from scene to scene, all of the characters and the backgrounds look the same, the colors stay consistent, and the effects are convincing.

The Animation Pecking Order

In the cartoon animation industry, there is a definite pecking order in the creative side of the business. The director is at the top and is primarily responsible for the creative side of the production. Below the director is a hierarchy of creative types, with different titles in different houses. Generally, there is an animation supervisor next, character animators below him or her, then key animators, tweeners, effects animators, background artists, and finally ink-and-paint people. (There is also an army of support people who check, composite, photograph, and do all of the myriad tasks necessary to create an animation.)

Once you're below the supervisory levels, each character animator is the lead designer for a particular character in the piece and draws the master images of how the character looks in different poses and from different angles.

The key animators draw each important pose for a scene or sequence and the tweeners (from *inbetween*) draw all of the images between the key images. The ink-and-paint people trace over the pencil lines drawn by the other artists and color everything with paint. The effects animators add the wind, motion lines, and other effects, and the background artists create, you guessed it, the backgrounds.

When we're working with a single computer, we can't have all those people helping out, so we rely on the power of the computer to perform many of the functions of the animation staff. The rest we do ourselves with the help of graphics tools built into a special kind of graphics program that lets us add the dimension of time to our creations.

A number of software companies have created this special breed of graphics package with the power to paint over time. On the PC platform, the most successful has probably been Autodesk Animator or Autodesk Animator Pro. These two packages originated in the mind of Jim Kent, one of the early graphics programmers on the Commodore Amiga and Atari ST platforms. (In 1994, Autodesk released Animator Studio to bring these programs into the Windows age.)

Programs like Animator Studio let you paint across a series of images. As you move your "brush," the pixels you leave on each image are in a different location. When the images are shown in succession, the result is animation. See Figure 1-9 for an example.

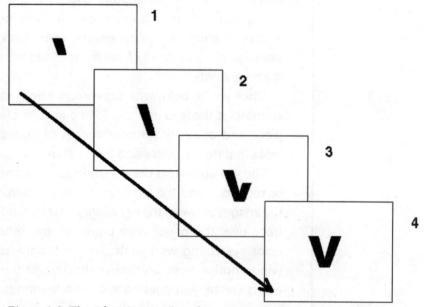

Figure 1-9: These four images show four stages of creating a V in a paint program. When shown from frame 1 to frame 4 in rapid succession, they would create the illusion that the V was being drawn on the screen.

Let's return to the baseball example we used earlier. We first defined two key positions where we wanted the ball to appear: the start of the throw at third base and the end of the throw at first base. These frame positions are key; in animation, they would be called *keyframes*. All that is necessary once the two keyframes are defined is to create the 13 inbetween frames. In the old days in a cartoon studio, an inbetweener would paint the ball, each time in a slightly different position on 13 successive frames.

Now, using a program like Animator Studio, we would simply define the length of the animation as 15 frames, create a movable ball on the screen on the first frame, activate the animation controls to recognize that we want to animate the ball, and place the ball where we want it on the fifteenth frame. The program then does the *tweening*, or calculating all of the intermediate positions of the ball and pasting a copy of the ball's image at each calculated point on successive frames.

This is fine, perhaps, for a little blob of a ball that moves in a straight line from one place on the screen to another. But what if we want to be able to see the laces on the ball and see it rotate realistically as it flies through the computerized air? If we used a paint program to paint the ball's laces as it rotated, we would have to paint by hand at least four and possibly more different views of the ball and then paste a copy of each in succession. This definitely increases both the complexity and the artistic ability required to accomplish this simple task.

There is a solution to this problem; it's called 3D.

3D Animation

3D modeling and animation provide the artistically challenged with a reasonable means of creating eye-catching animation. Most 3D modeling programs provide tools to make simple shapes (like our baseball), or you can simply buy models of more complex objects from companies that specialize in such things. If we wanted our third baseman to throw an elephant rather than a baseball, we could simply buy a model of an elephant. Or a spleen. Let's stick with the baseball; it conjures up fewer grue- some images than a spleen. To create our thrown-ball trick, we would follow these steps:

1. Create a 3D sphere as shown in Figure 1-10. It's an easy task in most programs.

Figure 1-10: In today's 3D programs, it's easy to create a sphere, as shown on the left, and to create a realistic baseball using a texture and bump map, as shown on the right.

2. Wrap an image of baseball laces around it, as shown in Figure 1-11.

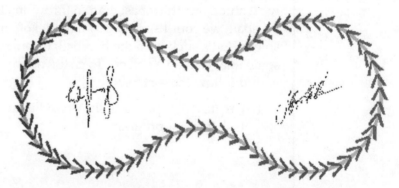

Figure: 1-11: This is the image map that is wrapped around the sphere in Figure 1-10 to create the baseball object.

3. Define our animation length as fifteen frames.

4. Place it at third base on frame 1.

5. Turn on the animation tools, give the ball a turn or two, and move it to first base on frame 15.

6. Tell the program to create and save an image of the baseball for each frame. (This is called *rendering*, and has nothing to do with hog farms. I think.)

The 3D animation program then does all of the tweening; it calculates the location and position of the ball on each frame, figures out how the light hits the ball and the position of the stitches, and whips up a series of images of the ball in flight. We can take a seventh inning stretch and go find ourselves a Nehi.

When the computer has finished rendering, we can view the finished animation with a file viewer, like the Apple MoviePlayer or Microsoft Media Player. If this animation is intended as part of a video game, we would deliver it to the programmer for incorporation into the game code.

One of the beautiful things about 3D modeling and animation is that if we don't like the results—or the programmer asks if we could "please do it again, but in 13 frames this time"—we don't have to repaint anything. We simply change the animation length, the lighting, or any other variable and tell the computer to re-render the animation. It's that simple.

3D—The Good, the Bad & the Ugly

3D animation is powerful. . . . 3D is predictable, repeatable, and reliable. . . . 3D is precise.

We touched on some of the good points of 3D modeling and animation in the last section, but there are more good points—and some drawbacks as well.

3D Advantages

3D animation is powerful. With 3D, you can create almost anything, and if you can't do it, you can either buy it or pay someone else to create it.

3D is predictable, repeatable, and reliable. Once you set up a scene, you can rely on the software to deliver the same results every time. This characteristic makes 3D a perfect partner for motion control cameras in filmmaking, where precise repeatability enables film technicians to create amazing optical effects. A 2D artist can never reproduce a work exactly without resorting to mechanical or printing techniques that rob the art of its originality and freshness.

3D is precise. Most software gives you the power to be exact, so that all objects in a scene are accurately sized and positioned and the speeds at which objects move is true. (Lighting is another matter; not all software reproduces real-world lighting precisely.) This characteristic makes 3D useful for scientific visualization, forensic animation, and even motion picture pre-visualization, in which directors test camera moves and positions and set accessibility in 3D before rolling the first camera.

> 3D can be expensive. . . . You can almost always tell when an image is 3D because it has an artificial look. . . . 3D requires a higher level of understanding of the real world. . . . 3D can be time-consuming.

3D Disadvantages

3D can be expensive. It requires a substantial investment in hardware, software, and talent to create state-of-the-art 3D animation. For example, to create *Toy Story*, the highly successful Disney/Pixar film of 1995, Pixar used 110 Sun workstations running 24 hours a day to render the 110,064 CGI frames. Each frame took anywhere from 45 minutes to 20 hours to render!

More Amazing *Toy Story* Numbers

Want more Wow! numbers from *Toy Story*? About 500 megabytes of storage were used to store the film's frames digitally, and all of the film data required a terabyte of storage. (That's 1,000 gigabytes or 1,000,000 megabytes of storage!) To give you some idea of the talent required, it took the programmers at Pixar nine months to write the shader program that described the way the boy's hair looked and moved.

If you're less ambitious than Disney and Pixar, you can create good animation for much less time and money than it took to create *Toy Story* levels, but don't expect to create broadcast-quality animation on less than workstation-level hardware running professional software.

Another minus is that nature is too imprecise for the precision of 3D. You can almost always tell when an image is 3D because it has an artificial look. To get the near-perfect quality of the animals in the Joe Johnston film, *Jumanji*, animators at Industrial Light & Magic had to add imprecise elements to simulate real-world variabilities.

Working in 3D doesn't eliminate the need for artistic talent. It merely removes the focus from the traditional 2D artist's talents and places it on visualizing and working in three dimensions. Sculptors do well in 3D, if they can get over the sterile, "can't touch the clay" environment of the computer.

3D requires a higher level of understanding of the real world, in part because 3D software is still in its infancy now. Even with the complicated professional software and immensely powerful computers available now, many times animators still must "cheat" and simulate a real-world effect rather than reproduce it on the computer.

We're now able to recreate wind, gravity, fire, fog, fountains, and other natural phenomena; some of the difficult tasks animators and software designers are laboring over include hair and fur, musculature moving under skin, human features and movement, and animal behavior and movement.

With some 26 separate muscles that move the human face, it's not surprising that no one has been able to reproduce their interactions on the computer, especially given the infinite variety of human faces! We're still having to simulate facial movements by positioning surface elements until they "look right."

3D can be time-consuming. Reflect on the numbers in the paragraphs on *Toy Story* earlier in this section. A little calculation reveals a stunning point: even if each of the 110,064 frames took only 45 minutes to render, it still took roughly *nine and a half computer years* to render all of the frames. That's why Pixar gathered together all of those Sun workstations into what is called a *render farm*. Without all of those machines working together, we wouldn't be seeing the movie for some years yet.

Moving On

In this chapter, we reviewed some of the basic principles of computer graphics and animation and reflected upon the meaning of reality in a computer-generated world.

In the next several chapters, we'll look at real-world science and art and see what we can learn to aid us in our quest for 3D perfection. First, in Chapters 2 and 3, we'll focus on the physical science and human anatomy and movement. Later, in Chapter 4, we'll look at the arts and see what there is to learn there.

Shall we? After you…

Understanding Your World

Understanding the real world is an impossibly tall order. No scientist, theoretician, philosopher, or artist can ever understand more than a small part of any area of human knowledge. But a good grasp of General Science 101 is necessary for you as an artist to produce effective 3D stills or animation.

Your work must not only be effective artistically, it must also appear to obey the physical laws of nature. But even if your goal is to create a fantasy world with its own set of physical laws, you still must at least follow the laws of your own reality.

As a 3D artist, you will probably concentrate on one or the other type of reality, either that of the real world or a reality of your own or someone else's invention. Some artists work in both, but most find a home in one or the other. Whichever way you go, however, you'll need to understand what we discuss in this chapter.

Initial Observations

Don't be intimidated. We aren't going to cover any topic in this chapter exhaustively. I just want you to have enough of a background so that you know what questions to ask of yourself or an expert when you sit down at your 3D workstation.

Right-brained vs. Left-brained

Artists are usually thought of as being right-brained, more adept at visual integration and composition than at linear, logical progression. Once trained, an artist working in noncomputer media can draw, paint, sketch, and sculpt without considering the logical steps required to get from a vision to the completed work.

Working in 3D on a computer is just plain different. At this stage of 3D software development, an artist must constantly be conscious of the mechanical requirements of the medium and the software. Most steps are not instinctive, although the software *is* generally getting better at anticipating the artist's viewpoint. But because of the enormous demands that 3D places on the hardware, it will likely be a substantial time before a powerful 3D application will have the intuitive qualities of, say, Fractal Design Painter, a remarkable piece of software that emulates a painter's tools.

At the apex of the pyramid of 3D modeling and animation programs are a handful of extremely powerful, extremely expensive, and extremely demanding programs. Each program has a unique interface and a 3D artist is hard-pressed to master one such program, much less be in command of all. But in order to produce their very best cinematic-quality graphics, the high-end 3D shops use at least two and often a combination of three or more high-end 3D programs. This can be a significant technical challenge to a 3D artist.

I don't mean to say that you can't learn to produce striking 3D images and animations using a single low- or mid-range product. But to do so, you will have to think more like a left-brained computer-type and less like a right-brained artist.

Keep Your Eyes Open

Still have that deerstalker cap from when you dressed up as Sherlock Holmes at Halloween? If you don't happen to have such Holmesian headgear, how about simply some sunglasses? Whether you choose to emulate Holmes or just observe the world unobtrusively from behind your Foster Grants, to work in 3D, you must be a keen observer of the world and the people around you.

Some call this observer's eye an *artist's eye*, but whatever you call it, you'll need it. If images or animation of characters is your milieu, you must take the time to watch people around you doing anything and everything. Whether it's wrestling with an inverted umbrella on a windy, rainy day or just slumping tiredly up the stairs at the end of the day, sooner or later, you'll need to call that image to mind to make your 3D characters live.

But what if you're sure that what you want to do is animate monsters and space aliens in video games? You can be sure that sooner or later you'll be called upon to animate some humanoid from another galaxy who is struggling with a recalcitrant blaster; you'll see that umbrella battle in your mind's eye and be halfway done with the storyboards.

Observing the world means more, of course, than watching people. Keep an eye on colors and light; how subdued the tones are under a gray sky or how rosy in a sunset's light. Watch how a baseball thuds off a padded outfield wall—or ricochets crazily from the bricks at Wrigley Field. Spend a day watching factory automation to get a feel for robotic movement. And you can lose hours watching your pets or, better still, zoo animals. How else do you think Disney's animators captured the movements of Rajah, the tiger in *Aladdin*? They spent hours watching and sketching live tigers, like the one in Figure 2-1.

Figure 2-1: To animate a tiger, study a tiger.

Time spent observing life is never time wasted. Watch it, record it, sketch it, file it away in your mind. But don't get yourself arrested!

In the Computer, It Ain't *Really* Real

It may seem obvious, but it seems worth a reminder at this point that what you see on the screen in a 3D program is not real. It's a mathematical representation of what *may* be real. And the end result of 3D work is not a reproduction of reality; at most, it's a simulation of reality. This distinction can be troubling to some and often gives trial lawyers fits worrying about whether a jury can distinguish between reality and a simulation.

When the animated 3D subject is a talking dragon, of course, (almost) everyone understands that it's just not real. When the subject is closer to home, closer to every day reality, however, some people begin to have doubts. They may wonder whether an animation of a collision between a bus and a tanker is real or a simulation? *An animation is not itself reality*, even if the vehicles' true movements were scrupulously entered into the program's animation controller. It's a simulation based upon reality.

This distinction becomes even more relevant when we seek to imitate natural phenomena in a 3D scene. Objects in a computer program are not real, solid, tangible things that can be taken from the screen and handled physically. Rather, they are mathematical models of things, and if the hardware, software, and artist are sophisticated enough, can look and even act like their real-world counterparts within that 3D scene. But every action and every similarity to real-world properties is created mathematically in the computer.

Illumination of a simple sphere by a light in a computer 3D scene is the result of a series of calculations, hidden from the artist, that determine the brightness and color of the simulated light; the distance between it and the sphere; the color, reflectivity, transparency, bumpiness, and other characteristics of the sphere; and the lighting model chosen for the process. To you, the artist, it's much simpler: you create and adjust a light, move it to where you want, and see how it lights the sphere, as in Figure 2-2. But you should never forget that there's a lot going on "under the hood."

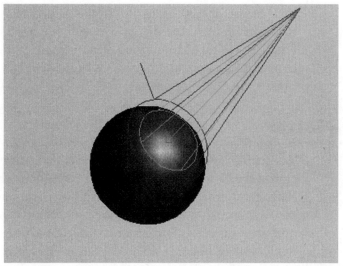

Figure 2-2: As simple as it may appear, even this scene of a sphere illuminated by a single light uses complex mathematics behind the scenes to provide the illusion of reality.

It's this computer need for mathematical precision that makes simulation of reality so difficult. Human and animal behavior, to choose the worst example, is far from simple. To begin with, no two human faces are identical. This amazing diversity is compounded by the complexity of facial movements. The variability and interaction among facial muscles and muscle groups make it impossible to reproduce a frown, a laugh, or any other expression easily in 3D—even using the most powerful computer workstation.

To make a 3D face frown, an artist must manipulate the surface defining the face, pushing here and pulling there to create the desired expression. Even the best facial animation systems now available are still nothing more than linked collections of mathematical animation controllers that have been created just for that purpose by stellar graphics programmers.

To be sure, as computer power increases and software becomes more sophisticated, more and more of this "tough stuff" that 3D artists now struggle with will be created nearly automatically by the system. Remember, the entire 3D graphics industry is little more than 30 years old. In the future, artists are sure to have more and more "artistic" power at their disposal, and the mathematics will be hidden more and more from the artist. But they can never disappear completely, because it is the math that makes the 3D engine work!

Matter

According to Webster's dictionary, *matter* is defined as the "substance that is considered to constitute the observable universe, that together with energy is held to form the basis of objective phenomena, that includes among its properties extension, inertia, and gravitation . . ." In other words, it's everything in the universe that's not energy. Since what we model and animate in 3D are almost always physical objects, we need to understand the nature of matter first.

The other part of the universe, according to the Webster's definition, is energy. Energy, including invisible phenomena like radiation and visible phenomena like light, is the universal complement to matter. As 3D artists and technologists, you work in a visual medium, so light and its effects must always be included in your scenes. Other invisible forms of energy like gamma rays can only be simulated in 3D, so it makes sense for us to focus our energies (so to speak) on visible light.

Extension

The first property of matter noted above is *extension*. Extension just means shape and form. Matter has a shape, either self-defined, like an elephant or defined by its confining container, like water. When you create a 3D scene, you almost always start first by defining the objects—the matter—that will fill your scene. You can build such objects within the program, import them from another program, or obtain them from an outside source. To be effective, 3D objects must have several characteristics:

- They must be accurate. Whether you're working close to reality or wildly far from it, the models must conform to the planned shapes.

- They must have the requisite degree of complexity for the task. Unlike the real world, objects in a 3D scene can be made up of a variety of mathematical approximations, including three- or four-sided faces, patches, NURBs (Non-Uniform Rational B-splines—aren't you glad you asked?), or metaballs. By adjusting the surface parameters, objects can be more or less complex (and more or less accurate, as well). See Figure 2-3 for an example of how two objects with the same basic shape can vary substantially in complexity and still retain much of the accuracy of the original model. The two teapots produce different results when rendered, as shown in Figure 2-4.

Figure 2-3: The complexity of a 3D object is under the control of the artist. The shape of the teapot on the left is defined by 1,024 triangular faces, while the teapot on the right requires 9,216 such faces. In general, they look quite similar, but examine Figure 2-4 to see the difference when rendered.

Figure 2-4: When rendered, the two teapots of Figure 2-3 look different, especially around the silhouette of the spout. Why are both surfaces smooth? We'll get to that in the section below on "Surface Texture."

Which teapot is preferable? The right teapot is much smoother, more attractive to the eye, and more accurately approximates the shape of the teapot. It is also *nine* times more complex. It will take much longer to display, animate, and so forth. If, for example, our 3D teapot will only be seen briefly on a table at the back of a scene in a low-resolution video game, we can probably get away with the angular teapot at left. But if we intend to use this model as the focal point of a four-color, slick-paper ad to sell teapots, well, it needs a whole lot *more* faces than it has and more dress-up work to make it presentable!

- They must have the appropriate number of sub-objects for the intended use. Typically, animated objects have more separately controllable components than static objects, such as arms and legs or wheels and doors.

- They must be sized correctly for the scene. If the storyboard calls for an attack by a 50-foot woman, then you'll have to deliver one.

Often, objects not created within a particular 3D program present artists with their biggest challenges. Some file translators do a poor job of importing external files, while others do an excellent job. Sometimes, it's almost more work to repair a poorly translated file than it would have been to create the object anew!

Elasticity and Deformability

Every object has a characteristic, elasticity, that defines how it interacts with other objects. A rubber ball is highly elastic, while an eggshell is not. Drop them both onto a rigid surface; the ball will bounce but the lack of elasticity in the eggshell will produce a mess instead of a bounce. Drop them onto a thick, soft feather bed, however, and:

- Neither the ball nor the egg bounce much.

- The surface of the feather bed will deform and not rebound.

- The inelastic eggshell won't break.

This illustrates several important characteristics that you as an artist must consider when working in 3D. Creating an effective 3D image or animation often depends as much on reproducing natural object interaction and surface characteristics as it does on the accuracy of the shapes of objects themselves. Our 3D feather bed need not be totally accurate, but if we drop a 3D egg on it and the bed deforms as we expect, it "sells" the effect to the viewer, as in Figure 2-5.

Figure 2-5: Thanks to the deformable surface of the feather bed, the egg didn't break. Of course, since this is a 3D image and not from real life, it wouldn't have broken anyway!

Another characteristic of elastic bodies is that they retain most of their volume when deformed. Squeeze a soft rubber ball between your fingers, and it spreads around the circumference to compensate for the pressure. Many 3D software products have this capability, called *squash and stretch*, built-in. It not only makes animating bouncing balls easier, but also lets you squash and stretch other objects, like animated cartoon characters. As we'll see in Chapter 4, squash and stretch is a time-honored technique of cartoonists.

Solid Modeling

In a computer 3D scene, nothing, of course, can be really solid. An object is usually described by its mathematically defined surface. A good example of this is the teapot shown in Figure 2-6.

Figure 2-6: Our better-quality teapot from Figures 2-3 and 2-4 with a hole scooped from it using a technique called Boolean subtraction. Notice that our fancy teapot is really just a shell, and in fact, if I hadn't told the program to render both sides of the material, we wouldn't even have been able to see the inside!

In spite of this "thin-skinned" approach, you will still see the phrase *solid modeling* used in conjunction with 3D programs. This means either that the program has a sophisticated package of mathematical functions that simulate the effects of physical laws or the program can simulate *solid materials*.

Solid modeling is especially important to engineers who can use the software to create a part, assign it material properties, and test its strength and other physical qualities without leaving the computer. High-end Computer-Aided Design (CAD) programs often include this capability. Most artists don't need their 3D creations to have the physical characteristics of stainless steel—they just want them to look like it.

Solid Modeling Precision

Solid modeling can be used to determine such physical characteristics as the center of mass of a 3D object, which can be important for certain types of animation. If you ever have a difficult animation project where you must precisely simulate the action of a complex system, consider using solid modeling as an investigative adjunct to your animation program.

Solid *materials* are more common than solid *modeling* in today's 3D packages. A solid material is one that is defined parametrically, that is, by mathematical equations with parameters (variables) that control its appearance. For example, you can simulate the appearance of a natural material like marble by controlling its component colors, vein width and frequency, and randomness, as shown in Figure 2-7.

Figure 2-7: The same teapot from Figure 2-3 and 2-4 with a solid, or parametric, material applied. Note that it seems to go all the way through the object, hence the term solid material.

Solid modeling, on the other hand, refers to the mathematically calculated physical properties of a real-world object *if* it was constructed as shown in the 3D program and *if* it was made of the specified material(s). Solid materials simulate the appearance of a solid object, while solid modeling simulates the physics

Inertia

Inertia is the property of matter that produces the results we described in Chapter 1:

- A body at rest tends to remain at rest.

- A body in motion tends to remain in motion.

- To change either *status quo* requires the application of an external force (with slight apologies to Sir Isaac Newton).

Inertia can't be seen, of course. It's the mass, the weightiness that defines how easy or difficult an object is to move or stop. If inertia didn't exist, our reality would be much, much different. Imagine a world where trees, people, and even molecules wandered off on their own without cause and stopped randomly wherever they happened to stop. It would be a very unreliable and unlivable world

Every object in the real world has inertia, either of rest or of motion (also called *momentum*). For most artistic purposes, you needn't concern yourself with mathematical calculations related to inertia. (After all, that's why you went into art and not physics in the first place, right?) You must, however, make your objects obey these laws or risk upsetting the sensibilities of your viewers. A "thrown" 3D baseball must continue in the direction it's thrown until gravity and air resistance (external forces) cause it to sink to the ground.

Remember also that the momentum of a 3D object in motion causes a reaction when it meets with another object. Depending upon the relative elasticity and deformability of the two objects, one will probably give: the eggshell will break, the feather bed will dent, the eight ball will head into the corner pocket, or the cartoon coyote will flatten his face against the cliff.

Objects in motion can be a great source of humor if the physical laws are handled properly. In Chapter 4, we'll examine the manipulation of physical laws in cartooning as one of its chief sources of humor. After all, where would Roadrunner cartoons be without Wile E. Coyote's ability to hang suspended in thin air until he looks down?

If you need to calculate precisely an object's momentum or resistance to air, or any of a million other engineering and scientific calculations, and you're not an engineer, consult one. My best advice to you is simply, "Make it look right!"

Even if your 3D work does not involve animation, creating a realistic still image requires that your objects obey the same laws. Figure 2-8 illustrates this: three of our famous better-quality marble teapots balanced in an impossible stack. If this is the look you're going for, that's fine—3D programs don't care a whit about what's possible or impossible in the real world. Just remember to be consistent.

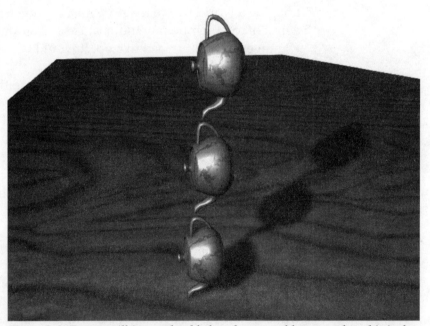

Figure 2-8: Even a still image should obey the natural laws—unless this is the look you're going for.

Gravity

Generally speaking, gravity is the force of attraction between objects. It exists as a property of matter between all objects, but requires substantial mass to be detectable. In something as small as an apple or a moderately sized superhero, the force of gravity is negligible, which is why superheroes don't attract apples to them.

To the artist, the depiction of gravitation—or gravity—is essential. Gravity causes trees to be wider at their bases, is a major contributor to the decline of the human physique, and keeps us all pinned to the surface of the earth. To overcome gravity by flying or lifting a foot, we must exert a force greater than the gravity that holds us down. And that takes energy: strength, muscle, power. Your work as a 3D artist must reflect this reality.

Keep your 3D objects firmly planted on the ground unless they exert a force (or a force is exerted upon them) to overcome gravity. If one of your 3D characters pushes off from the stage in a splendid *tour jeté*, make sure that he or she returns to the stage with the correct physical reactions. If the same balletic character has pendulous breasts or a bulging beer belly, these added attractions should also reflect the effects of gravity—and momentum—as the dancer moves across the stage.

If a cartoon 3D character hefts a monstrous, 1000-pound barbell, it should show. His muscles should bulge, his balance should reflect the new center of gravity, and his walking gait should change. If none of this happens, it just won't sell. You'll never convince your viewers that the barbell is heavy. (Remember a cartoon character lifting a balloon barbell? His physical reactions communicated immediately that the barbell was featherlight.)

Color (& Light)

There are two primary clues by which we recognize an object visually: shape and color. We can tell an apple, for example, by its characteristic irregular spherical shape, its stem, and the concavities at the stem and flower ends. Look at Figure 2-9—that shape spells Apple. Okay, Golden Delicious apple, even if we can't tell from the color.

Figure 2-9: An apple. Most people recognize it instantly just from the shape.

But what if you change the color of the apple just a bit, say, by applying orange and white hazard stripes as in Figure 2-10? Does it still look like an apple? Is it a new genetically altered safety apple? Or does the unnatural coloration completely destroy the illusion that this is an apple?

Figure 2-10: Is this a genetically altered safety apple or what?

3D modeling gives the artist unlimited abilities to create and control the color of objects and light. Depending upon the program, virtually everything can be changed. As we'll see later in Chapter 6, creating materials to color your models can be as simple or complex as you want to make it. But in order to define a color and lighting setup that will make an object look the way you want, you must first understand a bit about how we perceive color.

Light

Color begins with light; in absolute darkness, we can perceive no color. In the real world, most light radiates from a hot object, like the sun, a campfire, or the glowing filament of an incandescent light bulb. Light can also be produced by cold processes, however, as in lasers, fluorescent tubes, or fireflies.

Light can be made up of any combination of colors; put them all together and the result is white light. In fact, it's difficult to produce a light source that produces single-color light; lasers are the exception. When we look directly at a light, we perceive the combination of colors in the light. A red-tinted light bulb produces light primarily in the red part of the spectrum. Typical incandescent household light bulbs produce a broad range of light with a slight increase in the yellow area of the spectrum.

An object's color, on the other hand, is dependent upon both the color of the light falling upon it and the nature of the material of which it's made. If we shine a white light on a blue ball, the ball absorbs all the colors of the light except blue; it reflects the blue back toward us and we perceive the ball as blue. But if the light shining upon the object contains *only* colors that are absorbed by the object, we perceive the object to be black.

In Figure 2-11 nine spheres are arrayed, each with its own light. To avoid errors, each light was set to exclude all other spheres (this is another feature of powerful 3D programs: you can easily create lights that shine only on the objects you want). The left three spheres are a moderately saturated red, the middle spheres are a moderately saturated green, and the right spheres are a moderately saturated blue.

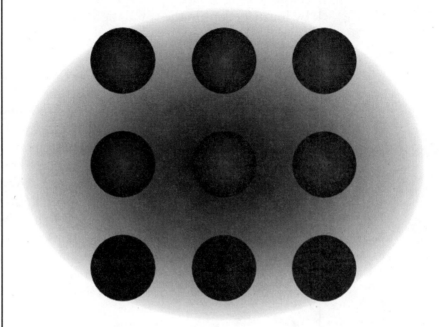

Figure 2-11: Each of these nine spheres are illuminated by its own light. The top three spheres all have white lights, the middle three spheres each have a light that matches the sphere's color, and the bottom three lights are complementary to the spheres' colors. In black-and-white printing, the color values of the top six spheres are fairly similar, but the darkness of the spheres in the bottom row illustrates the principle that an object's perceived color is dependent in part on the color of the light.

The top three spheres are lit by white light and the spheres in the middle row are each lit by a light that matches the color of the sphere. In both rows, the results are as we would predict: the color of the spheres is accurately depicted. The spheres in the bottom row are each lit by a light of the complementary color with no light component of the sphere color. The red sphere is lit by a green light, the green sphere by a red light, and the blue sphere by an orange light. Again, the depicted colors are as we expect: with no light component that matches the sphere color, the spheres are black. The slight variations in density are caused by imperfections in the simulation.

Object Color Components

Most 3D programs provide some control over the color of lights in a scene, and all let you control the color of objects. Depending upon the sophistication of the program, you may be able to adjust individually the effect of light in different areas of an object. The color of light in an area that is *not* directly illuminated is called the *ambient* color and is most affected by the ambient or average surrounding light level in the scene. Ambient light typically consists of diffuse reflections from other matte surfaces in the environment. It illuminates areas of objects not in direct light.

The color of an object in the illuminated direct is its *diffuse* color, and the color of any highlight is its *specular* color. These three different areas are shown in Figure 2-12.

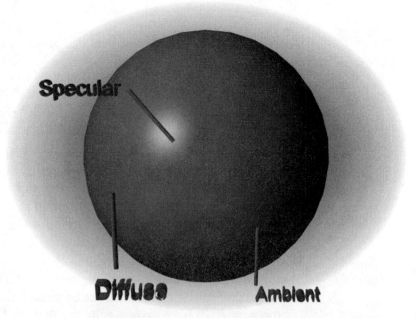

Figure 2-12: Three color components make up the lighting of an object.

Controlling each of these colors individually lets you simulate the appearance of different materials. For example, shiny plastic typically has diffuse and ambient colors very close in colorand a specular color that is much whiter than the other two. Highlights on plastic tend to be white, while highlights on most polished metals (not chrome or stainless steel) tend to be a lighter version of the diffuse color

Simulating Light in 3D

As illustrated in Figure 2-11, 3D programs generally let you control the color of each light in a scene, plus how and where the light falls. 3D lighting can emulate real-world lighting characteristics, such as how light falls off with distance or the special illumination from radiosity bounce lighting. It can also be totally artificial, like a light that excludes objects by definition

3D programs typically offer several different types of lights to simulate different types of real-world light. For example, an incandescent light bulb typically radiates in almost all directions from a point source, while the sun's light is essentially in parallel rays at the earth's surface because of the sun's distance. Because it's impossible to move a 3D light 93,000,000 scale miles from an object, make it bright enough to simulate the sun at that distance, and still retain an object scale that is workable, the sun's light is usually simulated by a source of parallel light from a point location. This produces realistic lighting and shadows while still being workable.

Shadows are cast by objects in most lighting situations where the light is strong enough and not diffused by atmospheric vapor, clouds, fog, smoke, or artificial diffusers. Shadows give depth and drama to a scene, and without them, an image can look flat and artificial.

Shadows are weak or nonexistent when clouds diffuse the sun's light; winter sun often produces faint shadows with soft edges. In outer space, with nothing to diffuse the light, shadows are harsh and deep with crisp edges. Many 3D programs let you adjust the depth of shadows and the softness of their edges to simulate different real-world conditions.

As a 3D artist, you must learn to recognize the type of lighting required to create a desired effect or simulate specific lighting conditions. Through careful observation of the real-world lighting you want to simulate, you can learn its light and shadow characteristics and then reproduce them on the computer. Pay close attention to the color of the light, the location, depth, and softness of its shadows, and the apparent distance between the light and the central objects. We'll discuss this more in Chapter 6, but for now, just remember to keep your eyes open!

Object Color Variations

Objects almost never have a uniform color across their surfaces. In addition to the variations resulting from light and shadow, the innate imperfectability of reality almost always produces variations in surface appearance. Merely adjusting the colors of a 3D object or light won't reproduce natural variation or artificial coloring. Let's say that you used a projector to project a slide of the desired surface color variations onto an object. This wouldn't be realistic for two reasons. First, if the object moved, the projected image wouldn't and the illusion would be destroyed. Second, those areas of the object that don't receive the direct light of the projector wouldn't receifve any of the coloration.

The main method developed to reproduce these variations on 3D objects is called *texture mapping*. We'll go into detail about mapping in Chapter 6, but for now understand that it means applying a 2D image to a 3D object, either by wrapping it around like Christmas wrap or projecting it like a slide projector, as shown in Figure 2-13.

Figure 2-13: Texture mapping. An image of the Carson House in Eureka, California, is texture-mapped onto two otherwise identical rounded cubes. The image is applied squarely to each side of the left cube, while it's projected onto the right cube from the front, upper-right corner.

For an artist, the key is, again, observation. Note how objects appear in the real world. Note combinations of intentional and accidental textures, and think about how you might create them for reproduction on a 3D object.

Surface Smoothing

Remember a few pages ago when we looked at the two teapots with different degrees of complexity? You probably noticed that while the silhouettes of the two differed, the surfaces looked virtually the same. This is the result of a mathematical process called *smooth shading*, which is used to convert the rough triangular mesh of polygonal mesh objects, as shown in Figure 2-14, into smooth-looking renderings.

Figure 2-14: Our two teapots with all of their triangular edges showing.

Changing the shading of the teapots in Figure 2-3 to *flat* or *constant shading* lets the faces show, as shown in Figure 2-15.

Figure 2-15: One shading option available in all 3D programs is called flat or constant shading. The program does not attempt to shade smoothly across surfaces.

Keeping the number of faces down is an economic fact of life for 3D artists. More triangular faces mean a closer approximation to the original model but slower production. Remember: if 3D is your work and not just a hobby, you'll need to balance image quality against computational time in order to survive commercially.

We'll get more into shading in Chapter 6, but for now, remember that, for better or worse, 3D rendering can smooth over many object surface irregularities you might otherwise expect to see.

Surface Texture

Objects in the real world are seldom as smooth as they are when smooth-shaded. Except for polished hard surfaces, all other real-world surfaces have dips, dents, dings, and blemishes. Since 3D programs use mathematical algorithms to smooth irregularities, how can you reproduce these variations?

There are several answers, including manually adjusting the position of the geometry itself—a laborious process, at best, that involves letting the 3D program push portions of the geometry around guided by a picture of the variations (called *displacement modeling* or *displacement mapping*), wrapping a picture of the imperfections around the object (another application of *texture mapping*), or using the same picture to simulate the way light would hit such an imperfect surface. This last alternative is called *bump mapping*.

Figure 2-16 illustrates the difference between bump mapping and displacement mapping. Both cubes have a Gila monster skin material texture-mapped onto them to give the characteristic colors. The cube on the left, however, is bump-mapped; it simulates surface bumpiness well on faces toward the viewer. But because it's only a simulation of the way light strikes a bumpy surface, it's smooth on the top faces of the cube. The right cube used the same map to displace or alter the geometry; it really *is* bumpy—all over! This is especially visible around the silhouette.

Figure 2-16: Two Gila monster cubes. The left is texture-mapped and bump-mapped, while the right is texture-mapped and displacement-mapped (exaggerated for effect).

Once again, working in 3D means making a trade-off between real-world accuracy and efficiency. Bump mapping is an efficient method of simulating irregularities or other surface variations, but can be inaccurate in many situations. Keep in mind that there is more than one way to (add a) skin (to) a bumpy cat!

Light Transmissibility

Finally, let's examine how light interacts with the surface of an object. We're familiar with all of these concepts, but let's list them explicitly. When light strikes the surface of an object, it can:

- Absorb part of the light and reflect the rest (Display color)
- Bounce off completely (Reflection)
- Pass through completely (Transparency)
- Pass some colors through completely and others partially (Transparency with tinting)
- Pass through but bend the light whenever it traverses a change in material (Refraction)

We've already discussed how the color of an object is determined by the combination of the color of direct lightand its partial absorption by the object. We're also familiar with highly reflective objects such as mirrors or chrome bumpers (remember them?). They reflect virtually all of the light that strikes them and display little color of their own.

Glass is the obvious example of a transparent material, and stained glass an example of tinted transparency. If you look through a glass marble, you'll see the world distorted by the passage of light from air, through the marble, and then through the air again. When light passes through a transition between two materials with different refractive properties, it bends; this is refraction. (Without it, I wouldn't be writing this book, as I need the refractive lenses in my glasses to adjust my vision to be able to see the monitor!)

Figure 2-17 illustrates refraction and two types of transparency. The glass ball in the center demonstrates the refractive characteristics of glass; the light rays reflecting from the checkerboard behind it are bent passing through both front and back surfaces of the ball on their way to the camera.

The bubbles on either side illustrate transparency, but there is a difference between them. The bubble on the left recreates the effect of a soap bubble: it's thinner in the center and passes less light at the edges. The right bubble shows the more typical transparency of a translucent object—it passes less light at its thickest point.

Figure 2-17: A refractive glass marble is flanked by a soap bubble on the left and a bead on the right. Notice the three different methods of depicting light through a mostly transparent object.

The lesson to be learned is clear: it's not always so easy to see through the simplest effect!

Moving On

In the next chapter, we'll look at another part of the real world: human anatomy and structure. Fascinated as we humans are with ourselves and our affairs, realistic character reproduction is one of the most dominant themes of 3D work. And even if you aren't animating a human, you still may be working with humanlike characters: witness the dancing car and gas pump in Chapter 1.

Human Anatomy & Movement

Did you have to take Biology in high school because you just had to have another science on your transcript? Or was it something you avoided like the plague because you *just couldn't stand dissecting frogs*? Count me in the latter group—I took General Science, Chemistry, and Physics, but stayed far away from the biology courses. Maybe it was the smell of formaldehyde.

But once I joined the 3D industry, I found that in spite of my general dislike of "slimy biological things," learning about them was absolutely essential to performing my job. The computer context kept them from being slimy, but I did need to learn how humans are constructed and how they move. And that's what this chapter is all about.

Why Humans?

I'm devoting an entire chapter to human anatomy and motion because, well, the most active, exciting, and challenging area of 3D animation today is *character animation*—simulating human form and actions realistically. We as humans, of course, are endlessly fascinated with our own kind (except for the occasional misanthrope among us, that is). We watch each other, talk with each other, study each other in endless college courses, and generally spend our time in the perhaps mistaken impression that what we humans do is the most important thing in the universe.

Our universal fascination with our own kind has produced a potential gold mine for talented animators who can mimic human movement.

Whether we are the center of the universe is a question beyond the scope even of this book (!), but our universal fascination with our own kind has produced a potential gold mine for talented animators who can mimic human movement. Look how much 3D business is devoted to depicting human movement; games of almost every genre typically include human protagonists or antagonists, movies with virtual stuntmen, medical visualization, and re-creations of murder most foul.

Keep in mind that I can no more explain human anatomy and movement in one short chapter than I could explain the "real world" in the previous two. Rather, look on this chapter as a general source for basic topical information; then examine the Resources Appendix for other sources of detailed information. I've tried to focus on the information most important to 3D modelers and animators, so don't look for an explanation of the structure of DNA in this chapter!

TIP

Remember always that there are no straight lines on the body; every part of the body has some curve or arc to it.

Instant Experts

In many ways, being a computer animator is a lot like being a trial lawyer. In both fields, you are called upon to become an "instant expert" in some arcane area, anything from the flow of sludge through pipelines to Labanotation (the dance notation system named for Rudolf von Laban) to finger-printing.

As a trial lawyer, I was often faced with the need to cross-examine—and, if possible, discredit—an expert witness testifying against my client. In order to do so, I had to quickly bone up on the witness's particular expertise as it related to my case, find any weak points, and figure out how to attack them most effectively. This sometimes meant learning the intricacies of gas spectrometry, the dispersion patterns of street lamps, or the effects of epoxy-based paint thinners on human physiology. Mind you, I never needed to learn all there was to know about any of those things; just enough to understand and analyze the facts in context and then cross-examine the opposing expert effectively.

Computer animators who specialize in forensic or other "real-world" animation often find themselves in almost the same situation. They often must re-create events far beyond their usual areas of expertise. A murder case, for example, might involve such arcane areas of science as blood spatter patterns and gunpowder stippling, the kind of scientific evidence that lends itself to visual presentation but that is seldom taught in, say, high school.

In order to prepare animations that depict such evidence accurately, effectively, and comprehensibly, an animator must learn almost as much about the subject as a cross-examining lawyer. Given the usual pressures of making a living, this means learning as *much* as possible as *quickly* as possible.

Even if you decide to avoid such grisly subjects in your career as an animator, if you stick with computer animation long enough, you'll almost certainly be called upon to animate a character or subject you know little about. It might be a dragon voiced by Sean Connery, a Coke-sipping polar bear, or how a camera dolly fits in a set. And that will mean that you must become an "instant expert" in how dragons, polar bears, and camera dollies move. If you're animating characters, most of all you'll need to know how *people* move, because that's what makes these characters accessible to the audience.

3D Character Animation

We can look at
an animated
figure and know
instantly that it
is animated
rather than real.

Infants are born into the world knowing little or nothing about humans (other than mom, of course). From our first breathing moment, we begin to learn how people walk, talk, sit, and stand; what their facial expressions mean; and how to interpret thousands of other subtle signs that help us understand their intentions and actions. We accumulate this huge body of knowledge principally through experience, and because it's begun at such an early age and is so necessary to our survival, we absorb it with little explicit analysis.

It's because of this vast experiential knowledge of human action and behavior that we can look at an animated figure and know instantly that it is animated rather than real. John Lasseter's baby in *Tin Toy* was a remarkable achievement for its time, but no one mistook it for a real baby.

Dragons, Toys & Dinosaurs (& One Pig)

In the current computer-animated genre, probably the most realistic re-creation of human speech and related facial characteristics is not a human at all, but Draco in Universal Studio's *Dragonheart*. The Industrial Light & Magic (ILM) team spent a year transferring Sean Connery's facial and speech mannerisms to this mythical last dragon on earth. It was a masterful accomplishment and when Draco spoke in 007's familiar Scottish brogue, the audience believed in dragons. (All right, *I* believed!)

When *Dragon-
heart's* Draco
spoke in 007's
familiar Scottish
brogue, the
audience
believed in
dragons.

Toy Story from Walt Disney is a good example of the current limitations in—and the direction of—character animation. The story revolves around the interactions of a group of toys in a child's room; human characters are involved only peripherally and usually from a toy's visual viewpoint. Why toys and not humans? Remember that it took a year to add the dragon to *Dragonheart*; extrapolate that time to a full-length movie like *Toy Story* and you'd find that creating an entire cast of realistic human beings in a completely computer-generated environment would probably exceed the combined CGI capabilities of Disney,

Industrial Light & Magic, Pixar, Boss Studios, and Pacific Data Images! In other words, it would be an enormous undertaking today.

Animating toys is just easier than animating people because viewers' expectations are lower. In the future, even in the near future, CGI will undoubtedly advance to the point where it becomes feasible to do a *Human Story*. After all, the advances over the past decade have been phenomenal. Until then, animators will find more success animating otherwise inanimate objects and lending them human characteristics because even an approximation is OK when it's not a real person.

The other area where CGI has been used successfully has been in the animation of animals. Steven Spielberg's Universal production of *Jurassic Park* pioneered the use of CGI dinosaurs good enough to occupy most of the screen without destroying the illusion of reality for the audience. It took the combined talents of many special effects magicians, particularly ILM's Dennis Muren and his CGI team. *Jurassic Park* was wildly successful and opened the door for such other productions as *Jumanji*, with its quite effective spiders, vines, and mosquitoes and less effective monkeys and lion. (Hair is another notoriously difficult subject to reproduce in CGI. PDI used smooth-furred polar bears in its Coca-Cola commercials and scored a hit. ILM was less successful with its hairy creatures in *Jumanji*.)

Rhythm & Hues had a different challenge in *Babe*, the story of an ambitious orphan piglet on a New Zealand farm. The animation in *Babe* was pervasive but subtle, limited principally to animating mouth movements and matching them to live film elements and dubbed speech. The accomplishments of Rhythm & Hues were evident in the success of the film; nothing spoiled the illusion for the audience. The charming story of *Babe* was combined with good direction and acting in a delightful production, and the near-invisible special effects enhanced the results. (Rhythm & Hues pioneered this mouth animation technique in *Hocus Pocus*, in which they made the witch's black cat speak.)

Hair is another notoriously difficult subject to reproduce in computer graphics imagery.

What a Character!

The common denominator of all of the successful toy, saurian, draconic, or animal characters was that they had character, or personality. The concept of character in a nonhuman creature is not new to traditional cel animators from the great animation studios like Disney, Warner Brothers, Walter Lanz, or Hanna-Barbera. But as 3D modeling has become more accessible to nonartists, its use has spread beyond the artistic capabilities or knowledge required to create effective animation. The result often has been mechanical animation with no character.

Before you can show character in your animation, however, you must first understand the basic structure of the human body. That's true whether you're creating an alien or animating a lovesick praying mantis. If you want your audience to identify with the character—or just to accept that the character has quasi-human qualities—you first must learn how a human is built and how it moves. We'll start with the skeleton, since it's the basic structure that both defines our size and shape and keeps us together.

> If you want your audience to identify with the character—or just to accept that the character has quasi-human qualities—you first must learn how a human is built and how it moves.

Artistic Basic Training

The vast knowledge you have already gained *just from living and observing* can provide you with much of what you need to create lively character animation—if you learn to tap it. Never stop studying people: how they move, sit, stand, talk, walk, cringe, strut, jump, fall, limp, kiss, punch, and on and on. (You may get a reputation as a voyeur, but if you tell your upset subjects that you're an artist, they may allow you a little more slack.)

Try sketching the poses and action you observed on paper. You may not be a skilled 2D artist, but the *act* of sketching helps you focus on the shapes and perspectives involved. Try and relate what you draw to 3D objects that you might create in your 3D modeling program. Then return to the computer and attempt to re-create what you drew.

➡

Traditional art classes are excellent for training your artistic eye and learning about composition, perspective, color, light, movement, tension, and so on. Few such 2D art classes, however, cross over into the world of computerized 3D art. In fact, if you want training in the creation of 3D shapes, take a sculpture class or two. The same techniques of visualization that help you create a three-dimensional sculpture also aid you in creating a 3D object in computerized space.

Once you have a 3D modeling program available to you, practice, practice, practice. Do the tutorials. Read the manual! Try every command and tool and explore its capabilities and limitations. Talk to other animators. Read the trade press. Go online and explore the Web; there is a wealth of knowledge and help out there.

The Skeleton Crew

The skeleton is a complex system of bones and cartilage held together by muscles and tendons.

Under all is land. (Whoops! Wrong book!) Under all of our *flesh*, at least, is the *skeleton*. It's a complex system of bones and cartilage held together by muscles and tendons. The skeleton provides the basic frame of the body (and protection for important organs), while the muscles, tendons, and fat are the upholstery that defines the overall shape (and provides motive power). Where two bones come together, there's usually a joint, which can provide some mobility in the linking.

The skeleton has more than 200 separate bones, as shown in Figure 3-1. It's amazing how this complex structure moves so effortlessly and in so many ways. The skeleton is easily noticeable on the surface of the skin and when the body moves. You can see the bones most easily in the head and where ribs, hips, scapulae (shoulder blades), clavicles (collar bones), knuckles, and kneecaps protrude.

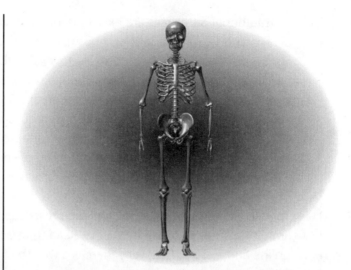

Figure 3-1: The unclad skeleton in all its glory.

Any deformities in the skeleton show through its "upholstery." For example, a shorter leg or even a hunched back caused by a spinal abnormality is readily visible, as shown in Figure 3-2.

Figure 3-2: Even though an abnormality may be at the spinal level, as it is with this character known variously as Olaf or Abby Normal, the results are visible at the skin level.

In the following sections, I'll describe portions of the skeleton that are typically more important to 3D animators.

Skull Session

The skull comprises 22 bones; eight are platelike, encasing the brain, while the rest provide the facial and jaw structure. Perhaps surprisingly, when viewed from the top, the head is not round or even oval: it's *ovoid* (egg shaped) with the smaller end towards the face.

Figure 3-3: The skull viewed from the top shows its characteristic ovoid shape.

The shape of the skull controls the structure of the facial features. In an infant, the lower jaw is almost even horizontally with the lower edge of the skull. As a person matures, however, the jaw angles downward, resulting in a longer look for the head.

TIP

If you must create a face from scratch, it's easier to start with a profile, because you can see defects more easily in the side view. You'll also need a front view (and a top view if you can get it) to produce an accurate 3D portrait.

A Spiny Story

The spine is the central column of the body. It provides support for all of the attached structures. The spine is made up of 24 separate bones, the *vertebrae*, separated by tough fibrous discs that provide cushioning and flexibility. The spine also protects the spinal column, the nerve "bus" that runs through the vertebral arch at the back vertebral bodies.

The spine is attached to the skull by the first and second vertebrae. The first vertebra is the *atlas*; it holds up the head like the mythical character who bore the world on his shoulders. The atlas also allows the rocking motion of the head both from side to side and also front to back. The second vertebra is called the *axis*; together with the atlas, the axis allows the swivel motion of the head, as shown in Figure 3-4.

The first vertebra is the *atlas*; it holds up the head like the mythical character who bore the world on his shoulders.

Figure 3-4: The atlas and axis together allow for all of the head's rotational movement.

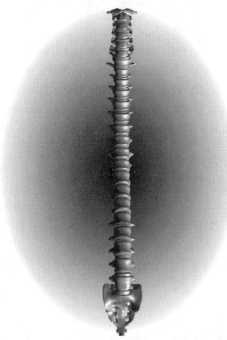

Figure 3-5: The spine is made up of 24 vertebrae separated by discs of tough fibrous tissue for cushioning and flexibility.

Spinal Notation

Vertebrae are typically identified by the region of the spine in which they're located and a number that identifies each vertebra. The three regions are the *cervical, thoracic,* and *lumbar.*

The cervical vertebrae begin at the base of the skull with the atlas (C1) and continue to vertebra C7 at the base of the neck. (The small protrusion on your back at the base of the neck is vertebra C7.) The cervical vertebrae provide attachment and movement for the skull and neck.

The thoracic region includes the 12 vertebrae that make up the chest cavity. Each vertebra has a pair of ribs attached to it. Vertebra T1 is at the shoulder-blades and T12 is at the lower-middle back.

The lumbar region includes the five vertebrae in the lower back, L1 through L5.

(Two other portions of what we think of as the back are not vertebrae. Below the L5 vertebra is the sacrum. The sacrum and the iliac provide the spine-pelvis connection. The coccyx is the tailbone, the remnant of our tailed days in the treetops. It's below the sacrum-ilium.)

· ➤

The cervical vertebrae are the smallest and most flexible of all the spinal vertebrae.

Ignoring thoracic movement is one of the most common errors in 3D character animation; it results in stiff-moving automatons, even when the rest of the body is properly set up.

The Neck & I

The cervical vertebrae are the smallest and most flexible of all the spinal vertebrae. They can move backward, forward, and from side to side. This flexibility lets you rest your chin on your chest, look straight upward to see a brachiosaurus dining in the tree-tops, or watch a fast tennis match from beside the net post.

Thoracic Park

The thoracic vertebrae are capable of the same movement as the cervical vertebrae, but to a much smaller degree. The ribs se-verely limit the amount of movement in the thoracic vertebrae, but there is still some movement. Ignoring thoracic movement is one of the most common errors in 3D character animation; it results in stiff-moving automatons, even when the rest of the body is properly set up.

Just Lumbar-ing Along

The lumbar vertebrae are the largest in the body and carry the most weight—the entire weight of the upper body. The lumbar vertebrae allow the most forward movement in the spine, al-though the stomach tissue may limit this bending. Surprisingly, the lumbar vertebrae allow little rotational or other motion.

These Are Spinal Curves

Far from being "ramrod straight," the spine actually has four curves, as shown in Figure 3-6. Two major curves are concave toward the front and allow room for the chest and pelvic cavities. The convex curves in the spine in the pelvic area assist in balance.

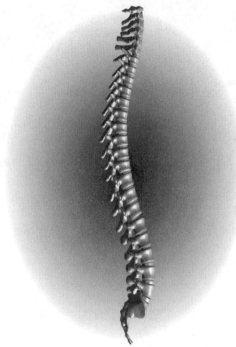

Figure 3-6: The spine is not straight. There are four distinct curves that help shape the body.

A Shoulder to Cry On

Usually, laypeople think of the shoulder as being a part of the torso; in fact, the shoulder, made up of the *scapula* and the *clavicle*, is separate from the torso itself, as shown in Figure 3-7. Only the ends of the clavicles attached by ligaments to the sternum (breastbone) are stationary. The rest of the shoulder is quite mobile.

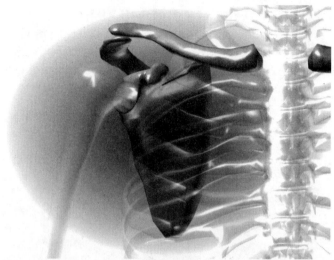

Figure 3-7: The shoulder is quite mobile. It consists of the scapula and clavicle.

Clavicles

The clavicles lie across the front of the upper torso from the top of the sternum to the top of the shoulder and typically slant downward slightly toward the sternum. The ends of the clavicles at the sternum are separated by about one inch, more or less. This separation forms the depression at the base of the front of the neck called the "pit of the neck."

The clavicles are attached to the sternum with ligaments. They attach at the other end to the acromion process of the scapula, allowing lateral movement for the arm. The ball and socket joint formed by the shoulder and upper arm is what allows the arm such a great range of motion.

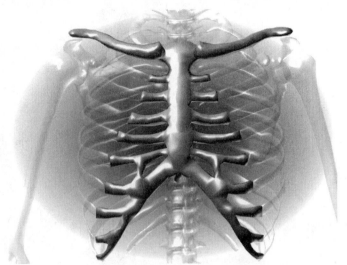

Figure 3-8: The clavicles are the front anchors of the shoulder joint. They're attached to the sternum with flexible ligaments to allow lateral arm movement.

Scapulae

The *scapulae* (plural of scapula) usually lie between the second and sixth or seventh rib on each side of the back. Each scapula is about as long vertically as the sternum is in the front. The scapula creates a socket for the head of the *humerus*, the bone of the upper arm.

When you stand with your arms down at your sides, the scapulae lie flat against your back. As you pull your arms forward, your scapulae are pulled around to the side of the back ribs. When you swing your arms out to the side, the scapulae swing to an outward position as well.

Even though the scapula must move in order to allow the arm to move, it does not move at the same time or speed. For example, if you raise your arm, at first the motion is almost entirely that of the arm. But when it reaches the horizontal plane, the wheeling of the scapula helps the arm continue its upward movement, as shown in Figure 3-9.

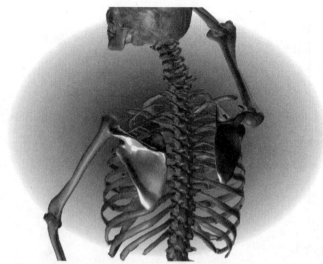

Figure 3-9: The scapula moves across the ribs, but at a different rate than the arm.

Pelvis Lives!

The *pelvis* is formed by the fusion of the hip bones, sacrum, and coccyx. The male and female pelvis are quite different, reflecting our genetic sex roles. Whereas the male pelvis is narrow and shallow, the female pelvis is wider and deeper to provide a birth channel in the mature female.

The side plates of the pelvis protect the inner organs, while the lower structures provide a place on which to sit. All of the upper body weight is transferred through the lumbar vertebrae onto the pelvis and then onto both femurs (or thigh bones).

The pelvis is relatively large in proportion to the rest of the skeleton. Yet, for its size, there are few points where it shows on the body surface. The pelvis points may show on a slim-figured person, but an obese person pretty well camouflages the hip points.

TIP

Remember, the navel is almost always on the same line as the top of the pelvis.

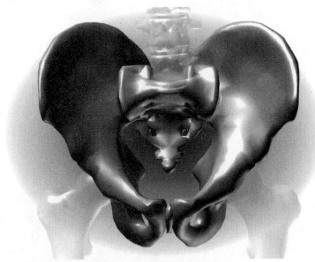

Figure 3-10: The pelvis.

Femurs, Lemurs & Less

The *femurs* are the largest bones in the body. The top end of the femur has a ball and neck and connects to the main shaft at an angle. The ball sits in a cuplike surface on the pelvis, creating a ball and socket joint, as shown in Figure 3-11.

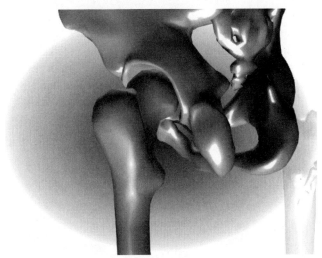

Figure 3-11: This is a pretty hip joint.

Failing to reproduce the natural angle of the femur is probably the second most common error in animating the human figure. Unskilled animators typically create straight thighs that swing from the sides of the hips, producing an automaton look.

Because of the angle of the ball and neck to the femur's shaft, the femur angles inward toward the knee. Failing to reproduce this is probably the second most common error in animating the human figure. Unskilled animators typically create straight thighs that swing from the sides of the hips, again producing an automaton look.

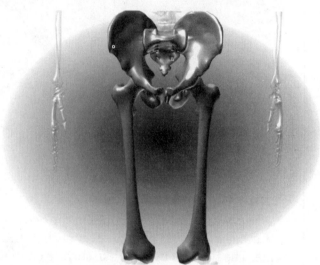

Figure 3-12: The femur angles inward toward the knee.

The lower end of the femur ends at the knee, as shown in Figure 3-13. The knees support all of the body weight other than the calves and feet. A knee has a little shock absorber pad inside called the meniscus, which is filled with fluid. This lets the knee give a little with added weight. Most 3D animation programs don't allow for this kind of flex, but it would be proper to account for this flex in heavily weighted situations.

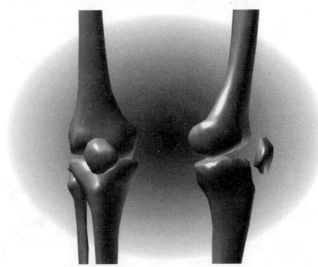

Figure 3-13: The "south" end of the femur forms part of the knee joint.

Tibias & Fibulas Forever

There are two bones in the calf, the *tibia* and the *fibula*. The tibia forms the knee joint with the femur, while the fibula is shorter. The knee is a hinge joint between the two bones, with the knee cap floating over it for protection, as shown in Figure 3-13.

The tibia-fibula combination allows very little rotation along the longitudinal axis. For animation purposes, it can be fairly thought of as a straight, simple rod with a hinge joint at the top and a complex ball joint at the lower end.

Sweet Feet

The lower ends of the tibia and fibula meet the feet in a complex system of small bones composed of three groups, the *tarsals*, the *metatarsals*, and the *phalanges*, as shown in Figure 3-14. Perhaps the third most common error in 3D human animation is treating the 26 bones of the feet as a single boxlike unit. The result is clumping, Frankenstein feet. The feet are a highly flexible and complex part of the human anatomy, and when they aren't constructed right or move incorrectly, it's really obvious.

Perhaps the third most common error in 3D human animation is treating the 26 bones of the feet as a single boxlike unit. The result is clumping, Frankenstein feet.

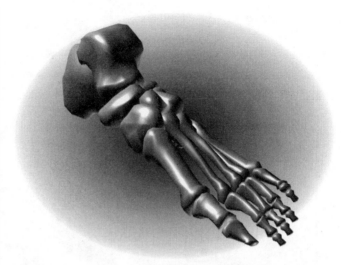

Figure 3-14: There are 26 bones in each foot, but many animators cheat by reducing this count to one!

Tarsals

The tarsals are the seven irregularly shaped bones in the ankle. They interlock to form movement support systems for the foot. In combination, they allow the foot to rock back and forth, tilt somewhat in and out, and rotate around the leg's long axis.

Metatarsals

The five metatarsals run parallel to each other and converge slightly toward the heel. They join with the ankle at the back and the toes on the front. The heads of the metatarsals are the ball of the foot.

The arrangement of the metatarsals creates the arch of the foot. The fifth metatarsal along the outside of the foot lies in the ground plane. The remaining metatarsals are positioned progressively higher in the foot, raising the first metatarsal the highest.

Phalanges

The 14 phalanges create the toes. Each toe has 3, except the big toe, which has only 2. The toes help provide balance and also aid in propulsion; as the foot bends, the toes do also to help propel the body forward. The toes are less flexible than the fingers, of course, but they do have some limited movement. You can see this when you stand on tiptoe—your toes spread out against the floor.

Yet another common error in animating the human form is failing to notice that the feet are not straight from front to back. They typically point outward a bit, even while walking. There's also a slight outward bend at the ankle to compensate for the femur ball angle. If there was no compensation, the sole of the foot wouldn't rest flat on the floor.

A Hand Out

There are 27 bones in the hand and wrist, as shown in Figure 3-15. In the wrist are 8 irregularly shaped bones called the *carpals*. The palm of the hand is made up of 5 long, slender bones with rounded ends called *metacarpals*. Finally, the fingers and thumb are made up of 14 short bones with the squared off ends called *phalanges*.

> Yet another common error in animating the human form is failing to notice that the feet are not straight from front to back. They typically point outward a bit, even while walking.

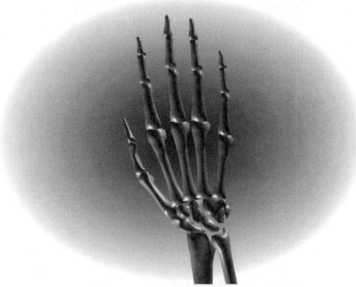

Figure 3-15: The hand and foot are constructed similarly. There are 27 bones in each hand.

Carpals

The carpals in the wrist fit together with each other, the metacarpals, and the forearm bones like a jigsaw puzzle. The joint at the base of the thumb has the most mobility, but there is also some mobility at the base of the fifth metacarpal (the little finger) and the *hamate* bone in the wrist. The rest of the wrist bones allow very little or no movement.

Metacarpals

The metacarpals make up the palm area of the hand. The four metacarpals directly under the four fingers of the hand cannot be separated or moved from each other. Only the first metacarpal under the thumb can be moved separately.

Phalanges

The phalanges make up the fingers. There are three bones in each finger and two in the thumb. They get a little smaller and more tapered as they get closer to the fingertips. The shapes of these bones influence the shapes of the fingers significantly. The phalanges allow no side-to-side movement, but the joints between the metacarpals in the palm and the first phalanges in the fingers do allow some side-to-side movement over the rounded edges of the metacarpals.

Of All the Gin Joints

Bones are connected to each other by joints that make the body flexible. There are three basic categories of joints: immovable joints, slightly movable joints, and freely movable joints. It's important to understand each type of joint in order to reproduce their action accurately. Of course, immovable joints are the easiest to reproduce—they don't move at all! The other types of joints require careful examination in order to understand their limits and flexibility.

Immovable Joints

Immovable joints like the plates of the skull, or the breast bone and the first ribs, protect vital organs such as the brain or heart.

Slightly Movable Joints

Slightly movable joints are like the discs of cartilage between the vertebrae. Even though these joints are classified as only slightly movable, the bend and arch of the spine is vital for fluid movement.

Freely Movable Joints

Freely movable joints include a number of different types that account for most of the mobility in the body. Table 3-1 summarizes the different kinds of freely movable joints. If you ever want to attempt character animation, it's important that you understand where each type of joint is found and its limitations; this table can help. There won't be a test at the end of this chapter, however.

It's important that you understand where each type of joint is found and its limitations.

Type of Joint	Example	Comments
Sliding joints	Wrists and ankles	Held in place by surrounding ligaments.
Hinge joints	Elbows and knees	Bend on one axis only; no rotation.
Saddle joints	Thumb at the wrist	Allow free movement.
Pivot joints	Elbow	Two bones moving within a ring.
Ball and socket joints	Hips and shoulders	Maximum movement.
Condyloid joints	First row of knuckles on the hand	Like ball and socket but no rotation.
Ellipsoid joints	Wrist	Modified ball and socket; contact surfaces are elliptical.

Table 3-1: Freely movable joints.

Each joint has a specific range that in many cases varies with age, physical conditioning, and disease. Such limitations are not usually built into 3D animation software, and that means that the animator must define the parameters of every joint—that is, how it moves and its range of motion.

Muscles & More

There are some basic formulas that describe the average human male and female body. They're just averages, but they are a good starting point when you are developing a character.

The first step is to understand how the body is measured. Usually, the human form is measured in head lengths, abbreviated HL. The average adult human is 7½ to 8 HL tall. Thus, the head size of a 3D character should always determine the length of the body, although the animator must also take into account the race, age, or physical deformity of the subject.

Some Obvious but Important Observations

Consider the differences between the sexes. Beyond the more obvious differences, men are usually taller, have wider shoulders, narrower hips, and tend to have more body muscle than women. Women tend to be smaller in stature with wider hips, narrower shoulders, and a smoother, rounder appearance.

I know, I know, you know this man or this woman who violates all of these descriptions. Of course there are such people, but I'm talking here about the norm, the typical, the average. As with any average, there are always variations toward the extremes of the bell curve.

Here are some more simple, *typical* measurements that are not only useful, but fascinating, to throw around on e-mail (the modern equivalent to the water cooler):

- Male shoulders are two HL wide; female shoulders are two head *widths* (HW) wide.

- Male hips are two HW wide, female hips 2½ HW wide.

- The typical shorter female height is usually the result of shorter thighs (up to ½ HL shorter); the upper arm is also shorter (up to ⅓ HL).

- With arms down, the elbow is usually located just above the waist, while the wrist is at crotch level.

- The head and torso constitute one-half the length of the entire body.

- The hand in the longest dimension is the same length as the chin to the middle of the forehead.

- The foot is the same length as the forearm measured from inside the elbow to the wrist.

- The head is five eye widths wide.

Muscling In (& Out)

The muscles surround the skeleton and internal organs and provide the means to stabilize, locate, and move the body. Muscle itself is made up of elastic fibers that contract and extend, while their ends are attached to bones with tough ligaments.

Most joints are stabilized by at least a pair of muscles that locate the mobile parts and hold them in position. When a nerve impulse instructs the joint to move, one or more of the muscles contract, while the opposite muscles extend. All of this muscular activity is visible through the skin, particularly in those with little body fat, like Ah-nolt in his prime. It's also much more apparent in a typical man than a typical woman, because of the additional fat layer between the woman's skin and muscles.

Face Facts

Whereas some of the muscles in the head and neck are typical in their action, others share a singular distinction: the facial muscles are the only muscles in the body that don't stabilize a skeletal joint. The facial muscles have one end attached to part of the skull, while the other end is attached to the skin, either directly or through another muscle. When a facial muscle contracts, it moves skin, not bone. When a facial muscle contracts, the skin is typically pulled back and bulges and wrinkles appear. It's this combination of bulges and wrinkles that we recognize as facial expressions.

It's the infinite number of ways in which facial wrinkles and bulges can combine that produce the astounding variety in facial appearance. No two people smile in quite the same way, frown the same, or make any two expressions precisely alike. Each person has a unique combination of musculature, skin, skeleton, and, yes, fat that produces a distinctive appearance. When a baby coos at a mother's smile, he's responding to a specific combination of wrinkles and bulges produced by his mother's muscles, skin, and fat. Nice thought, huh?

TIP

When designing or animating humanoids, 3D animators should keep facial anatomy in mind. To create two different characters, it's not enough to change just the skin tone!

There are still many more similarities than differences between faces: two eyes, two ears, one nose, one mouth, all placed in approximately the same arrangement. From this, artists and anatomists have been able to generalize about feature placement, as shown in Figure 3-16.

The first guideline is the vertical midline; it runs around the head vertically, down the centerline of the nose from crown to chin. The horizontal midline is located halfway between the crown and chin; this is the eyeline. Don't make the mistake of placing the eyes too high up on the head; they're really at the vertical midpoint!

The eyes don't lay in a straight line along the eyeline. This is one of the common errors made by non-artists. The inside corners of the eyes are on the eyeline, but the outside corners usually lie a little above the eyeline. The eyes are a distance equivalent to one eye length apart. The width of a normally opened eye is usually one-half its length, and the width of the iris is approximately one-third of the total eye width.

Don't make the mistake of placing the eyes too high up on the head.

The eyes don't lay in a straight line along the eyeline. This is one of the most common errors made by non-artists.

Make sure that you allow enough fore-head or your 3D character will resemble Tarzan's ape buddy.

The final two guidelines divide the face from hairline to chin into thirds. Locate the hairline in a normal, pre-male-pattern baldness position. Divide the region between the hairline and the chin into thirds. The top third is the forehead ending at the browline. Make sure that you allow enough forehead or your 3D character will resemble Tarzan's ape buddy. The nose begins at the browline and ends at the next line, the base of the nose. The distance from the inside corner of the eye to the top of the side nostril on the nose should be one eye length.

The ears lie between the top of the eye and the base of the nose. Finally, the mouth is below the nose (!) and no wider than the area between the center lines of the eyes. There's a wide natural variation in mouths, no pun intended, but it's also very easy to err.

There's a wide natural variation in mouths, no pun intended, but it's also very easy to err.

From the base of the nose to the bottom of the lower lip is a distance of one eye length. When the mouth is in repose or smiling, this measurement remains the same. In a laugh or yell with the mouth open, this distance naturally changes.

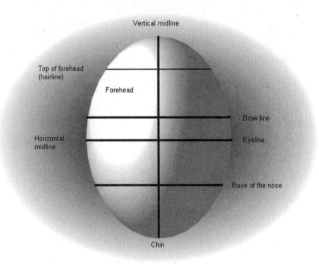

Figure 3-16: The face divided.

Much of the basic shape of the face comes from the skull. In many areas the outline of the skull is the outline of the face, as shown in Figure 3-17.

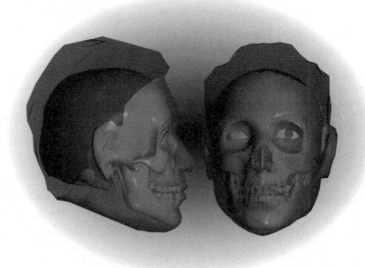

Figure 3-17: Although this might seem like an X Files image, it illustrates how much of the shape of the face is the result of the shape of the skull.

Head Cases

The head and face are the most difficult parts of the body to create realistically in 3D (or in clay or on paper for that matter). From the moment we're born, we see faces and learn quickly react to expressions. We soon know to look first to the face to try to detect attitude, mood, or intent. If a 3D re-creation is inaccurate, we know instantly that something's wrong, even if we can't identify exactly what's wrong. See Figure 3-18 for an example of a well-done face.

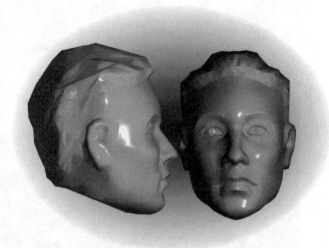

Figure 3-18: The head as it should look in 3D in profile and face on.

Depending upon how you define them, there are 26 muscles in the face used for expression, more or less, and most of those muscles are attached to the eyes, brows, or mouth. This high degree of fine muscle control naturally results in these three areas being the most expressive areas of the face.

The Eyes Have It

The eyes are probably the most intriguing facial feature. They convey a great deal of information and emotion. Even a bandit's bandanna covering two-thirds of his face still can't conceal what's revealed by the eyes. And marketers know that the eyes draw attention; that's why the models in advertisements look out at you.

Eyes are not symmetrical, as you can see in Figure 3-19. The peak of the upper eyelid does not line up vertically with the lowest point in the curve of the lower eyelid. As a result, the open eye is not a simple oval. The upper eyelid is more arched and appears to come down over the lower eyelid on the outside corner.

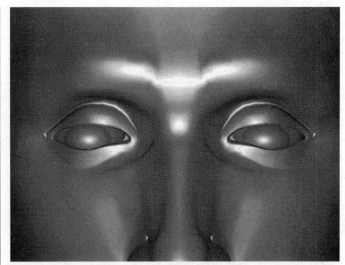

Figure 3-19: The lower eyelid is not a mirror image of the upper.

When the eye closes, it may look like the upper eyelid does all the work, but it can't move without *some* movement of the bottom eyelid. It is true that the lower eyelid has a much smaller range of movement than the upper. At rest, the lower eyelid usually just touches the lower edge of the iris and seldom moves below this position except in wide-eyed surprise or fear. Squinting (which accompanies bright lights or other ocular irritants), crying, or laughing, however, raises the lower eyelid far enough to cover part of the pupil.

In the typical alert, awake expression, the upper eyelid is just above the pupil, although this rest position can actually be anywhere from the top of the iris to just above the pupil. Interestingly, each eye has a characteristic rest position and always returns to it, so adjusting this can be another distinguishing factor when creating two 3D characters. By the way, if the upper eyelid touches the pupil at all, the appearance of alertness seems to disappear.

Where the eyeballs are "pointed" gives observers clues to the focal point. Everyone has been in a conversation and suddenly realized that the person you were talking to was no longer paying attention. What was your clue? Probably that the person's eyes had changed their focus from parts of your face to some distant point over your shoulder. We are very sensitive to interpreting such tiny changes. When the eyes look straight ahead, we interpret it as focusing at a distance, since closer focus always results in the two eyes turning inward, as shown in Figure 3-20.

Figure 3-20: Of these two audience members, which one isn't paying any attention to you? (And do they sell gum on TV in their spare time?)

Such a Mouth!

Twelve muscles are connected to the mouth, but only seven are involved in expression. Since the lips and surrounding mouth tissues are attached to the skull only indirectly, they have great freedom of motion and let us form many different expressions.

The lips define the mouth and can take an infinite combination of shapes: thin upper lip and thick lower lip, two thin lips, two thick lips, and so on. Perhaps no feminine feature has been so manipulated in this country than the lips. Almost every possible shape and color has been popular from bee-sting to collagen-injected, as shown in Figure 3-21. Changing the shape of the lips is a good way to create distinctive faces.

Figure 3-21: Lips come in all shapes and proportions.

We sometimes associate personality traits with lip shapes; thin-lipped people are thought of as mean, full-lipped people are emotional, accessible, and so forth. Consider this as a way to suggest personality through structure.

Neck, Anyone?

Necks seem to be always overlooked, especially by 3D animators. The neck is most often visualized as a cylindrical tube that is perfectly vertical; this isn't quite accurate. From the side, the neck cants forward, moving the face out in front of the body, as shown in Figure 3-22. This tilt is usually more pronounced in a woman than in a man, because of the greater degree of musculature in the man's neck.

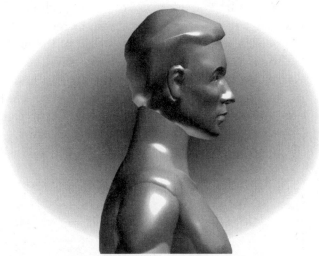

Figure 3-22: The neck cants forward, placing the face in front of the body.

From the front, the sides of the neck are not straight; the lines taper toward the head and vary substantially depending upon body type and sex. The female neck is usually more slender and graceful than the male neck.

Every Little Movement

With this quick overview of human anatomy in mind, let's turn now to the subject of human movement. We'll move through it rather quickly, again focusing on the aspects most important to 3D modelers and animators.

The Gravity of It All

The body maintains a delicate balance so that it can stand or move without falling. To maintain this equilibrium, a body—or an egg or building, for that matter—must maintain its center of gravity over its line of support at all times. In a standing human body, the center of gravity must be positioned over the feet.

If you look at an image of a body, whether it's a photograph, screen capture of a 3D program, or rendered 3D image, visualize a vertical straight line from the pit of the neck downward, as shown in Figure 3-23. If the body is in a resting position (that is, standing comfortably on both feet), this line of gravity should end between the feet. If the line does not end there, then the body is shifted in some way and is either in motion in the direction of the top of the line or about to fall right over.

Figure 3-23: The line of gravity runs from the pit of the neck down. A standing figure should have this line end between the feet.

Bend the body forward at the waist, as shown in Figure 3-24. In order to remain standing, either the feet must move or the legs must bend to shift the weight.

Figure 3-24: Bend one's figure at the waist and the weight must shift to compensate for it.

Body Language

Subtle facial changes alone can't communicate all our moods and feelings. Body language completes the set of visual cues. For example, slumped shoulders may indicate sadness, while an aggressive forward-lunging posture can signal anger.

The instinctive reaction to horror is to raise the hands to the face, while shyness usually results in a head-down posture with shuffling feet and hands clasped behind the back.

These subtleties of movement can help make or break a 3D project. They can also become crutches, with animators relying on stereotyped movements to carry the messages, because subtle movement is so much harder to do.

Moving in Arcs

Remember that the whole body is connected by movable joints— it's not fused into an immobile chain. It moves and turns, twists and bends in motion. Sometimes the movements are subtle and may be difficult to capture in 3D, but if they aren't there, the robotic appearance is a dead giveaway that it's not a real person.

Nothing on the human body moves in straight lines; rather, it moves in arcs. Think of the arm moving. It's composed essentially of two rods linked together and pivoted at their ends. It must move in arcs.

A simple step involves the feet, ankles, legs, arms, hands, hips, shoulders, back, and head! Not so simple! Even a simple turn of the head can be a complex matter. The head tilts down slightly as it turns, the eyes close as the turn begins, then open again, looking in the direction the head is turning. Watch someone turning his head next time!

Walking & Running

In a walk, one foot is always on the ground to maintain support and balance. The body weight shifts from one foot to the other, and there is a period where both feet are on the ground at the same time as the weight is transferred from one foot to the other.

Running uses the same basic movements as walking, but there is no period where both feet are on the ground or even a period where both are *off* the ground. Running is an unbalanced act, as the runner's weight is carried ahead of the feet. A runner must bring one foot in front of the last or fall down.

Moving On

Enough biology already! In this chapter, we explored the current focus on human character animation and how it's just a symptom of the age-old human quality of egocentrism. We delved into the difficulties of reproducing human movement accurately and then went under the skin to study the skeleton and muscles. Finally, we looked at human proportions, body language, and motion.

In the next chapter, we'll leave the body behind and pursue the arts. There is a great deal that 3D artists can learn from other branches of the arts. Every art form, from painting to cartooning to drama to video, contributes to the common language and body of techniques that make 3D a means to communicate and entertain. *This* will be fun!

Learning From Other Media

We now turn our attention to the traditional forms of art and entertainment that were the precursors of computer-generated imagery. These include painting, sculpture, motion pictures and video, cartooning, and the stage. (Yes, the art of pioneer animator Tex Avery is right up there with Michaelangelo—in this book, at least!)

For years—centuries—there has been cross-pollination among the media, as each borrowed techniques and concepts from the others. For example, use of pools of light that hid some details in deep shadow while brilliantly illuminating other areas was given the name *chiaroscuro* when the technique was first popularized in the paintings of Caravaggio and Rembrandt. Rembrandt's 1640 work, *The Holy Family*, shown in Figure 4-1, typifies chiaroscuro. Chiaroscuro lighting has since been borrowed by professional photographers and cinematographers, so much so that it's even sometimes called *Rembrandt lighting*.

Figure 4-1: Many of the works of Rembrandt Harmenszoon van Rijn were characterized by pools of light in large fields of dark shadow. This lighting technique has been borrowed by everyone, including Jimmy Durante!

In the end, all of this borrowing (also sometimes referred to fatuously as *my inspiration* or *returning to the seminal concepts*) has resulted in a widely accepted collection of concepts and techniques that have been applied throughout the arts and media.

Together, these concepts and techniques form a language that is available to artists to let them speak economically to their viewers, patrons, or customers. It's a form of shorthand that conveys facts or emotions in the most economical manner possible. (It's interesting to note that it's the artists who shun the conventional language of their art that seem to produce the most evocative and controversial works. Robert Mapplethorpe, Pablo Picasso, and Igor Stravinsky—to name but three—all shunned the artistic orthodoxy of their days and generated intense public and critical reaction to their work by so doing.)

In this chapter, we'll examine what makes up the visual language of 20th century Western culture by relating it to some of its diverse origins. Note that I'm not talking here about the technical aspects of moving CGI *to* other media. This is neither the time nor the place for learning about the differences between frame and field rendering, for example. I'm talking here about what the 3D computer artist can learn *from* other media. Call it the artistic input rather than the computer output.

Once again, I must caution you that I can't provide an exhaustive analysis of each of these topics. Entire libraries and industries are built around each of them. What I will do, however, is relate significant aspects of each of these media to the subject at hand: 3D imagery.

Sources & Inspirations

Great computer imaging borrows—or should borrow, anyway—from all preexisting media. It can be a powerful synthesis of the never-before-possible with the familiar, or devolve into the merely incomprehensible. Here are some of the areas from which CGI artists can learn:

- *From photography*: camera nomenclature, lens definitions, and concepts such as motion blur.

- *From film and video*: film's own language, shot selection and organization, and image framing.

- *From classic two-dimensional artistic media like painting*: composition, lighting, and color.

- *From classic three-dimensional artistic media like sculpture*: the understanding of viewpoints and the use of skeletons.

- *From cartoon animation*: exaggeration, anticipation, squash and stretch, and timing.

- *From the stage*: lighting for effect.

Let's plunge in first to the world of photography—a relatively recent development, but one with strong connections to the world of CGI.

Photography

The art and science of photography developed in the 19th century. It's all based on the fact that some silver compounds darken when exposed to light. That's it; that's the source of it all—one minor property of obscure chemical compounds. When this compound is bonded to a flat surface and exposed to the proper amount of light, an image is recorded that can later be developed and preserved using chemical processing. (Get that roll of film to the drugstore! Let's see how Aunt Myrtle's facelift pictures came out!)

Modern cameras are complex mechanisms containing beautifully ground glass lenses, tiny whirring motors, and unobtrusive but powerful computer chips. For our purposes, however, we can reduce everything to the lens that gathers and focuses light onto the film, the film itself, the *aperture* that controls how much light reaches the film, and the *shutter* that controls how long the film is exposed to the light—the *shutter speed*. These are the aspects that translate into 3D.

Photography & Digital Cameras

As I mentioned in a sidebar in Chapter 1, the current crop of digital still cameras are merely a variation on the photographic theme. They use a lens to gather light and focus it on a photoreceptive surface and a mechanical or electronic shutter to control when and for how long light is admitted into the camera or accepted by the receptors. The principal difference between a digital still camera and a traditional film camera is in the nature of this surface and how the image is stored and viewed thereafter.

In a film camera, exposure to light causes the film to react chemically. The film is kept in a light-tight canister until it's *developed*. In developing, the chemical changes are transformed into a visible image and treated to preserve them. If the film is a positive (a slide), the image can be viewed immediately. If it's a negative (with colors and tones reversed), another step is necessary: printing the image so that it can be viewed.

In the digital camera, an array of light-reactive electronic devices takes the place of the photosensitive film. The light image is converted by these devices into a series of electrical signals that are processed into storable data and held in some form of digital memory in the camera. To see them, you either "pipe" them to a computer or viewer via a cable or look at them on the camera's own viewing device, typically some sort of mini-TV.

A digital camera is a close 90s analog of a classic film camera with the exception I discussed in the first chapter: if image processing that distorts the data takes place before the image is first stored, then the similarity fails. For the purposes of this chapter, however, consider the two types of cameras the same. (However, if you want to feel more up-to-date, you may chant *an array of charge-coupled devices* under your breath wherever the text reads *film!*)

Light, Motion & Depth of Field

The shutter and aperture are two components of one equation:

$$\frac{\text{aperture}}{\text{area}} \quad \times \quad \frac{\text{exposure}}{\text{time}} \quad = \quad \frac{\text{total light striking}}{\text{the film}}$$

The aperture opens and closes like the iris of the eye, controlling the total area through which light can pass. The shutter controls how long the film is exposed to light passing through the aperture. To increase the light on the film, you can either increase the aperture opening to allow more light to enter or leave the aperture untouched and extend the exposure time. If you want to decrease the light on the film, you can do the opposite. (Digital cameras can also use an electronic shutter with no moving parts; rather than controlling how much light enters the camera, it controls how long and when the photoreceptors react to the light.)

The end result is that for every combination of camera, film, lens, and light, there are an infinite number of combinations of shutter speed and aperture that can produce an image on the film. You can open the aperture wide and crank the shutter speed up or close down the aperture and slow down the shutter to compensate. This range lets you tailor each image to reflect whatever you find significant in the scene.

For example, a bicyclist moving through a verdant park might be the most significant part of the scene to one photographer but be insignificant to another. The second might see instead an artistic composition of willows, a pond, and children at play in a sandbox… and incidentally a bike on a path. In Figure 4-2, several joggers are reflected in a foreground lake; this photographer chose the composition you see, but another would have chosen something quite different. Each would have chosen a particular combination of camera, film, lens, lighting, *and shutter speed and aperture.*

Figure 4-2: The joggers may be the most important part of this image to one photographer, while the overall tranquil composition was the drawing card for another.

Even if both used the same camera equipment and film, the two photographers would undoubtedly use different shutter speeds and apertures. Here's why.

Speed Bumps

As described, our park scene was generally static with a single moving object, the bicyclist. (The slow-moving kids in the sandbox don't count.) The first photographer—the action guy— would perhaps want to take a picture that captured the contrast between the fast-moving biker and the placid park. He would probably use a relatively slow shutter speed so that the biker would blur in the picture. This type of photo "defect" is known as *motion blur*. It occurs whenever the subject is moving faster than the camera can follow.

TIP

If the feeling of speed is what you want, use a slow shutter speed, don't follow the subject with the camera, and let the subject's motion blur its image. Keep this tip in mind, for it's equally applicable to 3D.

Motion blur has become so accepted in film and television that computer animators have had to add it to otherwise crystal-clear images in order to "sell" speed to the audience, as shown in Figure 4-3. (To see how to add motion blur artificially in computer graphics imagery, see Chapter 6.)

Figure 4-3: In Figure 4-3a, the saucer in the foreground is moving against a still background; only it displays motion blur. In Figure 4-3b, both the foreground saucer and the camera are moving; everything in the scene is blurred by the motion, but the foreground saucer is more blurred because of the combined motion of the camera and saucer.

That Telltale Too-Sharp Motion

When motion blur should be present but isn't, it's noticeable. For example, in 1963, special effects master Ray Harryhausen created a classic fight between stop-action skeletons and a live human crew for the movie, *Jason and the Argonauts*. It took Harryhausen and his crew more than four months to create the scene, but there was no digital imagery available to add motion blur to the moving swords.

The swords of Jason's crew blur because they were filmed live, but the skeletons' swords are crystal clear. It's a small defect in a great sequence, but it's conspicuous by its absence.

To prevent blur, you have two choices, depending upon the effect you want. If you move the camera—pan—at the same speed as the subject, it freezes the subject but blurs everything else, as shown in Figure 4-4. If you increase the shutter speed until it's faster than the subject's movement, everything's frozen except, of course, things moving even faster than your subject.

Figure 4-4: This image of a skier is a classic example of panning the camera with a (relatively) fast-moving skier to freeze him in crisp, clear visibility while the background blurs behind him.

Aperture & Depth of Field

Remember that in order to maintain the light level on the film, you must *increase* the aperture as you *decrease* the time the shutter is open. In other words, the higher the shutter speed, the larger the aperture must be. The aperture is usually measured in *f numbers*, which are actually fractions comparing the size of the aperture to the size of the lens. For example, an aperture of f16 produces an aperture that is one-sixteenth the size of the lens. Each decrease in f number (or *f-stop*) doubles the amount of light passing through. There is another effect of changing the aperture, however.

Without getting too technical, as the aperture increases (a lower f-stop), the *depth-of-field* decreases. Depth of field is the zone of a photograph that is in focus. It's measured from the camera out to the horizon. Anything outside this zone will be blurred to a greater or lesser extent, depending upon how far outside the zone it is.

Except in high-end programs like Softimage I 3D, depth of field is not explicitly adjustable in most 3D programs. It's a real fact of life in photography, however. When combining computer graphics imagery with photographed images, you must match the depth of field of the film or ruin the illusion. Notice in Figure 4-5 how the computer-generated rhinoceroses match the depth of field of the live-action shot.

Coordinating the aperture and shutter speed requires a delicate balance that must be struck for every photo. There's still another factor, however, that each of our photographers would consider: the focal length of the lens.

> Except in high-end programs like Softimage|3D, depth of field is not explicitly adjustable in most 3D programs.

Focal Length

The focal length of a lens describes one aspect of the design and construction of a lens. You'll seldom use this information directly, but it does determine several other aspects that are important to you: depth of field, magnification, and field of view. All other things being equal, a long (higher value) focal length lens will have a greater depth of field and higher magnification and a narrower field of view than one with a shorter focal length (lower value).

Figure 4-5: In this commercial by created Metrolight Studios, CGI rhinos chase a Mercedes-Benz sedan. Note the careful matching of depth of field to produce a seamless image.

Focal length is usually measured in millimeters, abbreviated *mm*. For a typical 35mm camera, a standard lens that reproduces human vision has a focal length of approximately 50mm. (The 35mm in this case refers to the image width on the film itself.) Anything above that is called a *telephoto* lens with magnification and depth of field above human norms and a reduced angle of view. If you've used a good set of binoculars, you've experienced these effects. You'd see that bird in the tree really, *really* clearly if you could only bring him within the narrow viewing angle of the binoculars.

Anything with a focal length less than the standard lens is called a *wide-angle* lens. It has lower magnification than the human eye, a reduced depth of field, and an increased viewing angle—hence the wide-angle name. Extreme wide-angle lenses can have a field of view approaching 180 degrees, producing a bubble or "fisheye" effect familiar to any reader of *Life*.

Lens focal length is, in part, a function of film size, so lenses for 35mm cameras differ in focal length, type for type, from those for, say, 2-1/4x2-1/4 or 70mm movie cameras. (A 2-1/4x2-1/4 camera produces a film image that is 2-1/4 inches on a side, while a 70mm movie camera produces an image twice as wide as a 35mm camera.) Focal lengths for 35mm cameras have become fairly standardized with a 50mm lens being the norm, but for a 2-1/4x2-1/4 camera, a 90mm lens is a normal lens. For 35mm cameras, 28mm and 35mm lenses are moderate wide-angle; 14mm and below are extreme wide-angle or fisheye lenses. At the other end of the scale, an 85mm lens is a mild telephoto that's excellent for portraiture. Above that are 100mm, 200mm, 400mm, 800mm, and even 1600mm lenses. The longer lenses are best used by nature or sports photographers, or detectives working on nasty domestic cases.

You may wonder what all this has to do with your career in 3D. Some 3D software uses standard 35mm camera lens sizes to define the equivalent simulated lenses. Knowing the equivalent lens size can help you achieve the look you want. Lenses on either side of normal distort images in different ways. Wide-angle lenses exaggerate the perspective, while telephoto lenses enlarge the subject in the frame and foreshorten the depth of field, compressing the apparent visual depth. It's these effects that are most evident; changes in depth of field are less so. In Figure 4-6a, two cubes on a picnic table are viewed through a 50mm lens. Note that there is no foreshortening and no depth-of-field effect apparent. In the second view, Figure 4-6b, the same cubes are shot through a 200mm lens from the same camera position. The depth of field is quite foreshortened in this image, and the cubes are not only enlarged, but seem to be right next to each other.

The third image, Figure 4-6c, illustrates the scene through an extreme wide-angle lens of 10mm. Note the wide field of view and the foreshortening of the cubes. (Note also that there is no depth-of-field effect.) Finally, the fourth image, Figure 4-6d, is through the same 10mm lens, but the camera is moved much closer to the cubes (*dollied in*—see the section on camera moves below); the foreshortening and distortion are apparent.

Figure 4-6: Four images of two cubes on a picnic table. The first is through a normal lens, the second through a 200mm lens and the last two through a 10mm lens. In the final image, the camera has been moved closer to the cubes to accentuate the distortion. Note that there is no depth-of-field effect in any of these camera simulations.

Film & Video

There's a strong symbiotic bond between film and video on the one hand and computer-generated imagery on the other. Much of the most astounding and remarkable work done in CGI has been done for these media. So it's no surprise that the CGI industry must borrow back from film and video their techniques and vocabulary.

A movie is composed of scenes; each scene is a dollop of plot that takes place at a specific time and place. In order to understand what's happening in each scene, the viewer must first understand where and when the scene takes place, who's there, any special conditions, and so on. In usual movie practice, a *master shot* is shown at the start of each scene. That's an overall camera shot that shows where everything is taking place. It's also called an *establishing shot*.

Think of how boring a movie would be if every scene began with an establishing shot. In order to catch and keep the viewers' interest, directors and editors sometimes intersperse scenes that begin with one or more interesting camera angles and subjects, then cut to the master shot to establish the context of the first shots.

On the other hand, if *every* scene began with an intriguing tight close-up of, say, a shadowed face with a teardrop hanging from one eyelid, a maggoty chest wound, or a sled named Rosebud, while it might not be boring, it would definitely be confusing. The master shot is there for a reason; moviemakers and animators alike shouldn't cavalierly abuse the shot order out of boredom or a misguided attempt to be particularly creative.

Camera Shots

In the shorthand of moviemaking, most other shots also have names. Some are used to describe camera angles and perspectives, while others are used almost like placeholders in scripts. The camera angles are also used to describe animation shots, as well as establish a common vocabulary for filmakers and animators.

Who Rules the Cinema Roost?

A script goes through several drafts, beginning with that first act of blissful creation by the screenwriter. By custom, the writer (that godly creature) must limit his description of camera angles and shots so that the director (the *ultimate* cinema god) can impose his own artistic sense on the production. (OK, OK, I admit a certain prejudice in favor of writers.)

Scene descriptions like "Angle on" and "Another angle" subordinate the screenwriter's own vision of how each shot should look to that of the director. These scene descriptions also help to break up long scenes and make the script more readable.

In Table 4-1, I've listed a number of shot names and descriptions with some indication of their typical uses.

Shot name	Meaning/Use
Angle on	A script placeholder that specifies the focus of the shot without directing camera location, angle, and so on.
Another angle	Like angle on, a shot of the same subject as the previous scene, but from a different angle. Used to provide visual interest and break up the script text.
Reverse angle	From a camera position exactly 180 degrees opposite the previous shot. Used to connect the actor with the action.
Close-on or Close-up (CU)	The subject matter fills the frame or dominates the image. Used to bring the attention in on one subject.
Extreme close-up (XCU)	The subject matter is viewed even tighter than in a close-up. For example, a close-up of a person might frame her face, cutting off her hair; an extreme close-up might show only her eyes. Screams at the viewer: "Look at this!"
Two shot	Two people in the shot. See Figure 4-7. Helps to establish relationship, position, and so forth.
Three shot	Three people in the shot. Like the two shot— a general shot that can be intercut with close-ups of each of the three.
Group shot	A group of people—more than three—in the shot.
Medium shot	Further back than a close-up, not as distant as a long shot. Typically a shot that includes the waist to the hat.
Long shot (LS)	A shot from a distance. A man on a horse.
Extreme long shot (XLS)	From far, far back. The man, the horse, and the mountain.

Figure 4-7: A two shot is of, well, two people, shot fairly tight, from the bust up: the soap opera standard shot.

Shot name	Meaning/Use
Aerial shot	Shot from above, typically from an aircraft or crane. A dramatic shot that is more than a master shot.
Point-of-view (POV)	From the eyeball viewpoint of one of the characters—what the character sees. Usually, the character whose viewpoint we're seeing is not in the shot, but be sure to watch *Lady in the Lake* (1947, MGM), in which the entire movie was filmed in POV. The character's hands and arms appear, as does the character himself in a mirror.
Reverse POV	The exact reverse angle of a POV shot. Usually used in conjunction with a POV shot, first to show what the character is seeing, then the character's reaction.

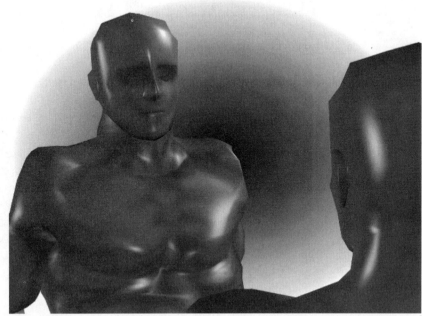

Figure 4-8: An over-the-shoulder shot helps viewers maintain the context of the scene.

Shot name	Meaning/Use
Over the shoulder	As if you're looking over the shoulder of a character. Often used to establish and maintain the context during a conversation. See Figure 4-8.
Reaction shot	Shot of characters or bystanders to show their reactions to an event. It's that horrified look when the T-Rex appears.
Zoom	A moving shot in which the field of view and the focal length of the camera change over time. Sometimes used to move from a master shot to a character shot, or vice versa.
Tracking shot	Moving shot that follows a moving subject or character through a scene, usually with a dolly. It can also be used to denote a shot that moves toward or away from a stationary subject. ➡

Shot name	Meaning/Use
Follow shot	Another name for a tracking shot, but not necessarily using a dolly. Keeps the focus on the subject.
Into view	A new subject is revealed by a moving camera. "The moving camera reveals…"
Into frame	A subject moves into a shot from offscreen. Adds a character without changing the previous shot.
Insert	Close-up, typically of an object, used to focus attention on a specific subject.
Montage	A series of shots are shown to build a mood or provide background. Typical are the "time passing" shots of calendar pages interspersed with leaves falling, and so on.
Split screen	Two images from different locations are merged into a single image onscreen. Long used to show both ends of a telephone conversation. See *When Harry Met Sally* (Castle Rock, 1989), where two simultaneous conversations are shown in split screen.
Pause or beat	A script term used to add a slight pause to control timing.
Freeze frame	A single frame is repeated, freezing the action. See the end sequences of the *Police Squad* television series for hilarious take-offs on freeze-frame endings.
Slow motion (slo-mo)	The camera speed during filming is increased above the normal rate, so that when the film is projected at a normal speed, the action is slowed down. Popular in *Disney True Life Adventures* and *Monday Night Football*.
Super (or extreme) slow motion	The same as slow motion, only more so. Good for *Straw Dogs* death scenes.

Shot name	Meaning/Use
Super	Image or text superimposed over (in front of) a shot or sequence. Most often used for credits.
Stock shot	Footage from the studio vaults, typically newsreel or other previously shot footage to provide background. Used to establish the time and place or to provide a context; also occasionally used as fill on low-budget productions.

Table 4-1: *An animator need not reinvent the wheel—moviemakers have already designed and named these camera shots to make communication easy.*

Storyboards & Scripts

The same shot concepts are directly applicable to 3D animation production. Remember, an animation production goes through most of the same processes that a movie does—although the food isn't as good. Both movie and animation productions begin with a script that is rewritten, honed, polished, reworked, and repolished until it meets the needs of the production. Quite often, an artist works along with the artistic team to provide visual aids that illustrate each shot and scene. These drawings are called *storyboards* and are especially important in action and special effects shots.

Once a script has been approved for production, it's then recast as a *shooting script*, in which a number is assigned to each scene. The team can then organize the production efficiently, including budgets, locations, catering, craft services, special effects, postproduction, and so on. This shooting script (subject always to further rewrites either on the set or overnight during shooting) becomes the bible for the production company.

Slating a Shot

The scene number and other pertinent data like the director, cameraman, and so on are displayed on a slate in front of the camera before and after each scene. This lets the film editor identify the scene later from the confusion of film that's almost always shot out of order.

Either a chalkboard or electronic slate is used to slate a shot. The chalkboard slate is shown upright at the start of a scene and inverted at the end. Video slates linked to the camera in a video production can show not only the scene information, but also the SMPTE (Society of Motion Picture and Television Engineers) time code from the tape itself for the start and end of a scene. This makes video editing much easier.

A well-designed 2D/3D animation production follows the same process. A writer writes the story. (A story? Yes, a story! 3D is more than just neat effects.) From there a team of artists, designers, animators, and writers collectively add visual details and modify the storyline, pacing, and so on as necessary until the script is final. Once again, storyboards are an essential part of the process. By the end of this process, the technical feasibility of all scenes has been blessed and the director and producer have agreed to the concept and direction of the project.

If it hasn't been done already, the script is now broken down into a shot list and the shots assigned to animators and teams. (I have not included the "dirty" work of budgeting, raising money , and so on in this "clean," artistic book.) It helps immensely if the animators doing the job—and everyone else involved in the artistic process—understand the concepts inherent in the camera shot descriptions in Table 4-1.

Camera Moves

In addition to the camera shots described in Table 4-1, camera movement also has a vocabulary all its own. Unless you want to emulate Andy Warhol or a Disney nature photographer sitting for days in front of a groundhog burrow, avoid a single long static viewpoint. Modern camera work takes advantage of every possible camera position and movement, using cranes, "helmet cams," Steadicams, dollies, handhelds, motion control, endoscopic cameras (for that *inside story*), and on and on.

These camera moves can all be duplicated in 3D animation software. The software packages that are easiest to use are those that duplicate the names for the movements, so that truck right, for example, can be accomplished without translation. In Table 4-2, I've listed all of the common camera move labels and how the camera moves. Once again, these are vital to understand if you're going into animation production.

Camera Direction	Movement
Pan left/right	Horizontal rotation of the camera about its vertical axis without any dolly movement.
Truck left/right	Linear horizontal movement. Perpendicular to the lens axis, usually done with a dolly or Steadicam®.
Dolly in/out Camera up/back Dolly up/back	Linear horizontal movement along the lens axis; the three sets of terms are interchangeable.
Tilt up/down	Vertical rotation of the camera about the horizontal axis parallel to the scene.
Tilt left/right (Bank)	Rotation of the camera about the lens axis.
Pedestal up/down	Vertical motion of the camera along the vertical axis.

Table 4-2: A camera shot specifies the subject, angle, and field-of-view, but a camera movement description tells how to move the camera during a shot.

Scene Transitions

The final piece of the scene puzzle involves how to move from one scene to the next. Camera shot descriptions describe the subject angle and field-of-view, and camera move descriptions tell how a camera moves within a scene. Scene transitions tell how to move from scene to scene.

In movies and television, most scene transitions are *cuts*; when one scene ends, another abruptly replaces it. This is the easiest transition to accomplish and usually the least distracting. Other transitions are designed to provide a specific effect, either softening the transition or achieving a special effect. In film production, these transitions must be added in postproduction, that period after all of the film has been shot, developed, and so on in which the finished product is assembled.

Most home video cameras, on the other hand, let the videographer fade up or down to a specified color. And video special effects generators (SEG) for home video are surprisingly inexpensive. In the hands of some, shall we say, less artistic amateurs, however, these cameras and SEGs can produce really horrendous results. Fading down to a brilliant red screen from a plebeian family picnic video is a surefire guarantee of audience bailout. Follow Reese's Rule of Graphics Restraint and you won't be banned from family picnics—at least not because of your video skills, that is.

Reese's Rule of Graphics Restraint

Just because you *can* do something graphically, that doesn't mean you *should!*

I don't care if you have 852 wonderful fonts on your hard drive, *don't* put them all on one page! And just because you can zoom a camcorder with the push of a button, pan a 3D camera as fast as your son can run, or tilt it 45 degrees "just like in the movies," *don't* do it in every scene!

Save the special effects for when they'll be special!

In Table 4-3, I've listed the most common scene transitions and their effects. Again, they translate well into 3D production.

Scene Transitions	Effect
Cut	An abrupt change from one scene to the next; where a fade takes place over a series of frames, a cut occurs from one frame to the next.
Fade in	The scene emerges gradually from a black or colored screen. Traditionally, all movie scripts begin with fade in and end with fade out, even if the movie doesn't.
Fade out	The reverse of a fade in; the current scene gradually darkens to black or to a solid color.
Crossfade	A slow fade from one scene to the next over a range of frames; it always involves at least one black frame between the two fades.
Dissolve	A slow fade from one scene to the next without the intervening black frame(s) of a crossfade.
Wipe	One scene pushes the preceding scene off the screen vertically, horizontally, in a spiral, or in some other manner.
Intercut	Where two different scenes occur simultaneously and form a single sequence, an intercut intersperses lines of action or events so that the parallel or contrast is apparent.
Match cut	A cut between two scenes that have the same object, scenery, or person in the same position; used to show passage of time or point up identity.

Table 4-3: Scene transitions tell the production crew how to get from one scene to the next. They're especially important for the editor.

Depending upon the destination of the 3D "footage," it's possible to accomplish many of these scene transitions within software. Again, the edit order must be known, and the animator must be confident in the exact transition point and the length of each scene. Still, it's handy to be able to accomplish cuts, fades, and wipes within 3D software. When the production has been nailed down, and all that is left is rendering, having an automatic postproduction facility in the computer can be a true luxury on long overnight renders.

Framing

Framing a 3D scene is just another aspect of visual composition, a subject that has been studied for centuries. (I'll take up composition a bit later in this chapter in the section on artistic media.) However, video, computer-viewed animation, and movies all present unique composition problems unknown to artists of antiquity. All involve:

- Screen-based presentations

- Moving media

- Multiple viewpoints

A screen, be it movie, computer monitor, or television, is nothing more than a means to view media within the *frame* of the screen's borders. The frame not only limits the extents of the image, it also creates psychological limits for the artist and his audience. An artist must not only keep his work within the frame, he must also keep the subject away from the borders or risk disturbing his audience.

The frame not only limits the extents of the image, it also creates psychological limits for the artist and his audience.

It's obvious that the subject must be *within* the frame or no communication takes place between artist and audience. Still, we humans are most comfortable with images that match our unspoken training in composition. We've all seen thousands of examples of print, television, movie, and computer images and have been trained to expect a certain balance and composition; when a new image varies from these expectations, we are uncomfortable at best.

The basic concepts of composition applied to print and still imagery are not new; they are centuries old. (The cave painters of prehistory also predated our accepted rules of composition; they apparently painted wherever they found a spot. Check out Sid Caesar in Mel Brooks's *History of the World Part I* as he presents an early critic's view of such untrained work.)

Artists from prehistory to the 19th century did not concern themselves with their models' movements. There was no way to preserve any movement, except to do as the cave artists did and paint multiple sets of legs to show running. Cinematographers and videographers, however, have had to develop their own rules to help maintain artistic balance and story continuity in a multiple-viewpoint presentation.

In these media, however, the term *composition* is replaced by *framing*, as each frame of film is a separate composition. For example, subjects move "into frame" and "out of frame."

Still artists not only can't capture movement, they also can't capture different viewpoints of the same scene simultaneously. Once a still artist chooses a vantage point, that's the end of it. But the director of a movie or video presentation changes shots as necessary to keep his audience interested, to focus their attention where he wants, and to convey emotion.

How Long Is a Shot?

Typically, a movie or television shot lasts no more than *eight* seconds! Establishing shots tend to be slightly longer, particularly with complex camera moves.

Few camera shots, however, are as long as the 8-minute tracking shot at the opening of Robert Altman's movie, *The Player*. During this lengthy (and some have said self-indulgent) shot, actor Fred Ward is even heard complaining of the "cut, cut, cut" mentality of today's movies and yearning for the tracking shot that opens Orson Welles's *Touch of Evil*! That shot was only 6½ minutes!

Good framing is just as important to the 3D artist as it is to the cinematographer or videographer. It focuses the audience on the action and helps provide visual transitions into and out of scenes. Bad framing jars the viewers and distracts them from the subject.

Every image should be framed properly, whether it's still or moving. Most of the rules that follow apply to both still and moving images, but they all apply to 3D. Here are some rules that can make framing easier:

- Keep the subject within the frame. Basic, yes, but essential!

- Give 3D characters "look space." In other words, if a character is looking toward the side of the frame, allow more room on the side he's looking, as shown in Figure 4-9.

> *Good framing ... focuses the audience on the action and helps provide visual transitions into and out of scenes. Bad framing jars the viewers and distracts them from the subject.*

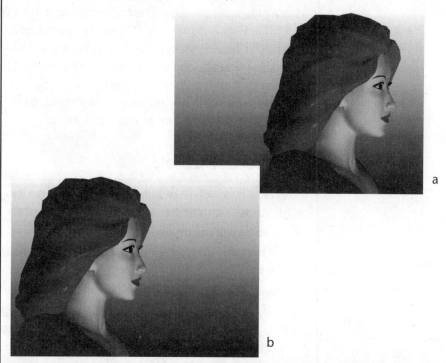

a

b

Figure 4-9: Look space is an important but subtle concept. Always give your characters a bit of room to look in order to keep the viewer's attention within the frame. The image in Figure 4-9a fails to allow look space, while the image in Figure 4-9b allows it.

- Don't shoot into the ear or up the nose of your characters.

- Always anticipate movement with the 3D camera so that a moving subject moves *into* the frame, rather than out of it. Again, this keeps the viewer's attention within the frame. Figure 4-10 illustrates this principle.

a

b

Figure 4-10: Movement should be into the frame as in Figure 4-10a, rather than out of it, as in Figure 4-10b. If necessary, pan ahead of the subject to keep ahead of the movement.

- Try to keep the camera position within a 180-degree arc around the subject, as shown in Figure 4-11. Constant reversals of viewpoint confuse viewers.

Figure 4-11: Follow the 180-degree rule. Keep the camera within a 180-degree arc around the subject matter.

- Avoid unnecessary camera movement and bizarre camera angles. If you can tell the story without the camera work distracting the viewer, so much the better.

- Keep your pans and zooms slow and seldom…unless you really want to make your viewers sick, that is.

- Maintain a human-height viewpoint unless you deliberately choose another to achieve a special effect. The "bullet's-eye view" or "arrowhead's view" is good about once in a 90-minute feature film. But when used for a reason, a different viewpoint can be effective; the low viewpoint of Steven Speilberg's *E.T. The Extra-Terrestrial* conveyed the child's—and E.T.'s—view of the difficult adult world.

If it's not obvious by now, I strongly believe that 3D artists must study movies and moviemaking to be good at their own craft. Even if you're thousands of miles from Hollywood, you can still learn a lot from a laser disk player playing a CAV disk (the kind you can freeze-frame) with a director's narration.

Artistic Media

The first part of art is always observation; the second, inspiration; and the third, technique.

Painters and sculptors have been working at their arts since the first caveman picked up an odd rock and thought, "This looks just like the woolly mammoth that chased Og." The first part of art is always observation; the second, inspiration; and the third, technique.

From the ancient visual arts we can learn much that is of use in 3D art. Although a great deal of time is spent by any 3D artist in just mastering the unusual tools, still more is expended in the effort to reproduce the results of "real" artists and sculptors, that is, those who work with chalk, oil, clay, bronze, and so on.

A fine arts background is, in fact, preferred by many computer graphics houses. It's easier, they say, to teach artists to use a computer than it is to teach art to computer technicians. But if you don't have training in fine arts, you can compensate by spending still more of your free time—when you're not watching movies critically or studying anatomy—looking at art. There's so much to learn from the masters!

Painting

Painting is the closest historical antecedent to our modern visual, electronic art. The lessons from painting, therefore, translate most directly to 3D. In particular, I'll touch here on composition, lighting and color, and form.

Matisse on Composition

"Composition is the art of arranging in a decorative manner the various elements at the painter's disposal for the expression of his feelings."

Composition

The concept of composition as a conscious element in painting was first posited by Leon Battista Alberti in 1435. To Alberti and his Italian Renaissance contemporaries, mathematics itself was divine, and its application to art was a natural extension of God's creation. (Tell *that* to the next graphics programmer you see in the office eating pizza in his shorts at 2 A.M.!)

In the last 500+ years, artists and others have studied composition and derived a number of principles. Here are some that are most applicable to 3D:

- Center the subject for most impact. If the focus of the work is pushed over against the frame, the viewer's eyes must search for it.

- Be conscious of the shape of the medium when planning a 3D scene. In old Italy, this may have meant checking the shape of the canvas; in our electronic media, it means being aware of the relative size and shape of TV, computer, and movie screens, as in Figure 4-12. The television screen, like the old standard theatrical movie, has a width-to-height ratio of 4:3, whereas most theatrical movies are released in a 1.85:1 format. In Europe, 1.66:1 is the standard, whereas such wide-screen formats as CinemaScope and Panavision use ratios of 2.00:1 to 2.55:1. High Definition Television (HDTV) is slated to use a 16:9 ratio.

- Symmetry, where subjects are evenly distributed on either side of center, produces a sense of balance and harmony. Asymmetric, or unbalanced, composition can subtly disturb the viewer; at the least, it is more dynamic than symmetrical. The two examples in Figure 4-13 illustrate the differences.

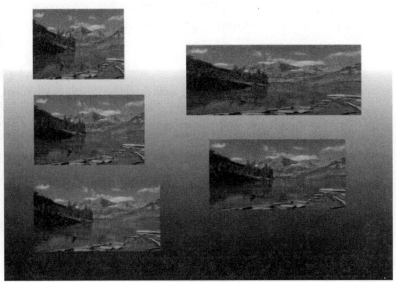

Figure 4-12: In these image formats, the TV or computer screen is at the top left. Below it is the European standard and below that is the U.S. theatrical standard. On the right are two wide-screen formats of 2.55:1 and 2.0:1.

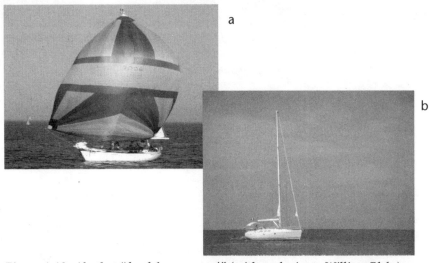

Figure 4-13: Ah, that "fearful symmetry!" (with apologies to William Blake). Balanced compositions, as in Figure 4-13a, are harmonious and static, while unbalanced compositions, as in Figure 4-13b, are dynamic and stimulating.

- Lead the eye toward the subject. Bright colors or contrast attract the eye and geometric shapes can direct it where desired. Figure 4-14 is a simple composition that should lead your eye to the text at the apex of the triangle.

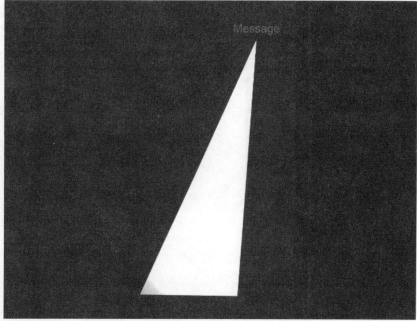

Figure 4-14: The bright white triangle attracts your eye, while its shape directs it toward the upper right. An old advertising principle suggests that the message should be at the apex of the triangle, not stuck down at the bottom.

- Use the diagonals to produce a feeling of depth and drama, as in Figure 4-15.

- Choose the perspective and horizon judiciously. Remember E.T.

Figure 4-15: Emphasize the diagonal to add drama to a composition and increase the sense of depth in an image. Note the strong diagonals that draw you into the scene and give a feeling of depth.

Light & Color

The judicious selection of colors and use of lighting values can add immeasurably (and subtly) to a 3D composition. Basic color principles apply just as much to 3D as to any other medium. Here are some basic principles that will assist you—and for more detail, be sure to review *Looking Good in Color* by Gary W. Priester from—who else?—Ventana Press.

- Yellows, reds, and oranges—warm colors—seem to advance toward the viewer, while blues and greens—cool colors—seem to recede.

- Colors can stimulate moods. Warm colors tend to produce happy, "up" feelings, while cool colors can be either restful and serene or gloomy and sad.

- There is a common association between color and good/evil that survives despite well-meaning protests from racial groups. For example, western heroes wore white hats or rode white horses, while the villains were black attired and mounted. Perhaps this association had its origin in the fact that humans learned very early to fear the dark places where carnivores lurked. When man became spiritual, the dark was thus naturally associated with fearful and evil things. As a 3D artist, you can use these associations to create positive or negative responses in your viewers.

Shape & Form

We all have natural responses to shape and form in humans, buildings, and everything else. Most people react more positively to attractive people than to those whose shape or features differ from the ideal. (Note that the ideal differs widely from culture to culture and race to race. If you are creating an image or product for worldwide distribution, be very conscious of these issues.)

Think of cultural stereotypes and you'll have a pretty good handle on how to shape your human characters to suggest particular qualities. Typical stereotypes of form and features include:

- Exceptionally muscular men and very shapely women are stupid. A cartoon superhero like The Tick is a classic example of the first, while Marilyn Monroe was often cast in roles that matched the second.

- Slight, bespectacled men are intelligent but cowardly. Wally Cox made a career of playing this character over and over.

- Teenagers with bizarre clothing, haircuts, or tattoos are druggies.

- Effeminate men are gay and masculine women are lesbian—but no one else.

Stereotypes are not fair and are a classic instance of prejudice, but you can use your knowledge of them to create surprising characters who play against their stereotypes.

Form and mass in architecture can also be used to stimulate an automatic response. A building can be graceful or ugly, inspire piety or disgust. I'll leave it to you to decide which response the building in Figure 4-16 inspires. While in the middle ages important architecture was built to glorify God, today most architecture is designed for efficiency, not spirituality. The natural result is cubic and plain; profitable, of course, but homely.

Stereotypes are not fair and are a classic instance of prejudice, but you can use your knowledge of them to create surprising characters who play against their stereotypes.

Figure 4-16: Most—too many—modern buildings tend toward the functional with little consideration for the esthetic.

Where a sculptor's work is viewed from all vantage points, the 3D artist delivers his work on a flat screen in two dimensions and thus controls the viewer's vantage point like a painter does.

When designing anything in 3D, be it machinery as set dressing, a vehicle, or an alien, consider first the response you want from your audience. Then scale and shape the objects or characters to match. For example, massive, oversized machinery or furniture that dwarfs the hero adds an element of desperation to his plight.

Sculpture

Working in 3D is similar in some ways to sculpting clay. Your fingernails stay much cleaner, of course, but the elements of 3D design are quite similar.

Like a sculptor, the 3D computer artist works with three-dimensional shapes and forms. But where a sculptor's work is viewed from all vantage points, the 3D artist delivers his work on a flat screen in two dimensions and thus controls the viewer's vantage point like a painter does.

Honesty in 3D

Sculpture is much more honest than 3D modeling. What the sculptor creates, the world sees with all its flaws. If the composition or balance is off, that can't be hidden. But because the vantage point is controlled by the 3D artist, he can "cheat" by hiding design or construction flaws. He can even stimulate a desired response in his audience by forcing an exaggerated viewpoint. The sculptor has little of this control available.

Not only does the 3D artist have incredible control, but the entire 3D process is itself one of simulation. Where the sculptor works in wood or clay, the 3D artist works in mathematical models with the surface visual characteristics of wood or clay illuminated by simulated light.

A 3D sculptor has much more control over the appearance of the materials and can change them in seconds. To move from stone to bronze in the real world is a Herculean task. Examine the two "sculptures" in the "museum" in Figure 4-17. They differ only in their material; it took less than ten seconds to change the marble to bronze.

Figure 4-17: Two sculptures in a museum share the same form, but differ in materials. It took less than ten seconds to change from marble to bronze.

Most programs let you move around a project while modeling in 3D, just as you would move about a sculpture in the studio. This is vital, because you must view your model from all of the potential angles to see it as the audience will. Sculptors use a turntable to do this on small projects; some 3D programs, like Softimage I 3D, actually use the term *turntable* for an interface device that serves the same purpose.

Another aspect of sculpture that has migrated to 3D is the use of armatures. An armature is used in sculpting as a skeleton on which to hang the clay or other soft compound. Bending the armature reshapes the clay. In 3D character animation, a jointed skeleton can be used like an armature to control a skin object. The skin can be defined mathematically in any number of ways, but the result is the same: the skin is deformed as the skeleton is moved. Figure 4-18 shows a 3D skeleton within a transparent mesh object of a baby.

Figure 4-18: Within the transparent mesh body of the dancing baby is a skeleton, called a Biped. This is part of a character animation system called Character Studio that runs within 3D Studio MAX.

Cartoon Animation

Animation can be used for anything from a simulation of genetic coding to toilet bowl cleaner commercials—think of Scrubbing Bubbles. Some of the best animation ever done, however, was done in the great cartoon studios under the direction of such masters as Walt Disney or Chuck Jones. Think of Mickey Mouse, Elmer Fudd, Bugs Bunny, Tigger, Marvin the Martian—the list of memorable characters goes on and on.

Cartoon animators developed a number of techniques that are—or can be—carried over to 3D animation. The joy that was at the core of the best cartoons was hard to capture in 2D; it's currently very difficult in 3D. In 3D, just re-creating real life has been so difficult that animators didn't even attempt to convey emotion. Some of the best work has been done under the direction of Pixar's John Lasseter. In *Luxo, Jr.*, he was able to imbue a pair of Luxo desk lamps with personalities and feelings.

Cartoon animation uses a number of techniques to convey emotion and stimulate response that are helpful in 3D. Although a good text on cartooning is valuable (and formal training even more so), I'll touch on several of the most common.

Exaggeration

Nothing is ever lifelike in cartoon animation. Whether it's a cartoon wolf ogling a woman in a Tex Avery classic or a rooster picking up his feathers for reattachment, exaggeration is the universal constant. Exaggeration can not only be funny, it also helps ensure that the audience gets the point. A weight falling on the head of a hapless victim is not just 200 pounds, it's *ten tons*. And he's not just bloodied, he's *flattened*. That's exaggeration.

Exaggeration has no place, of course, in factual animation. You would not be likely to have elective knee surgery if your doctor showed you an animation that suggested potential pain by having the knee throb to four times its size. But there is almost always a place in entertainment 3D for exaggeration. All of the animated elements in *Jumanji*, for example, were exaggerated, from huge, rapacious mosquitoes to vines that covered the walls in seconds. And the ultimate live-action/3D exaggeration was created by Industrial Light & Magic and Jim Carrey in *The Mask*.

Timing

There are several different aspects of cartoon timing that translate well to 3D. The basic subtleties of comedic timing are unteachable in print, but may I once again suggest that you watch others—this time, funny people. The late Jack Benny had perhaps the finest sense of timing in comedy. He seemed to know just when to pause and when to deliver a line or reaction. Watch old Jack Benny movies, and if you can find videotapes of his old CBS television series, you'll learn a lot.

Remember these principles:

- A gag is composed of a number of elements. First, you must *lead into* a gag or joke; that is, set it up and prepare the audience for what's coming. For example, Wiley E. Coyote must first take the time to set up his Acme-brand shoe rockets so that he can pursue the Roadrunner at supersonic speed. Then comes *the gag* as Wiley catches the bird in a cloud of dust, just as his rockets give out. As the dust slowly clears, we see the gag—he's once again suspended in mid-air, hovering unknowingly. Finally comes *a take* (comic reaction), as Wiley looks down, realizes his plight, and reacts with dismay. Then comes *the resolution* as he waves briefly and then plummets to the canyon floor with a distant puff of dust.

- Gag timing is not linear. Once Wiley has hit the canyon floor, there's a few seconds while he prepares his next attack, and we can prepare to be amused again. Remember to space the gags so that they don't collide with each other. It's terrible to be in the audience of a hilarious movie with gag after gag after gag, only to miss half because you or the audience is still laughing at the previous gag.

Squash & Stretch

An element of comic exaggeration is when something hits a hard surface, it doesn't just deform, it squashes like rubber and then *maybe* rebounds. A beanbag deforms but doesn't rebound; there's nothing funny in that! A rubber ball deforms and then rebounds—it can be a funny gag if done well.

A rubber ball can rebound because it stores much of the energy it absorbs in the fall and impact by deforming in such a way that its total volume doesn't change significantly. In 3D, this is simulated by squash and stretch, a scaling technique that preserves the total volume when an object is deformed. In Figure 4-19, both spheres are deformed by squashing along their vertical axes by 70 percent. The left sphere, however, has its volume reduced, while the right sphere was deformed using squash and stretch. As its vertical axis was scaled down by 30 percent, it was scaled up along its horizontal axes by the same 30 percent. Note the difference.

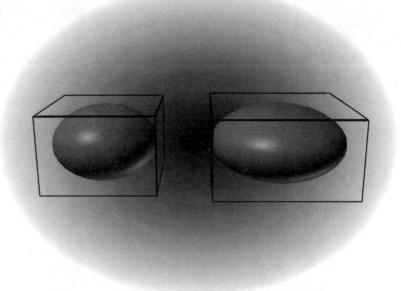

Figure 4-19: Both spheres were reduced in height by 70 percent, but the right sphere had its horizontal axes enlarged to compensate so that its volume remained constant. This is the principle behind squash and stretch.

The Stage

Before there were movies and television, there was the stage, drama, the *theater, dahling*. As a 3D modeler and animator, you can learn many things from the stage. Stage presentations are like movies and TV in that they are usually intended to be viewed from a single collective viewpoint (not including theater in the round, of course). Moreover, the principles of lighting developed in the theater are still widely used throughout movies and TV.

The *key light* provides general illumination from overhead, the *back light* helps to separate the subject from the background, and the *fill light*, low in front, helps to dispel any shadows on the actors' faces caused by the other lights.

Generally, there are three light sources used to illuminate a subject, as in Figure 4-20. The *key light* provides general illumination from overhead, the *back light* helps to separate the subject from the background, and the *fill light*, low in front, helps to dispel any shadows on the actors' faces caused by the other lights. This classic three-light technique is used everywhere, although special situations call for special techniques.

Figure 4-20: The classic three-light setup with key, back, and fill lights.

Sometimes the entire focus of the audience must be on a single actor. The answer is to darken the stage and use a single *follow spot* that follows the actor wherever he goes. Most good 3D programs let you link a spotlight to an object so that it focuses on the object (or actor) wherever it goes.

On other occasions, it might be necessary to simulate the look of moonlight coming through a window with a tree in silhouette. In the theater, a cutout of the desired silhouette, called a *gobo*, is fixed in front of a spotlight to cast the tree's shadow. Good 3D programs also let you link an image to a spotlight and work the same magic, as in Figure 4-21.

a

b

Figure 4-21: The image in Figure 4-21a acts as a gobo, casting a tree-shaped shadow in the scene in Figure 4-21b. This technique is a great mood enhancer.

Moving On

In this chapter, the last in Part 1, we examined entertainment and the arts and gleaned a few important concepts that are useful in 3D. We reviewed important concepts from photography, movies and television, cartoon animation, painting and sculpture, and the stage. By now, you should have a pretty good background that will prepare you for the real work that comes next in Part 2. In Chapter 5, we will look at the production process and review some of the equipment decisions that will confront you when you're *Doing the 3D Dance*.

The Practical Side of 3D

Congratulations, you've graduated from 3D Prep—you've read Chapters 1–4—and now you're ready to learn about working in 3D. In this chapter, I'll take you through some of the practicalities of the business, including the phases in a 3D production and some of the hardware you'll need. This chapter is a look at creating 3D images and animations from a different perspective, a step back from the theoretical material that's come before.

By now I'm sure that you realize that 3D is not only complex by itself, but is also the product of many complex, intertwined decisions that are made during a project's creation. For example, the hardware you have often determines the software you can use and the types of projects you can tackle. In turn, the projects you take on determine the nature of the creative process itself. A single still image can be created on one lonely computer in your back room or basement and output via the Internet to the client.

Almost at the other end of the spectrum from the single image is film effects work where perhaps a hundred shots must seamlessly blend with live action. You will need literally *hundreds* of high-powered computers, dozens of even higher-powered animators, and sophisticated film scanners and imaging equipment to compete with the big boys in this field.

Even above film effects work in terms of hardware requirements and technical sophistication is the field of scientific visualization of extremely complex data like DNA or nuclear research. For this, you need supercomputers with enormous storage and number-crunching ability and scientists with enough knowledge, ability, and education to even understand the results of the work.

In between these polar extremes are graphics houses that produce industrial animations, smaller effects pieces—in general, more sophisticated still and animated imaging than can be done by one person with one computer. Many focus on serving clients in a single field requiring special expertise, such as forensic animation or medical imaging, while other service bureaus work throughout much of the 3D imaging spectrum.

One of the factors that differentiates one type of 3D imaging from another is whether it is based in *reality* or *fantasy*. Although there are fields that must keep one foot in reality and the other in fantasy, such as advertising or film effects, most are either technically or artistically oriented. This dichotomy affects substantial portions of the production process, as we'll see.

Reality vs. Fantasy

In a reality-based production, special care must be taken to ensure that everything in the 3D environment is as accurate as you can make it.

I've harped over and over in this book about reality; what it is and how what you see on the screen may or may not be reality. In production, the dichotomy between reality and fantasy is more apparent. It guides the production processes down one of two paths.

In a reality-based production (that is, one that purports to display the real world as it is or was), special care must be taken to ensure that everything in the 3D environment is as accurate as you can make it. Environments, sets, objects, and characters must be modeled after the original counterparts, and the movements must be reality based.

In a fantasy-based production, the sky's the limit.

In a fantasy-based production, the sky's the limit. Everything is up for grabs, even the physics of the world in which the production is set. Characters needn't be humans or even humanoid—bubble people living in a plasma palace are probably easier to create and animate than recognizable human characters. In this fantasy world, viewers won't know what to expect at the beginning, and almost anything you do would be OK. Once you set up your world with its physics and behavioral ground rules, you must stick with them, of course, or risk disturbing or disappointing your viewers.

Movie effects, advertising, some video game simulations, and even some upcoming television game shows are a combination of 3D imagery with real world objects, settings, actors, or some combination of the three. The broad creative freedom usually associated with the fantasy side of 3D is limited by the strict needs of the combined production.

Production Phases

All creative human endeavors require careful planning for success and the production of 3D imagery is certainly no different. Animated velociraptors and space hero toys don't just happen—they're the products of long hours of planning and hard work, not to mention genius. To be able to plan a 3D production yourself, of course, you first must understand its phases. A typical 3D animated production includes these phases:

- Concept
- Story
- Storyboards
- Modeling
- Animation
- Rendering
- Laying off
- Postproduction

A typical 3D still production includes these phases:

- Concept
- Layout
- Modeling
- Rendering
- Image Output

In both kinds of productions, milestones must be established and approval loops must be set up to ensure that all parties understand who is to do what, when it's to be done, what the standards are to judge whether it is done correctly, and when payment is due for the work.

Concept

Every 3D production begins with an idea, a concept. In the entertainment realm, it might be:

- A great story line from a book.

- An idea induced by too many Jolt colas.

- Something weird suggested by a new capability or effect in a 3D program.

- Or even a type of game that the designers *really* wanted to try.

Then there are the ideas that come into the production group from outside:

- A movie company needs a particular special effect or maybe even wants to try 3D dinosaurs to complement the practical effects already scheduled. (This is the *Jurassic Park* scenario.)

- An edict may come down from marketing that "3D games are hot this year—we need one to compete."

- Or "Look at Joe Blow Games's racing simulation. We could do it better ourselves in 3D!"

- And in the realm of fantasy-reality (a new term that I've just coined—also known as advertising), a company wants to use 3D to dramatize the special benefits of a new toothbrush design.

On the real world side, the work may tend to be less exhilarating, perhaps because the ideas tend to come more from the business types than the creative ones:

- A trial lawyer may be facing a tough case with complex evidence that needs a creative solution.

- An aircraft company needs to come up with a way to show all of the maintenance shops around the world how to reassemble an airliner's landing gear properly.

- A real estate construction firm wants to show off their proposed new development, complete with houses, landscaping, and furnishings, in order to secure the investment capital it needs.

- A research scientist wants to use 3D simulation to better understand the intricacies of his work.

- A civil engineer needs to produce an exhibit that will show the city council how a proposed new street alignment will affect the neighborhood.

All of these ideas can result in a 3D production that will entertain, enlighten, or sell, as the case may be. Keep your mind open to new ideas—you never know from where they might come. You might even find a whole new career in landing gear animations!

TIP

A *great* creative concept is wonderful, but even a *so-so* concept that has guaranteed funding attached may be better!

Financing a new 3D production is not the focus of this book, but it can be as creative a subject as any we'll touch upon here. Suffice it to say that as an animator, you shouldn't make an open-ended commitment to any project, fantasy or reality, unless it's so important to your business or career that you're willing to fund it all the way to bankruptcy!

Story

After the concept comes the story. If you're working in reality, the story is dictated by the facts, the evidence, the statements, the terrain—whatever you have to work with. If the project requires that you create a 3D golf course, you may start from 3D data of the area if it's available, or terrain maps if it's not.

Similarly, a forensic animator or medical illustrator must begin with the scientific and other factual data he's given and work from that. (That's not to say that there isn't a great deal of creativity in these fields—it just takes different forms.)

In the fantasy side of the business, after the concept is approved—or after your buddies agree that you've got a cool idea—the next step is to flesh it out, turn it into a story. This may be a collaborative process in which several team members swap ideas and come up with a plot that is doable with the technology available.

Even a still image can have a story; it's the so-called *backstory* that brings the subject(s) of the image into the present. For example, an image with two 3D toys might depict them realistically in a toy box, or they might be "living" toys with a history of animosity between them. How they're modeled, posed, shaded, and rendered depends on how they're to be depicted.

Technology & Planning

The cutting edge of computer graphics production always seems to rely on software that is experimental and barely stable. Competition in the graphics business forces designers to plan projects around the availability of developmental software or even software that's little more than a twinkle in an engineer's eye.

Cutting-edge graphics houses and high-end 3D software companies share a special confidential relationship. The software company lets the graphics house use new software that's still in development, and in return, the software company receives the artists' feedback, rigorous testing of the software under production conditions, and "boasting rights" when their projects are released.

This intimate relationship helps both parties, but software development snafus can seriously impact graphics production schedules. When coupled with the time required for artists to get up to speed with new features, working on the "bleeding edge" can make planning a painful thing.

The more complex the project, the more complete the script should be.

Depending upon the complexity of the story line and whether live action or voiced dialog is required, a full-fledged script might be required with dialog, scene descriptions, and so on. The more complex the project, the more complete the script should be. Even a "simple" '90s-style arcade game requires extensive planning to produce the animations that frame the action, define the characters' movement sets, and so on.

Storyboards or Layout

I discussed storyboards in the last chapter as a means of visual planning. They are also the basis for preparing a production schedule. The storyboards help the producer, director, artists, programmers, and technical personnel understand the precise scope and nature of a project.

Storyboards provide a visual reference during production.

Based upon the storyboards, the producer creates a master shot list of all of the shots required to complete a project and then assigns each shot to an artist with the time and expertise to complete the work. The storyboards provide a visual reference during production for the camera shots, moves, and scene transitions. This lets artists located in widely disparate locations prepare graphics that will eventually be melded together into a single seamless project.

A 3D artist working on a still image generally works from a layout, a sketch that depicts the subject of the shot, the arrangement of the surrounding text, if any, video framing, and so on.

Approval Loop

The approval loop describes when and how work must be submitted for approval.

Seldom is an animator the sole judge of his work. Whether it's an outside client, the boss, or a director, someone usually has the right to approve or disapprove an animator's work. The approval loop describes when and how work must be submitted, by whom, and who must give the approval. (To make your lawyer happy, you should also attempt to spell out in the contract what the criteria for approval are. Make sure that there are as few grounds for future misunderstandings as possible.)

Production of a 3D project is not a trivial task. It requires days, weeks, or longer to complete. If all of the work that goes into a 3D project had to stand or fall based upon a single approval at the very end of the production, all of the work would be at risk. Thus, most agreements call for specific deliverables at specific dates with approval requirements that protect both parties.

The client/boss/director has an early chance to see the work and make changes before it's impractical. The graphics side is protected against late and unreasonable disapprovals, like "Sorry, I just think that the hero should be a little taller and have a green shirt." Or "Whoops! Looks like we gave you the wrong data last month. We sure can't use *this* animation!" Also, deliverables can be used to trigger progress payments, so that neither party is carrying the entire cost of the project from the start.

Pay Me Now, Pay Me Later

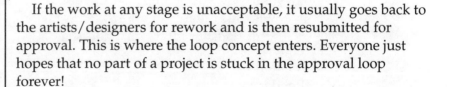

Typical progress payment points include:

- Concept

- Story/script

- Storyboards or preliminary design sketches

- Models

- Render tests

- Preliminary renders (low-resolution and/or low-color depth)

- Final renders

If the work at any stage is unacceptable, it usually goes back to the artists/designers for rework and is then resubmitted for approval. This is where the loop concept enters. Everyone just hopes that no part of a project is stuck in the approval loop forever!

The other side of the approval loop coin is where the client must provide data to the graphics house or artist so that the work can commence. Every agreement for reality-based 3D work must include a deadline for data submission. If it passes without the submission, all milestones should be readjusted, or the graphics house must be able to cancel the contract.

Modeling

The tasks involved in 3D generally can be divided into modeling, animation, materials, and character design and animation. Modeling is the phase that involves creating the objects and sets that will fill and decorate the 3D world. It can include the actors, the scenery, the text, whatever the production requires. It's something like cabinet-making by computer. It requires vision, precision, and an understanding of the future needs of the production.

Some 3D artists just seem to be good at modeling and less expert at writing shaders or animation. They are the natural choice for scene design and set decoration (all of the bits and pieces that dress up a set).

Some graphics houses use one tool for modeling, a second for animation, and a third for rendering. Industrial Light & Magic (ILM) traditionally has used Alias | Wavefront PowerAnimator for modeling, Softimage | 3D for animation, and RenderMan for rendering. Mind you, this is not an inexpensive combination, but with ILM's track record in commercial and film special effects, support is readily available.

Graphics houses without the track record and economic and artistic clout of ILM must usually make do with a single 3D package, or two if the budget supports it. Currently, the battle seems to be between Alias | Wavefront for high-end modeling and 3D Studio MAX (Windows NT), Electric Image (MacOS), and Lightwave 3D (Windows NT and MacOS) for mid-price work.

The same software is often used for animation and rendering as well as modeling, but Softimage | 3D seems to have the lead in high-end character animation. For ray-traced rendering, MentalRay from Softimage has the reputation as the best non-RenderMan output.

There are a number of low-end packages on both the Macintosh and Windows NT/95 platforms. While some are better than others for particular tasks, they are generally too limited for heavy-duty production work.

CD-ROM

On the CD-ROM, you'll find a variety of products tailored for particular 3D applications. Try them out and get a feel for how they work and what you can do with each. Keep on the lookout for reviews of 3D software in reputable magazines and on the Internet. I've included a number of references in Appendix B that will lead you to sources that can help you determine which low-end software is right for you.

If your budget allows, look for a product that is up-to-date and that allows expansion, either through an Applications Programming Interface (API) or Software Development Kit (SDK). Software developers that open their software to others for add-ons make it possible for you to buy a system that will grow with your needs.

As computer power increases, the more math-intensive forms of modeling become available at a lower and lower price. Mathematically defined surfaces like NURBs and metaballs (see Chapter 6 for discussions of both) have become available in addition to polygonal surfaces, even on mid-priced systems. This means more modeling power for the cost.

Smart modelers always keep libraries of objects they've built that can be reused in different ways.

Modeling always seems to take more time than you have allotted for it. Smart modelers always keep libraries of objects they've built that can be reused in different ways. For example, it would be very time consuming to create a detailed motorcycle, but once you've created one, you could use all of the interesting pieces to create variations of the single theme. This was one of the techniques used by LucasArts Games 3D modeler Richard Green when creating models for the game Full Throttle.

Think of a real-world use for 3D and the need for accuracy is obvious. Faithful adherence to accurate data is essential.

Modeling in reality-based projects requires the modeler to follow accurate drawings, data, or the actual objects or scene. Think of a use for 3D and the need for accuracy is obvious. Whether it's guilt or innocence, health or death, bridges standing or falling, roller coasters staying on the track or…well, you get the picture. Faithful adherence to accurate data is essential.

The Devil's in the Details

It's a funny thing about reality-based projects, but often their success or failure turns on the smallest detail. The roller coaster may have a grand, sweeping, breath-taking design, but if those rollers aren't quite the right size to keep the cars on the track, the great design isn't much good.

I've seen hundreds of court cases turn on the smallest details, often on things that are difficult to predict. That's one reason why forensic animation can be so painstaking. If a juror or judge fixates upon a single detail that is either inaccurate or missing from an animation, the party presenting that animation will probably lose the entire case.

Keep in mind not only the final *use* of the scene, but also the *position* of the rendered image within the scene.

Obtaining data for reality-based projects should be one of the prerequisites for taking on such a job. If a 3D artist must visit and measure a scene or site or laboriously re-create a murder weapon, the labor costs can be substantial. Factor this in when considering a reality-based project.

A final thought on modeling here is to keep in mind not only the final *use* of the scene, but also the *position* of the rendered image within the scene. If it's going to occupy just a few pixels of screen space off in the distance, all of the detail required for a foreground object is wasted.

Surfaces & Shading

In production terms, the more accurate you want a surface to be modeled and illuminated, the more expensive and time consuming it will be. At the bottom end of the scale is constant or flat shading of polygonal models. At the other end is ray-traced shading of parametrically defined surfaces with supplemental shaders for atmosphere, lens depth of field, and so on. In between are several types of polygonal shaders that have been widely adopted for their speed, relative simplicity, and availability.

Constant shading, as we learned in Chapter 2, applies a single color to an entire triangular or quadrangular face. The adjacent faces might or might not have the same color; if they do, the surface will appear smooth across the face between them. If two different colors are assigned to adjacent faces, the edge between them will be obvious.

The two most commonly used mathematical algorithms that allow a 3D renderer to shade across the straight edges between adjacent faces are both named after their inventors: *Gouraud* (pronounced *goo-roh'*) and *Phong*(pronounced *fong*). Gouraud shading is easier to compute and hence is faster than Phong, but Gouraud shading does not allow display of highlights. If you want highlights, then you must use Phong shading at a minimum. More accurate and time-consuming shading algorithms are available, such as radiosity and ray tracing, but Phong suffices for a surprisingly large proportion of everyday, mid-level 3D work.

Choosing a shading method is largely a matter of application. Where the end product will be composited with live film or video, the very highest quality shading at the very highest resolution must be employed. For fast smooth shading, such as in Internet applications, Gouraud is the current choice. For background objects, even flat might be acceptable.

Animation

As with modeling, animation is becoming a subspecialty of 3D graphics. A good animator, one who understands motion, timing, and the language of film, is quite valuable. Character animators are especially sought after, since the nuances of human movement are difficult to master.

Animation has become one of the more accessible parts of 3D. Animators now have available keyframe systems, skeletal control systems, and motion control that let animators create smooth, accurate, realistic motion with a minimum of work. (Again, character animation is the notable exception, although even that area has been vastly improved with footstep-controlled, semi-automatic animation systems for bipedal and multipedal creatures.)

Success in planning animation is largely the result of preparing good storyboards and following them. Usually, as work progresses on a project, other ideas, moves, or camera angles suggest themselves. The project evolves and changes, but the master script and storyboards still are the key.

The project evolves and changes, but the master script and storyboards still are the key.

Animation in reality-based projects is another instance where access to original, accurate data is essential. If the precise motion can't be determined or calculated, the value of the simulation is lessened. One of the hardest parts of forensic animation or accident reconstruction is recreating past events based upon either incomplete data, experts' conclusions, or witnesses' fallible memories.

Where the supporting data is fallible, the animator must protect himself against newly discovered evidence or changes in recollection. Near the beginning of my forensic animation career, I lost the final payment due me on a case because the agreement failed to address the issue of what happens when a witness changes his recollections. Don't make the same mistake if you take on this kind of work!

Rendering

Rendering is usually the most calculation-intensive part of the entire 3D process.

As you'll recall, rendering is the process of calculating and producing the final image or sequence from the model, shading, animation, and surface data. It is usually the most calculation-intensive part of the entire 3D process, because it's where all of the other parts come together.

Rendering is the last production step before laying off or other final output processes, and because it's at the end, all of the earlier production delays telescope the time available. This usually means rendering day and night, sending files off to be rendered elsewhere, adding more computers in-house, and using any other method that will add rendering capacity. It's crunch time where everything is on the line, whether the project is based on reality or fantasy.

In reality-based projects, last minute sometimes changes to *after* the last minute.

In reality-based projects, last minute sometimes changes to *after* the last minute. Forensic animators are familiar with the lawyer's call from the courthouse asking for changes to the animations based upon new evidence in the case. In almost every case, the answer is likely to be no because of the time required for rendering, laying off, and transfer to laser disk.

Typically, modeling, animation, and even simple shader or surface design can be done on relatively small computers. Of course, "relatively small" depends on the nature of the project; large projects still require large modeling stations.

Similarly, if a project requires that the artist build models or design animation over high-resolution video or film images, system requirements rise dramatically. Finally, complex shader or surface design usually uses many bitmaps to add visual detail; temporary storage space within the computer memory (a *buffer*) must be created for each. Proliferating buffers dramatically increases system requirements.

But it's in rendering that the demands are greatest. All of the techniques that add to the realism of a scene also add dramatically to the system requirements. Ray-tracing is a classic example of a computationally intensive rendering technique. In it, hypothetical light rays are followed (traced) from each point on an object through the scene back to each light, accounting for every reflection and refraction along the way. Even the description of the technique sounds burdensome!

To complete rendering of a lengthy project on schedule always seems to require just a bit more computer power than you have. You can add memory to a single computer, more computers, a partner in the rendering business, or in some cases more processors within a single system. I'll touch more on computer needs during rendering in the section on hardware, but suffice to say that you need ever more memory, more speed, and more storage.

The solution to the need for more computing power has always been to add more computers. Network technology and animation software development have allowed graphics professionals to link together many computers devoted solely to rendering. It's called a *render farm*. I'll return to the rendering system numbers problems in the "Necessary Equipment" section.

Laying Off

Laying off is usually the final task (other than billing) for a graphics house after rendering an animation project. The term means sending a series of images or animations to the delivery medium. Typically, this means to videotape. Laying off a series of still images from a computer to videotape is a time-consuming process, since each image constitutes a single frame or field on tape.

The bottom line with both rendering and laying off is that *everything* takes longer and costs more than you planned. And don't forget that there is a direct correlation between money and speed, and that's not just true on four wheels!

Postproduction

Postproduction straddles rendering in some cases. It refers to all of the processing that is required to edit scenes together, add special visual effects, composite layers of images, add sound, music, sound effects, and so on. Some of this work can be done in the computer system at rendering, but depending upon the delivery medium, other work is best done in dedicated effects or editing systems.

Planning for postproduction requires the services of experts in editing and postproduction plus a thorough knowledge of the capabilities of a modern *post house* so that you can decide what is the most economical division of efforts between in- and out-of-house. Just keep in mind that post houses usually charge for use of an editing suite and effects system by the hour, and it's not cheap. If you need an editor or special effects person to run some of the equipment, that's extra.

The final indignity is that because you have "Incredible Cosmic Powers" in postproduction, it's so creatively seductive that you'll probably double your budgeted time. (Apologies to Robin Williams in *Aladdin*.) Postproduction can be a definite budget buster unless you plan your work carefully and exercise steely discipline.

The final indignity is that because you have "Incredible Cosmic Powers" in postproduction, it's so creatively seductive that you'll probably double your budgeted time!

Necessary Equipment

The usual rule-of-thumb in computer graphics is that you'll need at least twice the computing power you ever thought necessary.

As I explained in the section on production phases, 3D graphics requires all of the power you can muster, computationally speaking, that is. The usual rule-of-thumb in computer graphics is that you'll need at least twice the computing power you ever thought necessary, even in your worst nightmares!

There are a number of selections to be made in hardware. The most basic one is the processor and platform you choose. After that, you must concern yourself with input, output, storage, and display devices. All are important and will affect the kind of work you can do and the markets you can enter.

Numbers

Let's begin at the low end. With a one-computer shop, you use that single computer for modeling, animation, and rendering—but you can only do one of those tasks at a time. While you're at the office, you do your modeling and animation; then, when you're ready to leave for the day, you set up your system to do unattended rendering and leave.

You may wonder why you can't just use one of the powerful multitasking operating systems that can divide processor time between two concurrent tasks, like Windows NT or UNIX, and do the rendering in the background while you model or animate in the foreground. That sounds reasonable, except that rendering is such an all-consuming process that even as a background task, it drowns every other task on the computer. Either the foreground task—modeling or animation—is so slow as to be frustratingly unusable or the background task—rendering—doesn't get done.

Another potential solution that comes to mind is to add more RAM to the one computer you have. Adding RAM is a good solution in situations where rendering slows down because a computer must resort to using virtual memory, but it's not that helpful in other cases where you have enough RAM. The bottleneck in rendering is the millions upon millions of calculations that must be made by the processor for each image. Once you eliminate the virtual memory slowdown, the speed of the processor itself is the culprit.

Replacing a slow processor with a faster one can help significantly, especially if you can move from one generation of processor to the next. Advances in this area are coming so quickly that replacing a year-old processor with a new one will usually make a noticeable improvement. I don't care what the *minimum* requirements are for your software of choice, you should be near the leading edge of the power curve to be competitive in the 3D market. You don't need to be at the bleeding, leading edge—just near it.

The best single solution today is to add a second system as a rendering station. You won't need a big monitor, expensive keyboard, or any other ergonomic components, since it won't be used for anything but rendering. What you will need is storage space and a plan to manage it as the image files pile up. I'll come back to storage in a moment.

A second significant improvement is to network your two computers together to speed up file transfers and avoid the need to use tapes or removable disks as a transfer medium. The "sneaker net" works with small files, but is doubly inefficient with large 3D files.

I should warn you that adding "just one more" computer is the first step down the long, steep road to being perpetually equipment-rich and cash-poor. Once you see the rendering speed improvement that adding one computer will make, you'll be hooked and become a "render baron!"

One of the most useful features of today's best 3D software is a built-in system to manage network rendering automatically. Such a system monitors the status of all render stations on the network and assigns rendering tasks to each as they finish the prior task. Some software like Softimage|3D with the Mental Ray ray-tracing renderer can divide a single frame into chunks, assign them to different computers for rendering, and then reassemble them when all the separate tasks are finished. Other software like 3D Studio MAX, assigns one frame at a time to rendering stations and then reassembles the frames into a finished animation.

Replacing a slow processor with a faster one can help significantly.

Adding "just one more" computer is the first step down the long, steep road to being perpetually equipment-rich and cash-poor.

One potentially significant cost factor in 3D is the cost of licensing the software for rendering. If you have to pay full price for a license to use software for rendering, it can become prohibitively expensive. The best solution is software whose license lets it be used on multiple rendering stations at the same time, but only on a single modeling station.

When the Cat's Away...

If you need every possible machine cycle for a major rendering project, consider using the administrative machines in your office as render stations during nighttime hours when the admin staff's off. Often, the staff machines are not as powerful as the 3D artists' machines, but you don't need the biggest, most powerful systems as adjunct rendering stations. They only need to be powerful enough to run the software and render without crashing. Even if an administrative computer takes much longer to render a single frame than your high-end rendering stations, any frame rendered without the cost of a new computer is a gain.

A side benefit of this concept is that your staff will also benefit from having more powerful computers. Not only will their work be done more quickly, they won't resent having last year's hand-me-down computers—the usual case in a technically oriented company!

You'll need one modeling station for every 3D artist unless they work shifts using the same computer—an efficient but frightening thought! Add a networked rendering station for each artist and you should be fairly efficient. Finally, add a server to manage the network traffic and store the output of all in a single location.

Operating Systems & Processors

Choosing an operating system and processor requires that you first choose the software you want to use; the platform is dictated by it. Here are some of the more popular choices:

- Alias | Wavefront PowerAnimator is only available on Silicon Graphics (Alias | Wavefront is a wholly owned subsidiary of SGI). See Figure 5-1.

- Softimage | 3D is available on Windows NT and SGI.

- Electric Image is only available on MacOS.

- Autodesk/Kinetix 3D Studio MAX is only available on Windows NT and Windows 95.

Hardware choice is a trade-off between cost and performance (see Figure 5-2). SGI systems are the highest performers for graphics as I write this, but the power comes at a substantial cost.

Figure 5-1: Silicon Graphics product family. Indigo2 IMPACT‰ 10000 screen image of Landreth faces, created by C. Landreth, courtesy of Alias | Wavefront. Onxy2‰ screen image of St. Peter's Cathedral courtesy of ENEL SpA and Infobyte SpA. O2‰ screen image of underwater camera courtesy of Katz Design. Image courtesy of Silicon Graphics, Inc.

Intel-based, multiprocessor systems are a worthy choice for lower-cost, less-than-supercomputer power. Other possibilities are the new MacOS clones or Alpha-based Windows NT systems; all offer a lot of power at reasonable prices. Again, look first at the software, however, then for the hardware.

Figure 5-2: Intergraph TDZ product family features one, two, or four Intel Pentium Pro 200 MHz processors and high-powered, hardware-accelerated graphics performance. These machines are the Rolls-Royces of PCs, although you will pay for this level of performance.

Memory

Memory is a relative thing, both in human and machine terms. Where word processing applications used to be content in less than 1MB of RAM, today's complex programs using a graphical interface need 8MB or more to accommodate both the operating system and the software. Graphics software is even more demanding. Count on having at least 64MB of RAM in every modeling station and double or quadruple that if your artists work in large scenes. Even a *gigabyte* of RAM is not unheard of when working with highly complex scenes for movie character animation.

Memory, however, is a bigger need at rendering time. If a computer runs out of real RAM space and must use a hard disk as virtual memory, rendering slows dramatically. Big systems that render big complex scenes can have as much as 4GB RAM. Yes, I said RAM, not disk space. The computers in the render farm used to produce *Toy Story* each had between 192 and 384MB of RAM per system. (My first RAM purchase in 1981 of 48K for $800 seem paltry by comparison, but, *boy*, was I ever thrilled then!)

Input Devices

Graphics input devices include the keyboard (yes, sometimes you have to type in data or object translations), a pointing device like a mouse or graphics tablet, a modem, CD-ROM drive, and even motion capture hardware!

First, you'll need a keyboard—everyone needs a keyboard, and if you spend any amount of time rapping those keys, invest in an ergonomic unit. I can't tell you how much better my wrists have been since I bought a Microsoft natural keyboard. It took a few days to get used to it, but it's really saved me. For Mac users, Apple makes a split, adjustable keyboard with built-in wrist rests. Try several different models and see which works best for you.

All graphics interfaces require some sort of pointing device. Get a good, three-button mouse if you're aiming for high-level 3D software. Many of the features in Softimage I 3D, for example, use the middle mouse button as one of the controls. If you have only a two-button pen and tablet, hmmm, it doesn't work. (Note that a three-or-more-button puck is also available for most tablets. It's like a mouse but better, and solves the missing button problem.)

A good, large tablet is wonderful for graphics work. I use a Wacom pressure-sensitive ArtZ II, and I love it. There's no wire on the pen and it's a natural, wrist-safe way to work. Try a tablet; you'll love it too.

I have included both a modem and CD-ROM drive as input devices, although they are technically a communication device and storage device, respectively. However, if you need to download data from a remote site or load a multi-MB scene into your 3D program, you'll definitely need one or the other.

Get the fastest CD-ROM you can handle, but also consider trading off load speed for the ability to *burn* (write) CD-ROMs. It's very handy to be able to store 600+ MB of your own data in a single place with random access. (A tape is a linear access device—you have to go through everything to get to the bit you want, while a CD-ROM or hard disk head can dance across the disk to wherever the data is.)

Modems are at a real crossroads now. Both internal and external modems with 28.8 kbit speed are available at almost every dime and stationery store. New 33.6 kbit screamers are hitting the market as this book goes to press. ISDN modems are finally more reasonable, but you'll incur additional costs for line installation. Cable modems that use your cable TV system have speeds much higher than ISDN; they're undergoing testing now and *may* be the answer, although whether they're the right answer for heavy users who need high speed in both directions is an unanswered question right now.

There are even satellite modem systems available to the general public that are faster than ISDN and less expensive. The next few years will be critical to development in the electronic communications industry. I won't predict where it will end, but just get the fastest, most reliable you can afford!

Output Devices

Most 3D animation is destined for either film, videotape, or computer-based output. Each has its own special hardware requirements and problems.

The most significant aspect of film is the very high resolution required to approach film's near-infinite resolution. Most CGI for film is rendered at 2K x 2K or 4K x 4K resolution; that's 2048 x 2048 or 4096 x 4096 pixel resolution. The images are then transferred to film using film recorders under the control of such sophisticated image management software like RIOT from Discreet Logic.

Transfer to videotape presents a different set of problems. There are five approaches currently being used to output CGI to video.

- *High-end computers with specialized graphics and storage capabilities can output either analog or digital video directly; this is the best solution, but also the most costly.* Note that the availability of this solution is dependent upon the complexity of the output image and the resultant size of the per-frame files. The more complex the images, the larger the file size, and the slower the playback rate.

- *Output to an optical videodisk.* Because most computer systems can't keep up with full-frame (640 x 480), full-color, 30-fps video output, the images must instead be sent one at a time to an external recorder. This can be an optical videodisk or a videotape recorder. The optical videodisk can record up to 24 minutes of video on one side of a 12-inch recordable videodisk, either at a full 30-fps rate or frame-by-frame.

- *Output to a videotape recorder.* Most people are familiar with the video cassette recorder (VCR) that lets consumers record their favorite TV shows. A professional videotape recorder can record at 30 fps, but it can also record a single frame at a time.

  To record a single frame requires the tape machine to back up to an earlier point on the tape, start playing to stabilize the speed, then at the correct frame, record the image that's present at the video input, then stop recording, stop the tape, and repeat the cycle. This is not only hell for a tape recorder, but it's time consuming at a point in the production cycle where time is always at a premium.

- *Output to a digital disk recorder.* These units are designed for video storage and store under a minute's worth of uncompressed video with near-instant access and full-rate video playback. They are expensive, but when you need it, nothing else works as well.

- *Output to a dedicated hard disk or array of hard disks with images stored in a compressed format.* The quality is not quite as good as with the uncompressed data stored on digital disk recorders or analog videodisks, but for many uses it's quite acceptable. And these devices can also *stream* (output continuously) video at a full screen size and full rate.

There are several other devices that you might consider in addition to those specified:

- A high-quality color printer can make your 3D output sing and can really impress the clients. In addition, you can use it to obtain a hardcopy approval for your files.

- A streaming tape device or high-capacity removable hard disk lets you move large quantities of data to another site for rendering or laying off.

You probably won't be sending many high-resolution color images with your modem, but in a pinch, and for single images for approval or special handling, it may become necessary.

Some applications, such as forensic animation or other fields where a permanent, durable, accessible record is required, the final output is on laser disk. Few graphics houses have the capabilities in-house to master a laser disk, but it's an easy task to ship a videotape or videodisk to a laser disk mastering facility. It just adds to the time required at the end of a production.

Display Devices

The display is your window into the computer. If you want to spend your time peeking through a gunslit of a monitor, that's your choice. But I tradeoff between 14-inch and 21-inch monitors and the difference is phenomenal. With a large monitor, you can see details without straining.

Bi-, Tri-, or Monofocals

As you age, your close-up vision is one of the first things to be affected. First you need reading glasses, then bifocals, then you start experimenting with trifocals, blended trifocals, and so on, just to be able to see a computer screen without getting a crick in your neck.

If you are finding it difficult to see the monitor clearly from a comfortable distance, go down to the mall over a lunch hour and have the local optometrist/optician make a set of single-vision computer glasses for you. Set the prescription so that you can see clearly at an arm's length, and don't try to include more than one prescription. Combine them with an ergonomic keyboard and you'll be able to work for long stretches without your arms or eyes giving out. Your butt, however, is your own responsibility.

If you want to spend your time peeking through a gunslit of a monitor, that's your choice.

At the least, go for 17-inch monitors; 21-inch seems about ideal, and although larger monitors are available, they're almost *too* large (and expensive).

Storage Devices

I remember when an 80K floppy disk was all the room I ever needed. Now, I find that some of my 3D scene files or databases run more than 10MB! Amazing!

At 30 frames per second and 2MB per frame, it takes very few seconds of animation to fill up a 1 gigabyte drive!

And rendered images can be just as enormous. Even compressing them may not help much. There's just so much data that preserving the quality you worked so hard to create means storing it as a full-blown image on a hard disk. And then another image and another. You know, at 30 frames per second, and even 2MB per frame, it takes very few seconds of animation to fill up a 1 gigabyte drive!

So you'll need hard disk storage and more hard disk storage. You'll need access to a server with arrays of hard disks, plus a CD-ROM burner to store your more important data in a nonvolatile form. You'll also need streaming tape backups for overnight backup of working files to make sure that you don't lose current files. And when you run out of space, you can also use tape to back up the finished product. In short, bigger *is* better.

Here's the current extreme example in CGI: *Toy Story*. Each computer in Pixar's render farm had three to five GB of local disk storage. There were also two large disk arrays with a total of 252GB of storage to accumulate images from the rendering stations. Since that still wasn't enough to store the entire movie, final images were recorded onto film and backed up onto tape drives.

What will you need in the future? Think in terms of gigabytes and terabytes (TB): even today, you can easily purchase huge disk arrays. For example, you can order STONE disk arrays from Discreet Logic that range in size from 31GB to 2.5TB, and they're but one of many producers of hard disk arrays.

Moving On

In this chapter, we looked at some of the nuts and bolts of working in 3D. We reviewed the production process, paying particular attention to the differences between reality-based and fantasy-based projects. We looked at hardware, and if you now are positive that high-end graphics is an expensive business, then you understood right! In Chapter 6, we'll look at some of the specific tasks and methods used in 3D to create CGI. It's another level of detail downward, so put on your diving suit and follow me!

6

Creating 3D Imagery

Now that the prep work is behind you, we'll look at the software *tools* that are available in 3D packages.

The *size* of the toolbox you have available in any piece of software depends greatly upon the software you select. If you buy the equivalent of a Homeowners' Emergency Repair Kit, you'll get very few tools, but they'll probably do a few tasks reasonably well. Now, if you buy the equivalent of a full mechanics' set from the Snap-On Tools guy who serves car dealers, then you'll have a tool for *everything*. In fact, you'll have tools for things that you didn't know could be adjusted!

The same thing is true of 3D software: the really, really high-end software includes capabilities you may never need, like camera shaders that directly simulate IMAX or Panavision cameras. But they also have tools—once you find and understand them—that can make all of your images sparkle.

Before you buy a program, carefully review what capabilities you need and the markets you're going to go after. Together with the budget, this will determine the software you need. Make up a short list of candidates and then find a dealer for each; go through a thorough demo with the dealer before buying a program. Ask all the questions you can think of and write down the answers—it'll save those sessions back at the office in which you say, "I *think* he said it'll do this."

Choosing Viewpoints

Choosing the viewpoint from which to frame a scene is the result of a combination of the storyboard (see Chapter 5) and the principles of composition (see Chapter 4). A scene can consist of several shots from different viewpoints that are edited together to create an interesting and informative narrative. It's the animator's job to find the precise viewpoints that are the most effective. It's amazing how slight changes in viewpoint and camera can change the look.

Most 3D programs allow you to use more than one viewpoint. In Figure 6-1, four viewpoints—camera views—are shown in separate viewports in 3D Studio MAX. Once you define different views, you can then either render the entire scene from each viewpoint and cut between them in postproduction editing (see Chapter 5) or cut between cameras during rendering and produce a finished epic right out of the box.

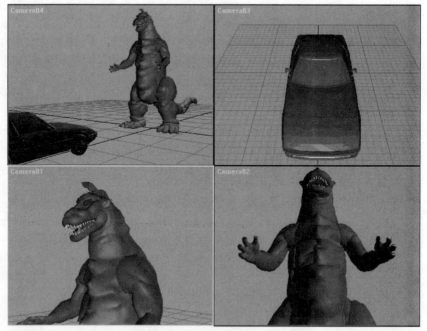

Figure 6-1: Four views of a Godzilla-like monster attacking a Mazda. From the top left in a clockwise direction, the four viewports show the master shot, the monster's view, the driver's-eye view, and a medium shot of the monster.

Whereas the "edit-in-a-box" method is exceptionally useful in creating a quick, edited version of a scene, complete with cuts, camera moves, transitions, and so on, one drawback is that if you need to adjust the timing of the scene—that is, if it runs long or short or just doesn't work—you may not have the frames available to reedit it.

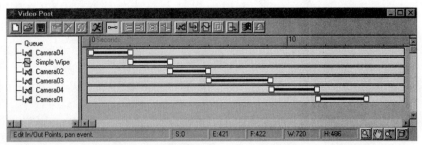

Figure 6-2: Editor-in-a-box. Whether it's called Video Post or whatever, a schematic view of the scene laid out against time, lets you do postrendering processing and set edit points during rendering. It's extremely handy, but can limit later edits.

You can move a 3D camera just like its real-world equivalent, except that because it has no size or mass, you can do things with it that would be impossible in the real world, even with a Steadicam. No place is beyond the camera's lens and every lens in the world is available. Professional-level programs like Softimage | 3D include preset camera shaders that are the equivalent of all standard lenses from fisheye to IMAX. Other, less-extensive programs only allow one camera at a time; if you're going to do professional work, avoid programs that don't allow multiple cameras.

Modeling

Virtually all 3D programs have *some* way to create objects. If they can't create objects, they can always load them from other programs or sources. Object-creation or modeling tools are usually broken up into different categories of objects.

The choice of which tool to use usually is determined by:

- The capabilities of the program you use.

- The type of object; round objects can be lathed, whereas rectangular ones can't.

- The use to which the objects will be put. Foreground animated objects typically require more careful modeling and a smoother, more deformable surface.

Primitives

Many 3D modelers begin with *primitives*. These are the basic three-dimensional geometric shapes that include cubes, rectangular boxes, spheres, cones, cylinders, tubes, and torii (plural of torus). Some programs also generate other more complex objects like geospheres or other polyhedra.

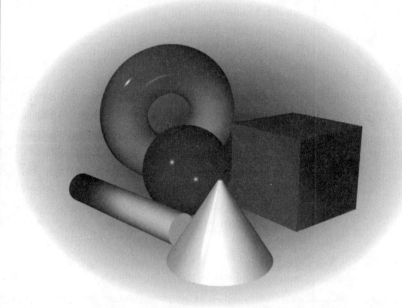

Figure 6-3: Primitives, primitives, and more primitives. These are the basic building blocks of 3D graphics.

These primitive shapes can be manipulated, added together, or subtracted from one another to form more complex objects. Individual components can be pushed, pulled, twisted, scaled, and linked to controllers to animate parts of a primitive. The abstract sculpture in Figure 6-4 was created from a cube.

Figure 6-4: Arte de primitivo. *This is what happens when you abuse a cube.*

Primitives are usually based on linear polygonal meshes and can have anywhere from tens to thousands of polygons depending on the smoothness required. They are by far the most common way to create objects.

Lathe

Lathe, spinning, or *surface of revolution* creates an object by spinning a shape around a straight axis. In Figure 6-5, the shape to the left was spun around a vertical axis at its left edge to produce the champagne glass in the center.

Figure 6-5: Lathing is an easy way to create smooth cylindrical or axial objects. The shape on the left was lathed around a vertical axis aligned to its left edge to produce the champagne glass and around a horizontal axis to produce the rocket nozzle thingy.

Lathing is similar to turning a piece of wood or metal on a lathe (from whence, obviously, it received its name). The components are the shape and the axis. Rotate the same shape around a different axis and you get a different result; the rocket nozzle thingy on the right in Figure 6-5 was produced by lathing the same shape around the horizontal axis.

Extrusion

Think of toothpaste squeezing out the nozzle of a tube and you know what extrusion is, as shown in Figure 6-6. The shape of the tube opening determines the cross section of the paste column (and sometimes additional openings give you neat colored stripes, too).

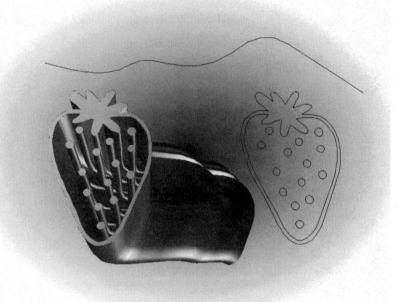

Figure 6-6: The strawberry tube you see on the left was created by extruding the strawberry shape to its right along the path above.

Extrusion requires two things: a single shape and a path, which can be straight, curved, or have complex twists and turns. If the path is complex and the shape is too large for the perambulations of the path, the surface of the resultant object self-intersects and can cause rendering problems.

Cross-section Modeling or Lofting

Cross-section modeling is similar to extrusion but uses additional shapes along the path. The result can be anything from a face to an objet d'art, as in Figure 6-7.

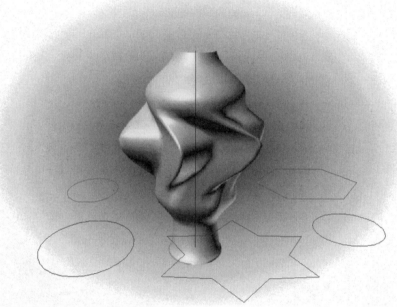

Figure 6-7: Cross-section modeling is similar to extrusion, but it lets you add a variety of different shapes along the path. By rotating them, you can create interesting objects.

The term lofting comes from the ancient art of ship building. Different programs use different labels for extrusion, lofting, and cross-sectional modeling. They all come down to using the same principle, differing only in the number of cross-sections allowed.

Booleans

Combine two objects and you create a third. Booleans let you perform logical operations, including union, intersection, and subtraction, on objects. The concept is named for 19th-century British mathematician and logician George Boole, who developed the branch of mathematics that bears his name, that is, Boolean algebra.

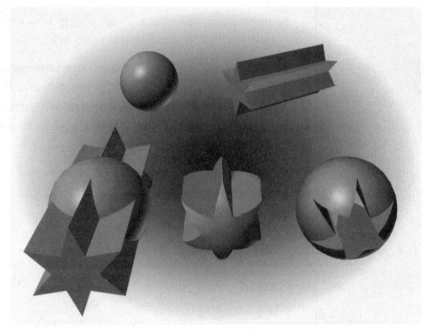

Figure 6-8: The three objects in the foreground were constructed using Booleans from the two behind them. From left to right, they are union, intersection, and subtraction.

Booleans are useful for creating larger, more complex objects from smaller, simpler ones and for carving out areas of one object using the shape of another. Booleans are also quite difficult mathematically and are a notorious source of problems with some objects and in some programs.

TIP

If you have problems performing a Boolean operation, try one of the following:

- Scale both objects up by a significant factor (say, 10), perform the Boolean, and then scale the result back down.

- Slightly readjust the position of the two components.

- Make sure that at least part of the two objects actually overlap, that is, occupy the same 3D space.

- Ensure that both objects have the same normal orientation. If one has normals pointing out and the other has normals pointing in, the Boolean will probably fail (although in truth I haven't tested this in all software). See the sidebar, "What's Normal."

- If the two objects are polygonal, *tessellate* them; that is, divide each of the existing faces into more and more regularly shaped faces. Boolean operations are most difficult with long, skinny faces.

Patches

Patches are one of the "coming things" in 3D modeling. They have many advantages over polygonal models, but take more horsepower to use. A polygonal or mesh object is defined by the locations of all of the vertices at the corners of its faces; a surface patch object, on the other hand, is defined by point locations and curve definitions. The most common form of surface patches used in 3D modeling is the *Bézier patch*, named after engineer Pierre Bézier.

Bézier patches are composed of a grid of Bézier curves, so let me digress a quick second to discuss Bézier curves. There are many ways to define a 2D curve, including the most basic, which is a series of vertices with straight-line segments between them.

The fewer the vertices, the poorer is the approximation of the curve. Conversely, as you increase the number of vertices, it more and more closely approximates the shape of the curve.

What's Normal?

In polygonal objects, every face has a front side and a back side. The front side is the one that the program normally renders and the back side is the one that is normally removed. A *normal* is a vector that represents the center and orientation of a front face; it's perpendicular to the face and located in the mathematical center. Normals are used for many calculations in 3D, from shading to Booleans to collision detection.

Normals are represented in most programs by small arrows that seem to grow from the faces, as in Figure 6-9.

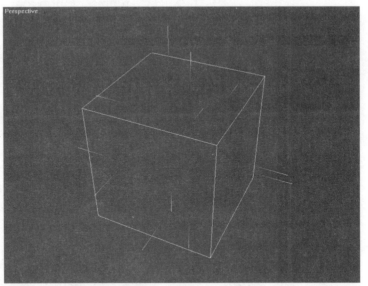

Figure 6-9: The shaded lines protruding from this cube are graphical representations of its normals.

Bézier curves define curves differently. Rather than approximating the curve by the brute force method of vertices and line segments, Bézier curves are defined by the locations of two endpoints and other two control points.

You may recall that I've mentioned NURBs several times in this book. NURB is an acronym for Non-Uniform Rational B-splines; Bézier curves can be defined as a subset of the family of NURB curves. Like Bézier curves, NURBs in general are very efficient tools for the representation of complex shapes. For example, to define a six-inch diameter circle using line segments, you would need hundreds of vertices and segments to make the circle appear smooth, yet using NURBs, you could define it with seven control points!

With a grid of 16 control points, you can define an entire curved Bézier surface. The control points form a lattice that can be displayed in all 3D programs that let you use patches. Also displayed is the surface representation that's produced by the arrangement of control points in the lattice, as in Figure 6-10.

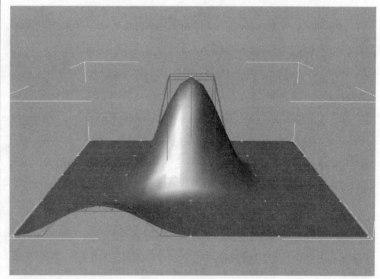

Figure 6-10: A Bézier surface patch consists of 16 (or more) control points in a lattice. Each can be easily moved about to deform the surface formed by the curves (see text). Note the vertex at the top of the "mountain" and its surrounding lattice. In the lower left corner, a vertex on the front edge of the patch is selected and its three control points can be seen around it as small boxes.

Patch surfaces are also called parametric surfaces. They can be easily and smoothly deformed, and it's easy to apply texture or other maps to them. But usually parametric surfaces must be reduced to a polygonal mesh to render them. Finally, although you can build up incredibly complex and useful models with patches, sometimes cracks can form at patch boundaries.

Blobs

Another "coming thing" in 3D modeling is blobs, also called metaballs, implicit surfaces, soft objects, and various trade names such as Metaclay, Metashapes, and so on. Blobs are not 3D objects themselves, per se, but mathematical representations of surfaces that can be converted into polygons for rendering. The surfaces have attraction and repulsion components that let the artist create anything from a muscleman to blobs of molten metal flowing together to reform into a Terminator.

Think of water droplets. Each droplet alone is essentially spherical, but when you get them close together, the surfaces begin to attract each other. Soon, the surfaces start to blend smoothly into one another. At first, they remain more or less distinct and form a sort of a dumbbell shape. But as the droplets get closer and closer together, they begin to form a single drop.

Blobs act a lot like the water drops. You can use them to create organic-looking, roundish shapes that flow together smoothly and perfectly, as in the body in Figure 6-11. They are now the tool of choice for creating organic body shapes over skeletons. Another good use for blobs is as the stuff of particle systems; with blobs, the particle drops of water in a fountain could run together, for example.

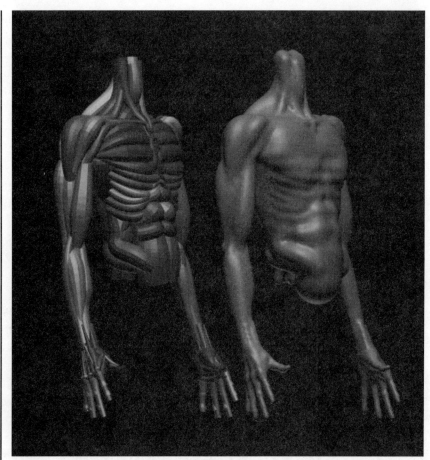

Figure 6-11: This body was modeled with blobs by Manuel Nguema using Metareyes 3.0.

Face Building

Back to the basics! This is the way that 3D modelers used to create objects. It's simple, really, but incredibly tedious. Each vertex is defined in 3D space with X-, Y-, and Z-coordinates; then each face is defined by three vertices, as in Figure 6-12.

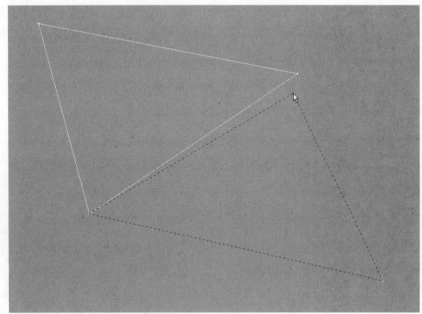

Figure 6-12: Four vertices let you build two triangular faces. I'm in the process of building the second here, having already instructed the program that the first vertex of the new face is at the lower left and the second at the lower right. The third is where I'm heading now.

The mesh representation of the patch surface in Figure 6-10 is a relatively simple object, but it is composed of 625 vertices and 1152 triangular faces. Would you want to define each of these manually? I thought not.

Morphing

Morphing is from the Greek word that means *form*; it's also the basis for the word metamorphosis, and that's just what happens in morphing. In computer graphics, it has come to mean any process that changes an image or object from one state to another. Two-dimensional image morphing first made a popular splash in Michael Jackson's music video for the song "Black and White." Three-dimensional morphing made its splash (pun intended) with the water creature in the James Cameron movie, *The Abyss*. Now it's everywhere!

In 3D, morphing lets you change the shape of a 3D object over time, creating an animated appearance as in Figure 6-13. It can be very powerful, but its uses have become more limited as more powerful animation tools (and the computers to handle them) have been developed.

Figure 6-13: The brick sphere at the top left is twisted over time into the shape at the top right using morphing. Objects representing stages of this transformation are shown below.

Particle Systems

Particle systems mimic real-world natural phenomena. Using an emitter and a stream of particles, you can simulate anything, including cigarette smoke, fire, explosions, water fountains, fireworks, clouds, BBs, snow, tornadoes, a swarm of bees, rain—almost anything that's composed of small particles.

Particle systems are based on chaos theory and produce tiny objects that behave according to the scene dynamics the artist defines. Particle systems can add incredibly realistic effects to an animation when combined with a physics system that simulates phenomena as electrical and magnetic fields, gravity, wind, and collisions with other particles and objects. A really good particle system gives the artist tremendous control over each system, but at the cost of considerable complexity. Perhaps in the future, particle systems will provide more prefabricated effects, but at the present time, the artist not only *can* control all of the subtle characteristics of a particle system, but *must* do so. The Softimage I 3D 3.5.1 particle system in Figure 6-14 is relatively organized and civilized for its level of sophisticated power.

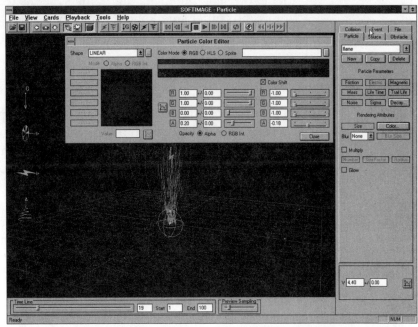

Figure 6-14: Particle systems range from the simple to the sophisticated. The Softimage I 3D Particle System is definitely on the sophisticated end of the scale.

3D Capture

3D capture is a different animal from what we've discussed above. If you have a real-world object that you need in your 3D world, 3D capture or *digitization* is the tool you'll use. Like motion capture that grabs the real-life movement of people, digitization brings the real-world shape of an object into a 3D program. It's often used in moviemaking to bring life masks of actors into the computer for special effects. (A life mask is an identical, wart-for-wart, life-size re-creation of an actor's face. It's made by first creating a mold directly from the actor's face, then using that to create the mask. It's like making a print from a photographic negative.)

3D capture lets you create accurate models without building them yourself. (Small 3D digitizing systems that let you digitize your cat or other small object can now be had for under $3,000. Like everything else in 3D, it used to cost five times as much!)

Imported Geometry

Sometimes you don't have the object you need, but it's available in the engineering department as a CAD (computer-assisted drafting) file. Many programs let you import geometry from "foreign" sources and convert it into entities that are familiar within the 3D environment. This is especially common in architectural and engineering firms, both civil and mechanical.

If you're desperate for a model late at night some time, and you don't have time to build it, head out on the Net and look for 3D sources. I've listed a number of resources in Appendix B, including several that can convert between file types. Check first what file types your program can import, then look for that type of file.

Some of the most common file types are .obj (Wavefront), .3ds (3D Studio pre-MAX), and .dxf (AutoCAD). If you are clever and lucky, you may be able to obtain the data you need in the format you want by using several freeware or shareware translators. For example, if you wanted to convert U.S. Geologic Survey .dem files to 3D Studio files, there is no freeware converter that can do it directly. But you can convert the USGS files into Vista Pro .dem files first and then convert them to .3ds.

When you purchase (or find) an object you want to use, don't forget to check the copyright to make sure that you can use it as you intend. You might need to obtain written approval from the owner of the copyright.

Commercial Sources

If you haven't the time, the resources, or the skill to create or capture your own 3D geometry or systems, there is still an option available if you need a particular object. A number of companies, like Viewpoint DataLabs International, Inc., specialize in the creation and marketing of 3D objects in a variety of formats. Each model is usually available in several complexity levels and priced accordingly. You'll find that, while they aren't cheap, the alternatives are even more expensive and time consuming.

Chaos & Fractal Geometry

Sometimes, you just want to create a nice landscape or clouds that you can use as a background for your project. There are several ways to do this, ranging from laborious face building to applying random noise to the vertical dimension of a patch model. Chaos and fractal theory, however, produce the most realistic mountains, clouds, vegetation, and other similar natural phenomena. Programs like Bryce from MetaTools are uncanny in their ability to generate realistic natural objects and backgrounds, as in Figure 6-15.

Figure 6-15: Is it real or is it Bryce? Only your modelmaker knows for sure. This landscape by Tim Stiles was created in Bryce 2 from MetaTools.

Data-defined

Finally, there's one last choice available. You can create an object in some 3D programs by importing a data file that originated in something like a spreadsheet or text processing program. This method can produce almost any conceivable shape, but the generation of the data itself can be incredibly difficult.

Typical uses for this method include modeling the results of scientific experiments and natural data collection. The results might be a 3D model that represents the distribution of pollutants in a water table, the migration of molecules by osmosis, the geographical range of the bighorn sheep, or localized geological formations.

Surface Materials & Shaders

In order to be visible in the final rendered images, all objects must have a surface, there must be light in the scene, and to be interesting, each surface must have a material or shader assigned. In the last section, "Modeling," I explained the different methods available to create (or obtain) surface models. Now I'll explain some of the variations in surface treatment that are available.

Shading

Basic shading concepts were discussed in the section entitled "Surfaces & Shading" in Chapter 5 and in "Surface Smoothing" in Chapter 2. Let's take another look at some of the variables that might affect the shading type and level you use in a scene.

First, let's briefly review shading types, as shown in Figure 6-16. For polygonal models, and polygonal meshes that represent the surfaces of patch or blob models, the lowest level of shading is constant, or flat. Each face is assigned a light level and the level is uniform across the face.

The next best shading is Gouraud. It's a smooth-shading algorithm that smoothes across the edges between faces. Light levels are computed only at the vertices, and the light level is interpolated across each face. It's fast and thus is excellent for online or real-time shading applications. It can't display highlights, however.

Phong shading is another smooth-shading algorithm that can smooth across edges and display highlights. In Phong shading, a normal (see the "What is Normal?" sidebar earlier in this chapter) is calculated at each vertex as the average of the normals of surrounding faces, and these normals are interpolated across the face. The light level is calculated for each pixel based upon the interpolated normals. It's obviously more processor intensive than Gouraud, since it recalculates the light level at each pixel, but Phong shading produces a better-looking image. Phong shading can accurately render bump, opacity, shininess, specular, and reflection maps.

The disadvantages of these three algorithms is their inaccuracy. They approximate the light falling upon a surface, rather than calculating it exactly. To be completely accurate, however, requires ray-tracing.

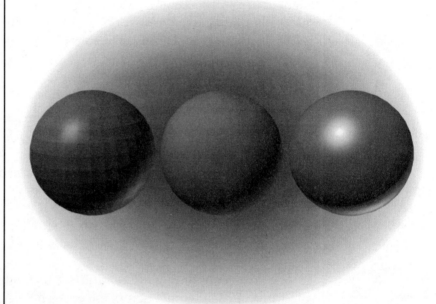

Figure 6-16: Shading levels: constant, Gouraud, and Phong.

Ray-tracing is a different method than the others. Where the first three shading methods looked at the light arriving at the object and calculated the light level from that viewpoint, ray-tracing begins with the viewpoint and traces rays of light backwards to the light sources. Some light arrives at the viewpoint directly from the light source, while other light is either reflected from or refracted through objects in the scene. When all of the possible light paths are calculated taking into account the nature of the object surfaces, the final image can be calculated. And it can be beautiful, as in Figure 6-17.

Ray-tracing is quite time consuming, and would be impossible if software designers didn't reduce the workload by limiting the extent of path testing done or approximating some of the values by interpolating between tested paths.

Figure 6-17: Ray-tracing may be slow, but it can produce beautiful images. This is a product of one of the nicest ray tracers, Softimage Mental Ray.

Wireframe is not technically a shading type, but uses one of the other shading types to display thin face strips at the edges of faces. It's handy for showing the structure of objects, although remember that the polygonal structure of a 3D model may have no relationship to the structure of a similar real object. Since it must still use one of the shading methods described above, it's not necessarily faster than full-face rendering.

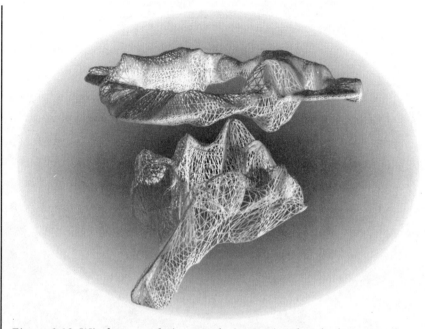

Figure 6-18: Wireframe renderings can be interesting, but don't necessarily save rendering time. Here's the atlas and axis vertebrae from Chapter 4 in wireframe.

One last shading method should be mentioned, although it is still computationally difficult enough to be rare. The radiosity method is a variation of ray-tracing, but concentrates more on the illumination of objects by reflection from other objects. Try holding a red ball near a white paper under bright light and notice that there is a red tinge to the white paper; this is what radiosity shading does.

Shading types can usually be mixed in a scene; those objects not requiring high levels of lighting accuracy can be shaded with lower-accuracy methods. This is particularly true of distant objects, that is, those that determine how the surface of your model will react to light. Usually, each material will have a shading level placed on it. In addition to that, you can specify how big the range of shading will be in your scene. Every object in your scene does not always need the same level of shading for optimal results. You can mix the amount of shading throughout the scene. The rule of thumb is the more shading there is, the more rendering time it will take to render the final picture.

Two last aspects of shading should be mentioned here: backfacing and two-sided materials. When 3D graphics was in its infancy and rendering was a new and slow process, bright engineers determined that they could save almost half the rendering time if they only rendered those faces that faced the viewer; that is, those faces whose normals pointed more or less toward the viewer. The process of determining which faces face where is called *backfacing* or *backface* culling. When you are working in wireframe within a 3D program interface, backfacing helps keep you from getting confused by seeing edges at the front and back of an object. At the same time, backfacing requires a bit more processing from the computer to determine which edges and faces to show and which to hide.

Two-sided materials are nothing more than turning that backfacing switch off at rendering. To the software, each face has normals that point both directions. Two-sided materials can be useful when your model springs a leak; that is, displays cracks between objects or patches that let you see through the back faces of the object's rearward-facing surface all the way back to the background. Applying a two-sided material to the back faces prevents you from seeing through the back faces. It can be a valuable quick fix, as in Figure 6-19.

Figure 6-19: The teapot on the left does not have two-sided materials, while the one on the right does. That's why the joint between the lid and pot is visible in the left pot but not the right. If you look carefully, you can also see through material inside the left spout.

Mapping

Mapping is the easiest way to simulate the real-world effect of natural surfaces. Over the last decade, more and more mapping techniques have been developed to use bitmap images to color and shape otherwise sterile 3D objects. Wood textures, foliage, and metal can all be simulated by wrapping digital reproductions of these surfaces around or through a 3D model.

As 3D programs have become more sophisticated over the past decade, they've added more and more material settings that let you control every aspect of the appearance of an object. You can set its diffuse, ambient, and specular colors; its shininess and roughness; its opacity, reflectivity, and refractivity; its bumpiness; and whether it glows itself. Each of these controls can also be mapped in a high-level program, giving you additional control.

Figure 6-20 shows the different types of mapping available in most software packages:

- *Texture mapping.* The basic process in which a 2D bitmap is wrapped around or projected onto a 3D model. It's applied in place of the diffuse color, although quality 3D programs let you vary the percentage of texture applied.

Figure 6-20: Mapping of all types. Clockwise from the top: texture, bump, opacity, displacement, specular, self-illumination, environmental, and reflection.

- *Bump mapping.* Uses the luminance (brightness) of the map image to simulate an uneven surface. However, bump mapping does not affect the edges or shadows; they are still as if the surface was absolutely smooth (which it is).

- *Specular mapping.* Maps an image into the highlight of an object. It's especially useful for putting an image into the highlight of an eye in closeup, but not widely used elsewhere.

- *Displacement mapping*. Differs from bump mapping in that displacement mapping is a modeling tool that uses a bitmap image to move the surface of the object. Again, the luminance value of the image is generally used. The edges and shadows produced by displacement mapping are accurate.

- *Opacity or Transparency mapping*. Two sides of the same coin. They use the luminance value of a bitmap to determine the opacity (or transparency) of a surface.

- *Self-illuminated mapping*. Simulates objects that have a light source of their own and appear to glow. The amount of "glow" is determined by the luminance value of the bitmap. Where the bitmap is dark, the glow is less. It's a nice way to add illuminated portholes to spaceships!

- *Environmental mapping*. Shows reflections of other objects in the scene. These are true (OK, *simulated* true) reflections, not simulated as in reflection mapping. The typical environmental mapping technique simulates placing a camera at the center point of the mapped object and taking six "pictures" of the surrounding scene. These six images are then mapped back onto the object as reflection maps. It's a time-consuming process, especially if there are a number of environmentally mapped objects in a scene, and even more so if one or more are moving!

- *Reflection mapping*. Fakes what environmental mapping creates. You can use any bitmap as a reflection map to simulate the surroundings around an object, and if you don't look too close, it will look OK. Take the reflection-mapped marble in Figure 6-20; it looks nice and shiny, and there's a vague reflection in its surface—except that the reflection doesn't match its surroundings. Compare it to the environmentally mapped marble at the nine o'clock position.

Lighting

Lighting can make or break a scene. It can cover up deficiencies in materials and modeling or highlight them. You can set a mood or destroy one. Be sure to review the section, "The Stage," in Chapter 4 for an overview of the classic three-light setup before going on here.

Most decent 3D programs let you specify the type, number, and color of the lights in a scene. What real-life photographer wouldn't love to have this much control in his studio? A good 3D program lets you turn lights on and off, change their size, shape, and location, change their color (use a gel, as in the theater), turn shadows on and off, set the softness of the shadow edge, set which objects will be illuminated by each light, and even use special dark lights to "suck up" excess light in certain areas! That's incredible control!

How you set up your lights will differ depending upon the effect you want to achieve. Most 3D programs offer several different types of lights that are designed to simulate real-world lights with a few notable exceptions.

If you are creating a 3D scene that takes place outdoors, you want to have realistic sunlight that appears to come from a distant source. Some programs don't include a sun simulator, forcing you to place a spotlight far away from the scene as a substitute. This sometimes fails for one of two reasons: either the light is not far enough away to make the light rays coming from it essentially parallel like the sun's rays, or it's so far away that it doesn't provide enough light.

A second source of lighting error is the lack of proper light falloff, that is, how the light amplitude declines with distance from the source. Most programs either allow no falloff or linear falloff; few include the inverse square falloff that reflects nature. If your work requires accurate reproduction of light levels, consider one of the high-end specialty programs that use a radiosity lighting method with accurate falloff.

Different types of 3D lights are used for different purposes. Here are some of the more common, as shown in Figure 6-21:

- *Spot or area lights.* Light sources that direct a cone of light onto your scene from a point in 3D space. Most 3D programs let you adjust each light's umbra and penumbra (hotspot and shadow edge) to set how much of the scene is in the bright center portion of the beam and the distance over which the edge of the light fades to black. Light from a spotlight radiates in a conical or prismatic pattern within the falloff circle or rectangle. Yes, you can define a 3D light to be other than a circle!

  Spotlights are good general purpose lights that can be effectively animated to follow a moving object or character. Well-defined spotlights can add drama to a scene.

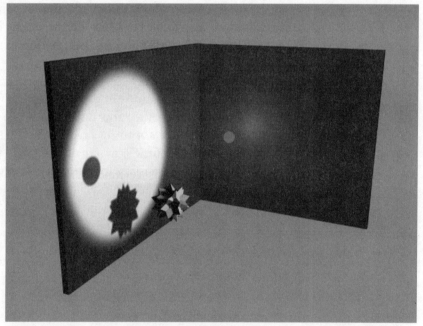

Figure 6-21: It's a cameraman's paradise. There are so many types of lights available in a sophisticated 3D program that you can create almost any lighting effect. Compare the soft-edged spotlight with the point light at the spot...and notice the dark spot caused by a "light sucker," a spotlight with a negative light value!

- *Point lights or omni lights*. Produce light in a 360-degree circle, like a light bulb. They are useful as fill lights or as general illumination.

- *Distant or sun lights*. Emulate the sun's rays; they are parallel through the scene and don't diverge from their source like point or spotlights do. Although their nominal source is usually shown as a point, in order to project parallel rays, they actually represent discs of light.

    The best type of sun lights also let you set the sun's direction and angle by specifying the date, time, and orientation and location on earth of the 3D scene, as in Figure 6-22.

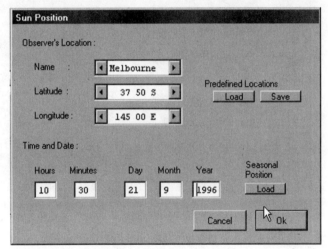

Figure 6-22: This is the ultimate sun simulator. Specify a location, date, and time, and the program does the rest. You can even use a predefined location and time of the year.

- *Projector or slide projector lights.* A special type of lights that let you add an image or animation "in front of" the light source to simulate a gobo (see Chapter 4) or a slide or movie projector, as in Figure 6-23.

Figure 6-23: This slide projector light works just like its namesake, but the visibility of its light beam comes not from the light itself but from an environmental effect called volumetric lighting.

- *Ambient or infinite light.* The indirect light in the scene. It lights all objects in the scene equally and has no source (although it may have an icon in the scene for convenience of editing).

Adding Motion

Up to now, whether you were creating a still or animation didn't matter—the modeling, shading, and lighting are applicable to both. Now, the roads diverge (in Robert Frost's yellow wood, so to speak). This section is about animation tools, not needed in stills unless you want to create motion blur.

In an animated sequence, you have a number of ways to animate objects. First, you could pretend to be back in the old cel animation days. Go to the first frame, set up the initial position of all your objects and then render an image. Move to the second frame, adjust the positions of all of the objects in your scene and render another image. Repeat this process 11,520 times and you'll have enough frames for a movie cartoon short! But don't forget to change camera angles and add camera moves for interest along the way! By the way, this is what stop-action animators like Wil Vinton's Claymation crew do all day—shoot a frame, move an arm, shoot another frame, move the arm some more. Me? I like computer animation!

Keyframing

"There's gotta be a better way!" said the weary cel animator. The solution to his and our woes is to get someone else to do it. In his case, the answer was in the personnel office; in ours, it's keyframing. Keyframing lets you set the key positions of objects at specific frames and then direct the computer to perform the adjustments and render the images inbetween.

Good 3D programs provide tools that make keyframing quite manageable. Setting a key in most is as easy as moving to a frame, adjusting an object, and then clicking on a button or icon. In 3D Studio MAX, all you need to do is turn on the Animate button, move to any frame, and make (almost) any change; keys are set automatically.

Even a simple animation can have a large number of keys, and all powerful 3D programs have something like the Track View dialog box in Figure 6-24 to manage them. Time is displayed horizontally in this dialog box and numbered in frames. The vertical axis lists all of the scene components; keys are shown as dots in the field to the right.

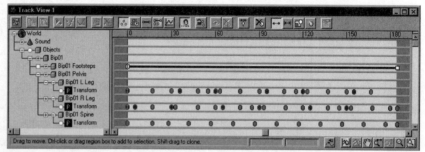

Figure 6-24: Called Track View, the timeline, dope sheet, or whatever, it still serves the same purpose: to present a tabular view of keys set in an animation. This window illustrates the keys set in a character walk animation.

One enjoyable part of today's 3D keyframing is that in a powerful program, you can keyframe almost anything: from the color of a light to the height of a mountain to the twist in a licorice twist. And you can adjust how the program changes between keys. In other words, does it change from one setting to the next abruptly, like turning on a light, or smoothly, like swinging a bat? The curves in Figure 6-25 show the movement path of an animated object through a 185-frame animation (note that it's a Bézier curve, complete with control points, also called handles!); where the curve changes direction, the object movement changes as well. This is a nice feature for adding character and uniqueness to animations or to smooth out rough movements.

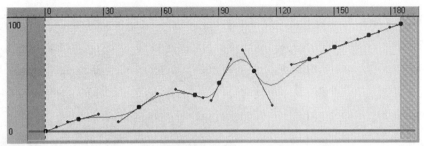

Figure 6-25: Good old Bézier curves are used to control how the program changes from one key setting to another. Simpler controls may include "ease in" and "ease out" to smooth the transitions from setting to setting.

Data-driven Animation

If you need a precise re-creation of actual (or hypothetical) events, you will probably use some form of data-driven animation rather than keyframing. In data-driven animation, a stream of data derived from samples, experiments, motion control, or a data file is fed into the program and assigned, channel by channel, to the controllers that move or change settings in an animation. Obviously, this takes a great deal of forethought and setup to produce worthwhile results, but when done properly, it can be spectacular.

Other animation methods may be faster than data-driven, but when technical accuracy is necessary, data-driven animations are the only reliable way to produce technically accurate and realistic re-creations for industry and courtroom use.

Others

As computer and software power grows, more and more built-in specialty animation tools are added. Particle systems, described earlier in the section on modeling are also animation systems that, in fact, produce their most spectacular results in motion. Other animation controllers include character animation systems that let you place footsteps to control the gait, pace, and attitude of a skeleton and skin deformation controllers that let you add a skin to the skeleton and deform it realistically. The baby in Figure 6-26 is an example of these two types of animation controllers.

Figure 6-26: Inside the mesh skin of the baby, shown translucent here for clarity, is an animation skeleton that is itself controlled by placing footsteps.

Manipulating Objects

It's nice to have the control to manipulate each and every object in a scene separately, but it's not *always* so nice. Say you needed to pose a 3D model of a human skeleton with all of its 200+ bones in a nice dance pose. Would you like to move each and every one of those bones separately and keep them all in correct relationship to the others? I thought not—it's a nightmare!

Hierarchical Linking

One of the things that computers do well is keep track of things. Today's powerful 3D programs let you set up a linking system to keep track of what bones, say, are connected to what other bones, and how they move in relation to each other. (The foot bone's connected to the ankle bone, and the ankle bone's connected to the shin bone…your computer sings this to itself, by the way, but millions of times per second!)

Objects are linked in a hierarchy in which one is the parent of a second, and the second is the parent of a third, and so on. In a skeleton, for example, this hierarchical linking might begin with the pelvis as the root object, the great-great-great-whatever grandparent of the tiniest phalanx in the little finger.

Now let's say that you want to move and pose the skeleton. You can grab the pelvis, our root object, and drag it around and all the rest of the bones move with it. This is called forward kinematics. Everything stays in the same relationship as it was before. Similarly, if you rotate the upper arm, the lower arm bones stay connected.

Now, once the skeleton is in position, you want to be able to grab one hand and move it into a nice, graceful pose while the pelvis stays still. This presents the computer with a complex series of equations to solve in order to compute the positions of all of the bones in between the finger and the pelvis. This is called inverse kinematics.

The hard part of hierarchical linking is the setup. Each link in a hierarchy must be created and the nature of the link defined. Is it a sliding joint? A rotating joint? Are there limits to its movement? Where is the center of rotation? Are there axes around which it can't rotate or slide? Once you get through the tedious work of setting up joint parameters, however, the rest is fun. It took most of a day to link and set up the skeleton in Figure 6-27, but once it was done, I had a ball creating odd and unusual poses quickly.

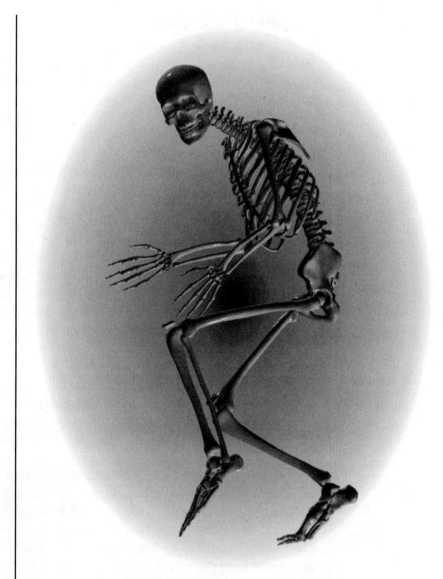

Figure 6-27: Moving and posing a skeleton requires that all of the bones be linked in a hierarchy and that you use forward and inverse kinematics, techie words for simple ideas.

Motion Capture

For many kinds of complex character movement, it's very difficult to achieve realistic motion quickly. Moreover, for the many
computer artists who came from computer backgrounds rather
than art, human movement is a relative unknown (and not just
because of the long hours at the keyboard). The solution to this
problem is *motion capture.*

Motion capture has been described as the science of analyzing
the movements of the body in motion. First used to help professional athletes perfect their performances, it's now used for
everything from Ninja video games to walking dinosaurs. Even
Moxie, the animated host on the Cartoon Network, is animated
through motion capture.

The two most common methods of motion capture today work
on the same basic principle. Actors wear either sensors or light
reflectors strategically placed on their bodies and perform predetermined actions. These motions are detected either by video
cameras placed in an array around the actors or via magnetic
sensors. Three-dimensional data from each sensor is then fed to a
computer that integrates and records it. It's then applied to the
skeleton of a 3D character.

Special Effects

The final pizzazz in a scene often comes from the addition of
special effects. They can include atmospheric effects like wind,
clouds, or smoke created with particle systems; fog; dust in the
air; motion blur; lens effects; glow; or other added sparkles
(sometimes called "gleams and glimmers"). I discussed particle
systems above briefly, but Figure 6-28 is an example of a scene
rendered in Softimage I 3D using Mental Ray to recreate the
effects of fog in Hawaii.

Figure 6-28: Atmospheric effects make a big difference in the quality of the final image. This was produced in Softimage | 3D using Mental Ray, their ray-tracing renderer.

One of the results of assembling camera lenses from separate lenses produces visible flaws in a photo taken toward or near a light source. These flaws are called *lens flare*; we have become so accustomed to seeing it that if it's not there, we miss it. (It's a bit like smog, but few people miss smog when the air is clear in Los Angeles.) The image in Figure 6-29 shows a nice lens-flare effect that was created in 3D Studio MAX using RealLensFlare.

Figure 6-29: Lens flare is the result of design flaws in compound lenses, but it's so effective to "sell" the idea of a real photograph that it has become a big 3D gimmick.

In the movie business, it's common to add special effects to the film after it's exposed and developed. The process is called *rotoscoping*. In 3D graphics, you can add all kinds of effects to an image. In Figure 6-30, a glow effect is added to an alien robot scene to enhance the look of the "lasers" firing. In Figure 6-30a, the scene has been rendered without glow. In Figure 6-30b, glow has been added as a post-processing effect, right in the 3D program.

Figure 6-30: In 6-30a, the scene has been rendered without any post-processing or rotoscoping. The self-illuminated and translucent laser blasts look tame. In 6-30b, a glow filter has transformed the pedestrian lasers to hot stuff.

One last effect that can be very effective and has become much more accessible is volumetric or dust lights, also called a volume shader. This effect lets you add a visible atmosphere to light. You've seen it in Figure 6-23; here it is in Figure 6-31 times three from three different colored lights.

Figure 6-31: Volumetric lights add a look of depth and realism to an image. It can be set up to resemble a smoky room or, as here, colored lights in a mist-filled room.

Moving On

In this chapter, we reviewed some of the principal tools available in 3D programs to model, color, and animate 3D scenes. In Chapter 7, we'll take a look at how to combine 3D imagery with other media, including sound, photos, and so on. It promises to be a very swinging time, so come on along.

7

Integrating 3D With Other Media

If you're a 3D aficionado like me—or have become one while reading this book—3D graphics provides you with entertainment and enjoyment all by themselves. But there's more to the world than 3D; this chapter is about how it's combined with other media for a variety of uses. I won't detail *how* it's used—that's the subject of the next chapter, but I will discuss some of the technical aspects of 3D that must be addressed before it can be combined with other media.

The discussion in this chapter is a bit more technical than most of the others. It deals with the tricky subject of how to integrate the product of this Brave New World of 3D (apologies to Huxley) with more traditional media. We're not back in the days of cutting and pasting with rounded-end scissors and yummy white paste. We're well past the pre-computer publishing paste-up tools of liquid wax and X-Acto knives. We're in the digital realm, where everything is easier…and harder.

Integration of digital images with other media is like most other creative work on the computer: It's relatively easy to produce mediocre images, but to produce excellent images, you must plan carefully, think about what you're trying to accomplish, examine the results each step of the way, and look at all details of the final image. At first blush, an image may seem perfect, but if your work is to be seen by many people, someone will be sure to spot all the flaws.

Planning is key. You must always begin a compositional project by breaking it down into its basic elements. Begin with the purpose of the project, and proceed through each part of the process. We'll look at one such project in this chapter; when we're done, you'll see what I mean.

Computer-generated imagery can sometimes be as conspicuous as a forgetful chameleon in an Easter basket. Other times, it can masquerade as part of a photographic setting. The difference is not always just the skill of the 3D artist, although that's certainly a major factor. Intent is the key—does the artist want his work to stand out or blend in?

The answer to this question determines how the artist approaches his work. If the 3D work can stand on its own or look different from its artistic environment, then the artist has a freer creative hand. Fitting 3D art into a photographic image or movie requires that the artist be creative, but primarily in the sense of a chameleon—the creativity is not supposed to show.

In this chapter, I'll look at four aspects of integrating 3D into other media: perspective, appearance, motion, and sound. (Note that it's possible to use sound to trigger or control 3D motion; that's not what I'm talking about here.)

Compositing Techniques

There are several alternative methods available for compositing 3D CGI with preexisting imagery. The principal difference is in whether the compositing is performed as a part of the 3D rendering process or done afterward in another program. If the foreground 3D objects must interact with the background imagery, such as by casting shadows or creating reflections in background objects, then the compositing should take place in the 3D software.

If the shadows, reflections, or other interaction can be faked by hand in effects software, then the compositing can be done in software designed specifically for this purpose. Software such as Adobe AfterEffects or Adobe Premiere are well designed for such tasks.

Opacity
information is
usually stored
as an image
component
called an *alpha
channel.*

In order to assemble foreground 3D CGI and a preexisting background *after* rendering, the CGI should include a mask component so that the compositing program can determine which areas of the CGI are transparent, opaque, and translucent. This information is typically stored either as a component part of the main image stream or as a separate image stream. In either case, the opacity information is usually stored as a 256-level grayscale image component called an *alpha channel.* In Figure 7-1, a rendered 3D vase is shown beside its alpha channel mask.

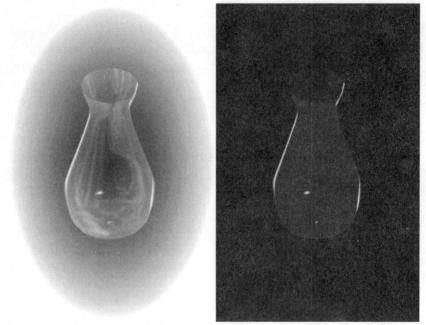

Figure 7-1: The 3D vase on the left has a translucent glass material applied. On the right, the compositing mask, or alpha channel, which was generated simultaneously by the 3D software, is shown.

It is possible to use an image processing program like Adobe Photoshop to generate a compositing mask, but it's much easier if the 3D software can do the job in a single step.

If the live action is to be composited *over* the CGI, as with a virtual or synthetic set, it may be easier to use *color keying* or *blue screen compositing* like ChromaKey or Ultimatte to assemble the elements. Creating a blue screen composite image begins by photographing the foreground image in front of an evenly lit, bright, pure blue background. All of the blue in the picture—including any blue objects in the foreground—is replaced during the compositing process with another image, known as the *background plate*.

Blue screen composites can be made optically for still photos or movies, electronically for live video, or digitally for computer images. Until recently, all blue screen compositing in movies has been done optically and all television composites have been created using analog (as opposed to digital) electronic circuitry. Figure 7-2 shows an example of blue screen compositing. The foreground element is on the left and the composite is on the right. By the way, blue screen is used to put your local weatherman in front of a map pointing at Idaho as he talks about the weather in Maine.

Color keying has other, even more creative uses—in *Forrest Gump*, color keying to remove Lieutenant Dan's legs. Colored fabric was wrapped around his lower legs for the post-amputation scenes. The colored areas were then removed frame by frame after transferring the film images to digital media, followed by hand clean-up using digital paint tools.)

Some software provides compositing tools that can assemble layers of images and processes while the 3D geometry is still available to generate effects like shadows, glows, lens flare, reflections, and so on. This capability can be a godsend during a long rendering session. One version is shown in Chapter 6 as Figure 6-2, the "editor in a box."

ChromaKey is the technique that puts your local weatherman in front of his map pointing at Idaho as he talks about the weather in Maine.

Figure 7-2: The foreground actress was videotaped in front of a blue screen (above), and a matting tool called Ultimatte was used to composite it with background video to produce the image below. If you can move everything to video, there are many nifty tools readily available.

Matching Perspectives

In order to combine 3D with other media—or even a prerendered 3D scene—you must match the perspective of the existing image.

Perspective is defined in *Webster's Third New International Dictionary* as "the technique of representing on a plane or curved surface the space relationships of natural objects as they appear to the eye." Every photograph, movie, video, and 2D or 3D computer-generated image is created with a particular perspective that represents how the subject looked to the artist or photographer who created it. In order to combine 3D with any of these media—or even a prerendered 3D scene—you must match the perspective of the existing image.

I can't begin to teach you the principles of perspective in this book, of course, but any good art text or beginning art course can teach you what you need to know in fairly short order. Suffice it to say that in order to match the perspective of an existing image, you must either have precise data that defines the perspective or be able to derive what you need from an examination of the image. Figure 7-3 illustrates the terminology of traditional artistic perspective; all of this data must be defined either explicitly or implicitly. You must define:

- Picture plane—the area of the image.
- Station point, center of vision, and line of sight—the viewpoint, target, and line between the two.
- Horizon and vanishing point(s)—the "edge of the world" and where objects seem to disappear.
- Ground plane—the surface on which the observer stand.

In most jobs as a 3D artist, you won't receive this kind of data. But you should hopefully receive data that defines where the camera is, precisely how it's pointing, and the film and lens combination that defines the FOV. If the job involves animation, you'll also need any camera moves or setting changes and the frame at which they occur. With this information, you can simulate the real camera with a computer version.

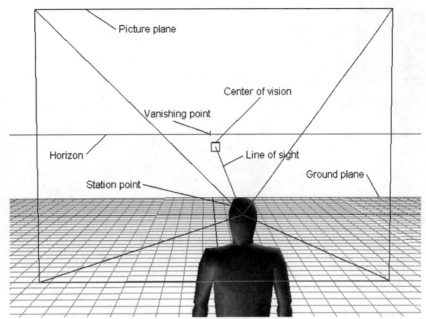

Figure 7-3: The components of traditional perspective. In order to match new 3D geometry with an existing image, you must either have access to data that defines these components or be able to derive them from an examination of the image.

If you must work from an image, the task is different, but not overwhelming. The best way to see how it's done is to take a look at a concrete example and work through the problems one at a time. We'll be dealing with problems of perspective matching in this section and appearance matching in the next. Both are necessary to create a workable illusion.

Let's assume that our task is to produce a composite image of an elephant defiling the reflecting pool before the Taj Mahal for a signature image of a tacky new curry-flavored vodka. The agency supplies you with the background image, shown in Figure 7-4.

Figure 7-4: The client wants us to put an elephant in the pool in front of the Taj Mahal to pitch a new curry-flavored vodka. Well, don't knock work, I guess.

The first thing we do is check our 3D archives for an elephant. We find the nice pachyderm shown in Figure 7-5 and carefully pose it according to the agency's sketch.

Now we have to examine the background image and determine its perspective so that we can match it in our composite image. This is a pretty easy job; it's a straight-on, single-perspective image and the horizon is easy to determine by extending nonparallel lines. The critical lines are shown in Figure 7-6.

Figure 7-5: Our own pachyderm, posed and ready to wade.

Figure 7-6: The background image with important perspective lines drawn in.

Depending upon the tools included in the 3D program, matching a perspective can be either an easy and quick or a tough and tedious task.

It's helpful to use the marked-up version of the background image to adjust the perspective of the foreground element. We can then replace it with the clean image for the final rendering. Using the tools built into the 3D program, we can then create a grid and use it to match the perspective of the background image.

Depending upon the tools included in the program, this can either be an easy and quick or a tough and tedious task. The best programs for this work let you select a quadrangular area on the ground plane in the background and use it to derive the perspective of the 3D camera. Short of this, you may need to manually adjust the camera position, angle, FOV, camera target location, and so on to achieve a match. When making adjustments manually, it's awfully easy to make just one adjustment too many and end up skewed (so to speak).

Once the camera is positioned and aligned to produce a true perspective, the grid is moved into place, as in Figure 7-7, where it's used to align the vertical location of the elephant's feet.

Figure 7-7: The grid is located where we want the elephant's feet to be. Note how its perspective matches the background.

Now all we have to do is drop in the elephant and we're done. Take a look at Figure 7-8 and see the result. Something's missing in the image, namely the shadows and reflections that should match those already there—we'll talk about how to add these critical elements in the next section.

Figure 7-8: Our elephant's in place, but, boy, does it look drab—no shadows, no reflection. It looks just like what it is: a 3D elephant plopped onto a 2D image. The client won't like this.

Matching Appearance

It's essential to match perspectives between 3D CGI and other media, but it's also vital to match appearances. Real-world objects and people have exceptionally complex appearances; thousands of diverse hairs and minute skin flaws and features produce an appearance that is just plain impossible to duplicate with today's computers and software. At the same time, however, with a great deal of effort by artists and CPUs, it's possible to make many 3D objects fit in well enough with live action to be usable.

With a great deal of effort by artists and CPUs, it's possible to make many 3D objects fit in well enough with live action to be usable.

While bump mapping changes the surface appearance of an object, it doesn't affect the edges or shadows.

Realism

The most significant aspects of a realistic appearance are the accuracy and smoothness of the silhouette or outline, the texturing of the rendered surfaces, the lighting, and the interaction between the 3D objects and other parts of the scene.

As we saw in Chapter 6, combining different kinds of mapping can produce wonderful surface appearances. But recall the discussion about bump mapping: while it changes the surface appearance, it doesn't affect the edges or shadows. Look at the sphere in Figure 7-9; the Phong shading algorithm has done a wonderful job of camouflaging the true faceted nature of the object, but the silhouette gives away the game.

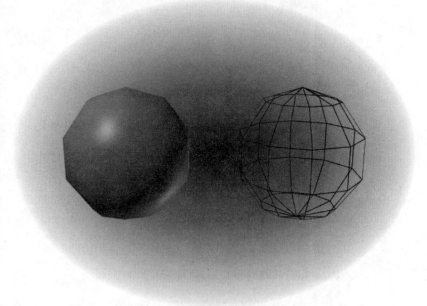

Figure 7-9: The surface of the "sphere" on the left is smooth, but its silhouette gives the lie to the surface. It's no smooth sphere, as its wireframe brother on the right reveals.

The answer, of course, is to bump up the complexity of 3D objects until their silhouettes take on the desired appearance. And to create a complex surface appearance, you can keep adding texture and other kinds of maps until you get the look you want. In *Toy Story*, Buzz Lightyear required 189 separate texture maps when he wasn't dirty and another 45 when he was! It's that kind of complexity that made it necessary to use 117 Sun SPARCstations with 192 to 384MB RAM *each* (and 294 processors total) to render the film!

That Flat, Cartoon Look

Sometimes, you don't want a realistic look; if you're rendering 3D art for compositing with cartoon-style 2D paintwork, you must take an entirely different tack.

At the present time, this kind of work is done principally for stylized video games like LucasArts Entertainment's Full Throttle. The technique is relatively simple. It combines color reduction with a line-drawing algorithm that draws edge lines like a cartoonist would. In Figure 7-10, the cube on the right has been processed with a cartoon filter, while the cube on the left has not been processed.

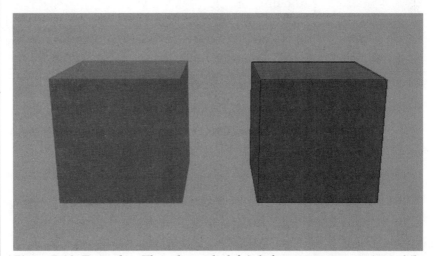

Figure 7-10: Two cubes. The cube on the left is before cartoon processing, while the cube on the right has been processed for compositing with 2D paintwork. Note the automatically generated edge lines and flat, even shading.

This look can be achieved in several ways. The most tedious method is to load each frame into an image processing program and manually edit it. This allows you the most control, of course, but will probably also produce inconsistencies from frame to frame, as well as drive you bonkers. Mind you, the inconsistencies might be a blessing rather than a curse, as it may add a desirable "hands-on" look that reduces the cold, computer look. As to whether being driven bonkers is a blessing; well, many of the tedious tasks required to produce animation have this effect!

It's much easier to use a shader or filter built into the 3D program to control the rendering and/or process each frame automatically immediately after rendering. What you sacrifice in control with this method, you more than make up for in time.

Lighting

Lighting is also critical to matching the look of 3D to other media. Returning to our elephant example, remember that our first effort looked flat and inaccurate because our elephant neither cast a shadow nor created a reflection in the pool. These defects are important because while viewers might not know *what's* missing, they'll recognize that something is and disbelieve the illusion.

The first step is to study the shadows in our background image; you'll note in Figure 7-4 that the sun is low and to the right, creating weak shadows that run from the right to the left. We'll add a shadow-casting light to simulate this sunlight and a special type of 3D geometry called a *matte object* that can receive shadows but not obstruct our view of the background. Figure 7-11 shows this geometry and the direction of the light coming in from the right.

Figure 7-11: We've added a light to simulate the sun and a "shadow catcher," a matte object that can receive shadows but be otherwise invisible in the scene. The matte object is placed where we want our shadow to appear.

When we render the scene shown in Figure 7-11, we can see several defects in our setup, as shown in Figure 7-12.

Figure 7-12: We've added a shadow, but it may not be an improvement. It's too dark, at the wrong angle, and just seems to lay there instead of draping across the landscape like a good shadow should.

First, the light is not aligned the same as the sun, producing shadows that don't match the angle of those in the photograph. Second, the shadow is much too dark. Third, the shadow doesn't follow the contours of the landscape but just overlays the whole left foreground like a big dark blob. We'll adjust the light position and shadow brightness and try again.

You can see the results of the adjustments in Figure 7-13. The shadow angles are better and the shadow brightness more closely matches the existing shadows. But the shadow still doesn't lay right along the landscape. We'll add a second shadow catcher to conform the shadow shape to the background landscape.

Figure 7-13: With the light position and shadow brightness adjusted, it looks much better, but the shadows still don't match the landscape.

Adding a second shadow catcher to this scene is relatively easy—we only need to match the raised walkway along the left edge of the pool, as in Figure 7-14. The landscape beyond the walkway is just about at the same height as the water, so we can leave the first shadow catcher to add shadows at that height.

Figure 7-14: A second shadow catcher conforms the cast 3D shadows to the shape of the walkway. Figure 7-14a shows the new shadow catcher and Figure 7-14b shows the result—much better!

Our final step is to add an object to create a flat reflection in the pool. Depending upon the software, this can be done using our first shadow catcher, but for the sake of clarity, we'll add a third, as in Figure 7-15.

Our final image in Figure 7-16 shows our elephant merged into the scene. The reflection and the shadows help to sell the idea that the elephant is actually a part of the Taj Mahal scene.

Figure 7-15: The white object creates a flat reflection at the height of the water's surface. This is the final piece we need for our exercise.

Figure 7-16: Our final image shows what may just become the signature image of Ponderous Pachyderm Vodka ("Two drinks and you'll move slowly too!"). The reflection and shadows help sell the idea that the elephant is actually in the pool.

Matching Movement

I've shown briefly how to solve the perspective match problem with still images. It can be tedious, but its problems are not insurmountable. Moving perspective matches are something else again. For decades, movie production companies prevented having to match camera moves in composite imagery by "locking down" the camera. But modern cinema just can't live with a single-position camera, even in one scene. The result has been a variety of solutions for different situations.

One alternative is to use a *motion control* camera that's controlled by a computer. Originally perfected by John Edlund and the ILM team for *Star Wars*, it's moved beyond the special effects stage to more general use on the sound stage. The motion control camera makes it possible to repeat a camera move precisely as many times as necessary and store the camera path and other data as a digital file. This information can then be transferred to high-end software to control a digital camera and move it identically through the 3D scene.

Where it's not possible to use a motion control camera, it's still possible to derive a camera path and other important data from the filmed or videotaped images themselves. For example, 3D-Equalizer software from Science.D.Visions, shown in Figure 7-17, can reconstruct a camera motion path in 3D space and export it to high-end 3D animation software.

Matching object or camera movement is not a trivial task. Without the help of a computer somewhere in the process, it's pretty much a trial-and-error process. Limiting camera moves to smooth, consistent, linear single moves can make the task theoretically possible, but it won't be easy even then.

The motion control camera makes it possible to repeat a camera move precisely as many times as necessary and store the camera path and other data as a digital file.

Figure 7-17: 3D-Equalizer from Science.D.Visions can reconstruct a camera motion path from the images themselves.

Matching Sound

When a live-action movie or video is created, the dialog is initially recorded simultaneously along with the images. Later, after the movie is edited together, dialog may be rerecorded to enhance it, and other dialog, music, and sound effects are added. The reverse is true in the typical animated movie—the dialog or music is usually recorded first and the animation is timed to the dialog. It's easier to match the animation to the dialog than vice versa.

Working with digital sound is a definite advantage for an animator. First, it's possible to edit digital sound to adjust the length without changing the pitch. In other words, you can speed up dialog without your actor sounding like Alvin the Chipmunk! You can also, of course, slow dialog down in the same way.

Second, digital audio can be viewed along a timeline and compared to the keyframes that define the animation. It's a relatively simple task to move the keys to match pretimed sound; much easier than the reverse. In Figure 7-18, a waveform of a .44 Magnum report is displayed above a track that displays the keys for movement of a bullet. Note that the bullet has a beginning position, a position defined at the start of the sound, and a position at the end. The first and second keys ensure that the movement when it comes will be sudden; the third key establishes a destination for the bullet object.

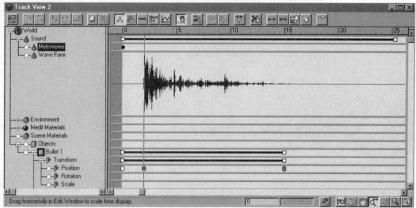

Figure 7-18: A visual representation of the sound of a .44 Magnum being fired is shown at the top of this dialog box, while the keys defining the movement of a bullet object are shown below. Seeing it all in one place makes timing easy.

If we wanted to use cartoon techniques, we could also add a squash key just before the shot and a stretch as it speeds along its way to elongate it. Seeing the sound helps to determine where these keys should be placed. If the timing of the shot sound must be adjusted, it can simply be slid along the timeline.

Moving On

We've looked at different ways of integrating 3D with other media, learned about blue screen, the alpha channel, creating shadows where none exist, making reflections for elephants, and moving a bullet to match the sound it never made. Rather a full day, I'd say. In the next chapter, we'll look at how 3D has penetrated almost every area of commerce, science, engineering, and entertainment. And that's another full day…

8

Applications

In this chapter, we'll look at *how* 3D is used and give you some tips on how to succeed in these fields. 3D is such a versatile tool that its uses seem to be as broad as anyone's imagination. People use 3D to visualize what never was, what could be, what's being built, what was built millennia before, and what occurs in an instant or over a century. Animation and still images created in 3D can inform, persuade, instruct, entertain, and even titillate. Applications for 3D are almost as broad as applications for computers themselves.

You can think of 3D applications as falling into one of three areas according to their goal: inform, persuade, or entertain. There are obvious crossovers between these areas. For example, advertising is intended first to persuade, but is also informative (although it's difficult to find the informational value in some advertising). Advertisers have also found that if you *entertain* while you're attempting to *persuade*, the second task seems much easier.

Inform

As we're often told, this is the Information Age; information is a *very* valuable commodity. Today, the communication, classification, and interpretation of information seems to be one of the principal activities of most human enterprises. Businesses, governments, charities, schools—everyone—is determined to accumulate, massage, and use all kinds of information, including much that we may not want used.

There are many legitimate and beneficial reasons to accumulate and use information; used properly, it increases the efficiency of a system and lets the decision-makers rule with wisdom. To that end, 3D can assist in making information more understandable and thus more timely.

Business Graphics

In the earliest times, information was communicated and classified in its raw form—words and numbers. But information itself has become increasingly more complex and comprehensive since the first reports of early chariot production figures. ("Antonius, Claudius, and I made four chariots last year.") Organizations became larger and the amount of information available increased exponentially. Advances in communications also ensured that as the complexity of the information increased, so too would its quantity and the speed with which it arrived. ("Boss, the second batch of buggy whip invoices from the Midwest just came in the mail.") Today, information arrives in huge quantities at high speed and often requires instant analysis and reaction. ("Sales of giant prunes in the six southern markets are not matching predictions; we'll need to lower the special 'This Week Only' price another six cents.") Raw data, like that in Table 8-1, is just not enough any more.

Sales Region	Jan	Feb	Mar	Apr	May	Jun
Region 1	100	98	96	80	89	99
Region 2	100	102	104	108	110	109
Region 3	100	100	104	104	106	103
Region 4	100	99	98	97	96	99

Sales Region	Jul	Aug	Sep	Oct	Nov	Dec
Region 1	101	125	131	131	142	139
Region 2	109	108	107	109	110	112
Region 3	100	98	99	101	103	105
Region 4	103	106	108	110	110	111

Table 8-1: For generations, tables like this were the only methods most people had to analyze data. It takes a sharp eye to discern trouble spots, bright spots, and trends.

Alternatives to the display of raw data were developed over the years by mathematicians, statisticians, and others for whom analysis was especially significant. The 2D graph shown in Figure 8-1 is an example of a relatively primitive form of data display that is still quite helpful. Charting capabilities like this have been available even to desktop computer users for a decade.

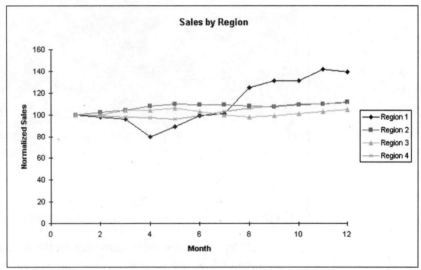

Figure 8-1: A 2D graph makes the relationship of the sales data from Table 8-1 clearer. Beginning with a normalized sales figure of 100 at the start of the year, it's easy to track the percentage gains over the previous year.

Adding a third dimension to the display of information really makes the interrelationships between elements clear. And the fact that you can create a 3D chart like the one in Figure 8-2 with a couple of mouse clicks in Microsoft Excel is an example of just how far consumer software has come. Note how the use of 3D communicates the information for each region quickly and illustrates trends clearly. While the 2D line graph in Figure 8-1 also shows this information, 3D is not only more dramatic, but also communicates the information better.

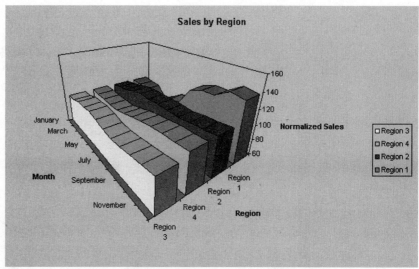

Figure 8-2: A few mouse clicks, a little fiddling, and the data in Table 8-1 is displayed in three dimensions. It clearly shows who's up, who's doing OK, and who's getting a visit from the boss next week.

TIP

Use 3D to communicate information faster. It's easier for adults to judge the relative size of three-dimensional objects than to sort through intersecting 2D lines.

Most business graphics are no more complex than the examples shown here. But other types of information are more complex, more subtle, and change in more than one aspect over time. This requires more complex analysis and a more complex display. For example, a field of pollution sensors as simulated in Figure 8-3 might be dispersed throughout a water table at preprogrammed levels. The data returned by these sensors would not only show the dispersion of a contaminant at any one instant, but could also reveal its source.

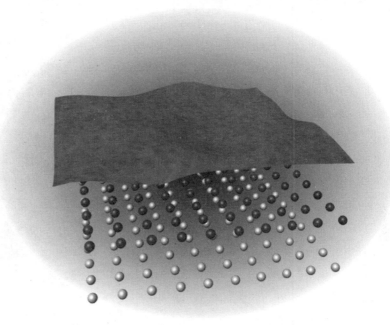

Figure 8-3: Correlating and analyzing readings from 200 groundwater pollution sensors that change over time would be a major task. But careful analysis could assist you in finding the source of the pollution.

The easiest way to show changes in data over time is animation. This is particularly true when the data has a natural physical dispersion, as in the simulated pollution scenario in Figure 8-4. And if the data has a three-dimensional component, 3D animation is the obvious solution.

TIP

Use 3D animation to show changes in data over time. Where the data has a natural dispersion, or if spatial dispersion would assist analysis, 3D aids immeasurably in comprehension.

Figure 8-4: The dispersion of pollution at an instant in time can be captured in a 3D image derived from the sensor data, but to show the dispersion over time, you need 3D animation.

Software & Internet Interfaces

Another use of 3D that has become more and more important in the past few years is its use as components of a software or Internet interface. Despite the increasing standardization of user interface tools, there's still some room for innovation. MetaTools has been in the forefront of innovative interface design; check the interface for the Spheroid Designer, part of Kai's Power Tools, in Figure 8-5. OK, it's not Microsoft standard!

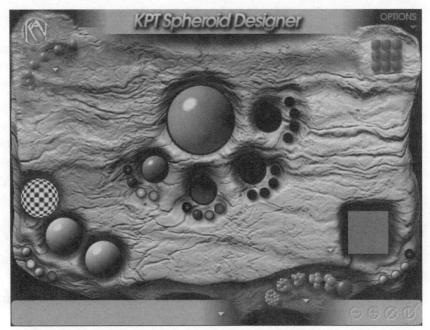

Figure 8-5: Spheroid Designer from MetaTools (part of Kai's Power Tools) is a good example of innovative 3D interface design. It may not meet Microsoft's or Apple's interface design standards, but it works, and works well.

With the incredible expansion of the Internet and the development of Virtual Reality Modeling Language (VRML) and Virtual Reality Behavior Language (VRBL), 3D promises to add both new content and new methods of navigation to the Web surfer's domain. By using VRML and VRBL to create virtual worlds in which participants can move, Web site developers can produce a far richer and more exciting environment by adding the new dimension of mobility. But there's a fly in the VRML ointment: 3D is more complicated than 2D and puts a greater burden on both the server and Web surfer. See the sidebar for a brief discussion of the issues and solutions.

Maintaining 3D Animation Display Quality

To be effective, 3D animation must be displayed at a frame rate that matches the original target rate. Below approximately 7 frames per second (fps), animation looks jerky; it begins to be acceptable at 10 fps.

If the speed of any component in the display pipeline is slow, the quality of the animation will suffer. For animations delivered from a local source, such as a CD-ROM or hard disk, the pipeline consists of the storage device, the computer bus, the graphics or central processor, video or system RAM, the display card, and the monitor. If any one of these falls below the minimum speed for display of that animation, it suffers and the illusion it's supposed to foster suffers as well.

Online animation adds the element of distance between the storage device and the rest of the pipeline. Since the communications link can seldom keep up with the rest of the components, you must either reduce the size of the 3D imagery, its complexity, or the nature of the data that's being transmitted. If you choose to put the rendering burden on the server, then it must send a stream of rendered images to the display—a very slow and inefficient process.

The better strategy is to create a language that sets up specific parameters for defining 3D objects—that's VRML. This lets the server send a series of basic parameters, which are then interpreted and rendered into a virtual 3D world by the client station. Since the brunt of the processing work is placed on the client, rendering speed is dependent more on the receiver's hardware than on the speed of their Net connection. This will typically produce a frame rate that is much higher than with server-rendered images (although still not terribly realistic).

At the present time, virtual worlds are really available only to a relatively few people with access to communications pipelines with the speed and bandwidth to create the sense of immediacy that's necessary to an interactive 3D environment. For the 3D artist, VRML work requires special tools and special care to minimize the burdens on the system while still providing a worthwhile 3D experience.

TIP

If you'd like to try creating a VRML world, explore Pioneer version 1.1 from Caligari on the Companion CD-ROM.

Architecture, Design & Engineering

Architecture, design, and engineering have the following in common that make them perfect applications for 3D:

- Need for visualization

- Strong use of computer tools

- Precision

Despite persistent derogatory comments from right-brained people about the alleged lack of creativity in engineering, all of these fields are about creativity. But it's not the creativity that uses pastel chalk and an artist's pad; it's the other kind—the kind that produces toasters that work, houses that withstand earthquakes and hurricanes, and faucets that are quiet and drip-free as well as graceful. Professionals in these areas often turn to 3D to make their jobs easier, to communicate their work to others, and to present it in the best light possible (pun intended).

The products of all three fields can be so complex as to defy understanding by the casual observer. For example, a typical building may have dozens of systems to heat, cool, humidify, clean, and distribute the air; control perimeter and interior access; signal security; and provide electricity, water, natural gas, steam, compressed air, computer network access, video, lighting, and so on. The set of plans that communicate the information necessary to build such a building is as complex as the structure itself. It's no wonder, therefore, that architects have always turned to 3D to convey the sense of their work. Up until the last decade, however, that 3D was almost always in the form of wood and plastic scale models with little puffy sponge trees and tiny silhouettes of pedestrians.

Moving from physical three-dimensional models to 3D models has let the architect view his project from any viewpoint, even inside—a very difficult vantage point to achieve in a small-scale physical model. *Everything* can be adjusted and controlled in the 3D version of the building, from surfaces to lighting to time of day. 3D lets the professional test and examine his own creation under all conditions.

One popular architectural 3D concept is the *virtual walkthrough*. In a virtual walkthrough, the architect moves a 3D camera along a path through the building, giving the viewer a feel for what the building will be like when finished. In Figure 8-6, an interior created in ArchiTECH.PC is shown. The power of 3D for visualization is obvious.

Figure 8-6: Looking down a 3D staircase in ArchiTECH.PC. It's amazing how much feel you can get from an image.

TIP

CD-ROM

On the Companion CD-ROM is a demonstration version of a powerful architectural 2D and 3D program, ArchiTECH.PC. Try it out!

Architecture, design, and engineering are also well suited to the use of 3D because all three professions are so well invested now in Computer-aided design and drafting (CADD). It's hard to find a T-square or drafting board anymore—the computer's power and precision have taken over in virtually all of these kinds of firms.

One result of the CADD invasion has been that a firm's technical files are now stored on computer. If the design or engineering software is not itself capable of visualization, the files can be readily exported to software that is. Two of the most popular file formats that allow the exchange of data between programs are the Autodesk Drawing Exchange Format (.dxf) and the Initial Graphics Exchange Specification (.iges) from the National Institute of Standards.

TIP

If you want to work in engineering, design, or architectural visualization, make sure that your 3D software imports and exports files in at least one of the common exchange file formats.

Finally, these fields require precision. That's one reason computers have become so popular: computers are precise. In fact, they're so precise that they have a hard time dealing with anything that's *not* precise. It's a big deal when scientists are able to give computers the kind of "fuzzy logic" that lets humans make connections between disparate topics that are not obvious.

The precision of computers is also necessary for 3D—the software is still not able to respond to a human instruction like "Give me a two shot at sunset in November in San Francisco with a light fog." No, current 3D software requires that you place the simulated camera *here* and its point of interest *there* and set the light, the fog, and the actors precisely where they must be. Using a source file from a nice, precise CADD program gives the 3D visualizer a leg up.

For example, Figure 8-7 shows a portion of a processing plant with attendant piping. The scene file was imported from a CADD program into 3D Studio MAX, a 3D modeling and animation program, and rendered there. It's not an intensely complex file, but there are still almost 21,000 faces—more than I'd want to construct, even using primitives and other shortcuts!

Figure 8-7: Thanks to the luxury of widely accepted file exchange formats, engineers and visualizers have a way to pass scenes back and forth. This image had its origins in a CADD program, but was rendered quickly in a 3D program.

Scientific, Medical & Legal Visualization

Scientific, medical, and legal visualization are similar in many respects to the fields of architecture, design, and engineering. The purpose of all is to communicate complex or confusing concepts and information to others in a form that's more easily understood. In the first two, it's the information itself that's complex. In legal visualization, however, it's not just the complexity of the information; the nature of the forum makes the information even more difficult to understand.

These just aren't simple areas in which to work. Prior training and experience in a related field is an absolute necessity. Scientific visualization is done by professionals with degrees in the subject fields or by artists working directly with them. It's easier to teach 3D to a biologist than to teach molecular biology to a computer artist.

Scientific Visualization

Science itself has progressed far from its precomputer roots. Scientists are now able to explore hitherto unknown areas of the universe, both cosmic and microscopic, and the visualization of scientific concepts in 3D lets scientists communicate information about these realms to their peers and to laypeople. Even basic principles that are well accepted today, such as the earth orbiting the sun, are frequently more quickly understood when presented in 3D. Just imagine if 3D visualization had been available during Galileo's 1633 inquisition for heresy. It might not have made a difference to the overzealous Roman Catholic tribunal, but it sure sounds like an interesting movie concept!

Figures 8-8 and 8-9 are two examples of scientific visualization at the microscopic end of the scale. The 3D images are not only striking themselves, but also illustrate how the Internet and 3D visualization have made it possible for research institutions to assemble exceptionally valuable visual research tools that can be accessed from anywhere in the world.

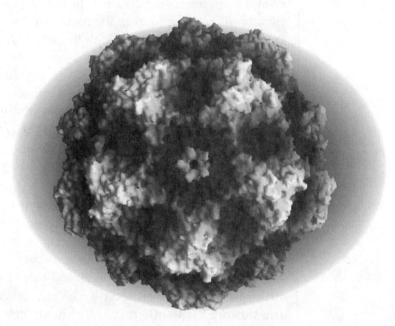

Figure 8-8: This image of the canine parvovirus was created using radial depth cue rendering by Jean-Yves Sgro. It may look like a cabbage to you and me, but it shows how powerful 3D scientific visualization can be. (Image © 1994 by Jean-Yves Sgro.)

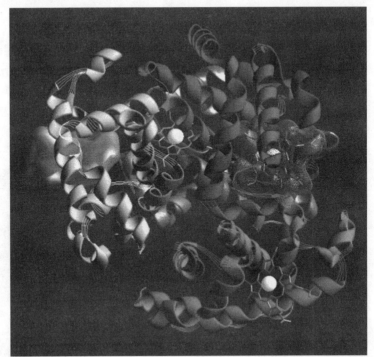

Figure 8-9: A complex protein, 1HHO_oxy-hemoglobin_1, is shown in this image. (From the SWISS-3DIMAGE image database and used with the permission of the Geneva University Hospital, the University of Geneva, Switzerland, and Dr. Manuel C. Peitsch of the Glaxo Institute of Molecular Biology.)

Medical Visualization

Medical illustration can be thought of as part of the larger field of scientific visualization. Its subjects always relate to medicine or the anatomy or functions of the body. It's a complex field with a long history, but it has been changing rapidly over the past decade or more. Where it was almost exclusively found in the academic world, medical illustration has also found uses in the advertising and legal professions. Man has studied anatomy since the first caveman peered at the entrails of his late lamented friend and wondered what all that "stuff" was.

We know more now, of course, but most of us could make little more sense of all that "stuff" than the caveman. For example, could you identify a pancreas? I know I couldn't! Yet the medical illustrator is constantly required to communicate all kinds of abstruse medical information in a manner that clarifies the information being communicated. To be a medical illustrator requires a skilled artistic hand, a trained eye, a thorough understanding of anatomy and general medical knowledge, and collaboration with a subject matter expert. In Figure 8-10, renal normal anatomy is effectively illustrated using 3D. All of the parts and their physical location and relationships are clearly displayed.

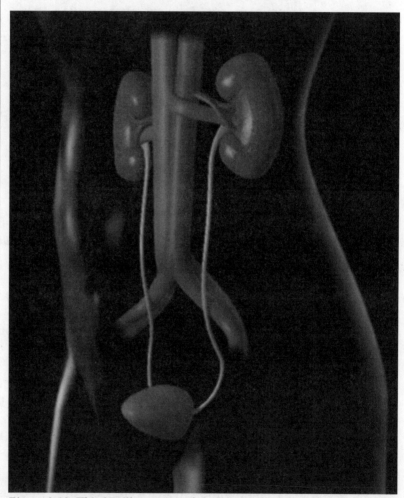

Figure 8-10: This 3D illustration of renal normal anatomy was prepared by medical illustrator Mike De La Flor of the University of Houston Medical School–Houston. (© 1995 UTHHSC.)

The use of 3D solves some of the illustration problems but does not make the process automatic. For example, although standardized 3D organ models are available from such 3D "organ banks" as Viewpoint DataLabs International, Inc., they must be painstakingly modified to depict an abnormality, injury, or disease process. Often, it's easier to draw the subject in 2D. Compare the 3D illustration in Figure 8-10 with the 2D illustration in Figure 8-11. The 2D image would be economically infeasible in 3D.

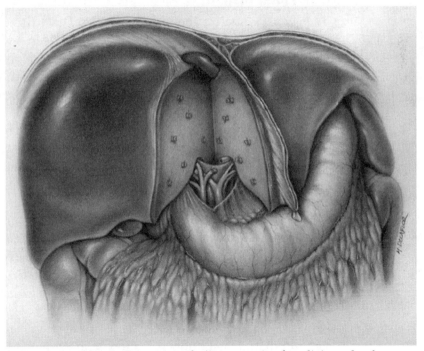

Figure 8-11: This 2D illustration of a liver resection for a living related transplantation was also created by Mike De La Flor of the University of Houston Medical School–Houston. It would be virtually impossible to re-create in 3D. (© 1995 UTHHSC.)

Medical and scientific images are often constructed from various kinds of digital imaging data, such as magnetic resonance imaging (MRI), computer-assisted tomography (CAT), or nuclear magnetic resonance (NMR) spectroscopy. Today's wide availability of powerful computers has made it possible to analyze processes and conditions that occur within soft tissues that are transparent to X rays. With these techniques and 3D imaging, fewer biopsies and invasive surgeries are required.

Legal Visualization

Legal visualization is an odd field. The artist must not only be able to work with subject matter experts in a wide variety of fields—as diverse as the subject matters of lawsuits and crimes—but also be able to describe their techniques in such a way that jury members can understand. Add to that the complexities of the trial court environment, with its strict rules for examining witnesses, stilted language, and antagonistic relationships, and it can be a minefield for an unprepared 3D artist.

As I mentioned much earlier, I was a trial lawyer for some 13 years. I often had to present complex or confusing evidence to lay juries who either didn't want to be there in the first place or were not able to receive evidence in such abstruse niceties as digital signal processing, blood spatter, or fingerprinting. It often required hours and days of testimony from experts just to present the foundation for and explain the meaning of such evidence. In fact, it was this problem that caused me to go into 3D animation in the first place!

Over the past decade, the use of legal visualization, or forensic animation as I dubbed it a few years ago, has spread widely. It's been accepted in many kinds of cases in courtrooms throughout the country. The subject matter of legal visualization can be simple—cars and trucks—or as complex as any scientific subject. It's seldom boring and it also offers the thrill of being on the witness stand under the hostile examination of a lawyer who needs to destroy your credibility to win his case.

There are three types of legal visuals: tutorials, illustrations, and simulations. Tutorials present information of a general nature, such as how an alcohol breath-testing device or variable-pitch airplane propeller chip operates. It's presented as a visual aid to the judge and jury of facts that, while in need of explication, are generally agreed upon between the parties. Illustrations are the most common form of legal visuals; they illustrate the testimony of an expert or lay witness and are offered in support of that testimony. The animation or still image can't stand alone.

The last type of legal visual is the simulation. In a simulation, the computer plays an equal part with the witnesses in determining what occurred. For example, the speed of an automobile pre-collision can be determined by combining evidence of skid marks, its weight, coefficient of friction of the pavement, and so on. Feeding all of this evidence into a computer so that it can calculate the speed and create a 3D animation of the event would be a simulation. Simulations are relatively rare, because so much of the 3D process is subject to examination and proof and so little of the subject evidence is accurate enough: "He was going *about* thirty miles an hour." Or "It was pretty dark out."

One of the special advantages of using 3D for legal work is that once the scene is set up according to the witnesses' statements, you can then choose any other vantage point from which to view the incident, as in Figure 8-12. Often, this is very effective in nailing down or disproving the claims made.

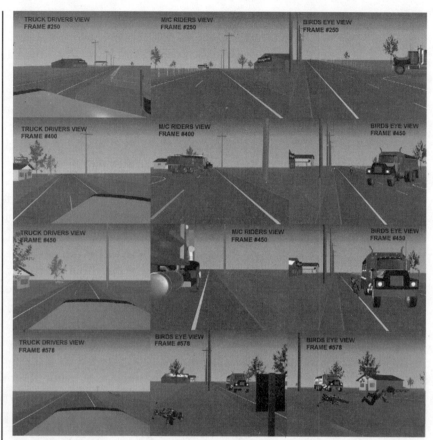

Figure 8-12: This series of images are frames from a forensic animation created by AEGIS, Inc. The availability of multiple viewpoints can be critical in understanding events. The images in the left column present the truck driver's view; those in the middle column (with the exception of the last image) present the rider's view; and those in the right column with the last image in the middle column present a bird's-eye view. (© 1996 AEGIS, Inc.)

Computer-based Education

Computer-based education has become a hot field recently, and not just because computer makers see it as one of their best hopes to sell computers to parents. It's an effective method of providing structured information and drills that can be gauged to the child at the keyboard. 3D has no special place in educational software that makes it preferable to 2D. Of course, with 3D, an educator can present three-dimensional information, can make the display of information attractive and engaging to all age levels, and can make it possible to visualize unseen areas of the world. But these capabilities are part of what makes 3D so useful in many fields.

Figure 8-13 illustrates how 3D can be used in educational software. A.D.A.M. Software has won many awards with their two-dimensional explorations of the human body. Earlier versions of their "A.D.A.M. The Inside Story" software used illustrations painstakingly hand-drawn by medical illustrators exclusively, while the most recent version, the 1997 edition, adds a 3D exploration tool called Cybervizz 3D with anatomical 3D graphics derived from cadaver data (yecch!).

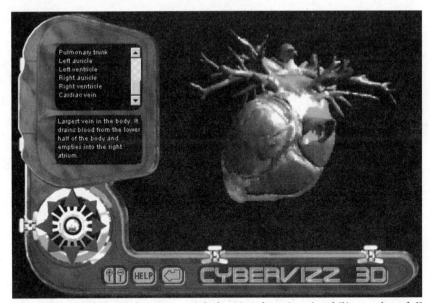

Figure 8-13: While 3D has no special place in education, its ability to show full three-dimensional representations of objects makes it a good tool for many uses. (© 1996 A.D.A.M. Software, Inc.)

Persuade

The second major use of 3D graphics is to *persuade*. While many of the informational uses described in the previous section are actually used in an attempt to persuade *someone* of *something*, the critical difference between using 3D to inform and using it to persuade is one of intent. (You see, those three years of law school were good for something!)

Scientists seeking grants may put together a multimedia presentation for the granting authority that includes what were originally informational 3D imagery. And lawyers don't present evidence, 3D or otherwise, just to *inform* a jury, but to *persuade* it. Finally, business presentations of every kind are made to persuade others in or out of the company to adopt a particular course of action.

TIP

Whenever you are called upon to put together a *factual* presentation, consider the setting, audience, and intent of the presentation. If you approach it as an exercise in *persuasion*, you may be more successful.

Advertising

Advertising has become a fertile ground for 3D use. Those with products, services, or ideas to sell have always combined information with persuasion to seek customers or converts. Sometimes, the informational aspect dominates; other times it's the persuasive. Whichever is dominant, however, advertising must first attract before it can do either. And 3D has found a niche in attracting attention. Whether it's the festive air of dancing candy, the power of an armed and dangerous mouthwash bottle, or a car causing a field of corn to pop, 3D can be a powerful attractor that holds the viewers' attention while it conveys the persuasive message.

Other commercials may not be as glossy as those mentioned in the last paragraph but still make effective use of 3D. Toothbrushes have become one of the battlegrounds in the 3D commercial wars with several manufacturers trading 3D brushing demonstrations. This may seem puzzling at first, but it reflects one of the advantages of 3D: its effectiveness in simulating events, even in a setting of a mouthful of dirty teeth—not an attractive environment for a sales message.

◄ **TIP**
. . . .

When considering an ad concept, remember that you can tailor reality to match the message. I don't mean fraud here, just the creation of "symbolic" plaque to be "brushed away" by a 3D toothbrush. Use 3D to sell the idea without necessarily depicting all of the uglier aspects of reality.

. . . . ►

As we saw with our mock Vodka advertisement in the last chapter, the use of 3D in advertising isn't limited to television commercials. It's as common in print as on television, although it's usually used more subtly in print. Objects like our elephant are placed into environments that make them more attractive or more striking.

◄ **TIP**
. . . .

To grab the viewer's attention, use 3D to create unusual combinations of elements.

. . . . ►

Advertising agencies and their clients know that before you can persuade, you must first claim the attention of the audience. And since the public is still fascinated by the use of 3D, it makes a great vehicle for attracting their attention. Still, the best uses of 3D in advertising are those that begin with a great concept and end with great execution, like the dancing Gummy Life Savers or the sport utility vehicles that climb buildings, move from season to season, or overcome every possible obstacle in thirty seconds.

The image in Figure 8-14 was created by Artewisdom, a U.K. graphics design firm to convey the concept that the named companies are the "Holy Grail" of computer design. One quick look at the image is all that's necessary to gain the concept; it works.

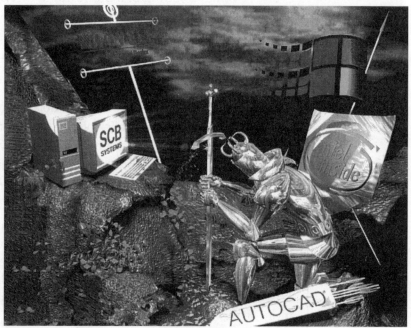

Figure 8-14: A knight has found the "Holy Grail" of computer design. (© 1996 Artewisdom, Ltd.)

It's a great challenge to communicate an idea within the thirty seconds of a television commercial. What 3D contributes is to make it possible to depict the impossible or improbable in a way that seems absolutely real and without risking any stunt performers!

TIP

Add 3D to the conceptual mix and it absolutely destroys the boundaries of "what's possible" in advertising.

Flying Logos

Television uses 3D animation to death. Almost every station or network break, movie series logo, or sports opening sequence is now created in 3D with zooming numbers and swooshing shapes. The ostensible reason for all of them is to *inform*—you *do* need to know that *Monday Night Football* is about to start, and the FCC mandates that you be told which station you're watching every 15 minutes. And of course you want to know which teams are playing or whether you're on ABC or Fox. But do you really need 3D football helmets that smash together to tell you the team names? Not really—the primary purpose of that animation is to *persuade* you that the upcoming contest will be a real battle, one worthy of your attention.

The use of 3D in television openings ("opens") is an example of what's come to be called *flying logos.* Anyone can produce a 2D image with the station call sign and channel number. Even the cheapest consumer *character generator* can add 2D text onto a video signal with the quality of Figure 8-15. A character generator, or CG, is an electronic device that, well, generates electronic characters—text.

Figure 8-15: Attractive, isn't it? This is the bare minimum: plain text from a CG, or character generator, added over the video using a keyer, an electronic device that combines two or more video signals.

With 3D, the call sign and channel number can be extruded 3D text that flies in from out of the frame and zooms to a halt in an attractive position in frame. Figure 8-16 illustrates a simple flying logo, one with "gleams and glimmers." The latter are the sparkles and highlights that always seem to appear on flying logos to show just how sparkling the coming program is. Gems and precious metals gleam and sparkle; we've automatically come to associate these flashes of light with high value.

Figure 8-16: A simple 3D flying logo with the station call sign, channel number, location, and a nice little gleam added to the 22.

Flying logos can be used in any video or multimedia presentation; they're both informative—even if marginally so—and audience grabbers. Many high-tech business presenters today make heavy use of flying logos to help keep the attention of their audiences.

TIP

Use flying logos to grab the attention of audiences. And add gleams and glimmers to suggest excellence and value.

Entertainment

The third area in which 3D has found a home is entertainment. The power of 3D to create the impossible and put the viewer in places he's never been has found a ready home with the creative types producing entertainment of all types. Perhaps the most spectacular and most visible successes have been in the movie industry. Virtually every major movie over the past decade has had some computer-generated or computer-enhanced effects. Consider these movies from the past decade: *Toy Story, Lion King, Beauty and the Beast, Hunchback of Notre Dame, Jurassic Park, Judge Dredd, Mission Impossible, The Abyss, Terminator, Terminator II: Judgment Day, Alive, Casper, Dragonheart, The Flintstones, Indian in the Cupboard, Jumanji, The Mask, Twister, 101 Dalmatians*, and *Forrest Gump*. Not all are great movies, but all featured computer-generated, and in most cases 3D, graphics.

Some of the most remarkable uses of 3D are those that are indistinguishable from the live action. In *Forrest Gump,* for example, the feather that floats behind the credits was generated by Industrial Light & Magic and composited into the film images. For all the world, it looks like a real feather, albeit a very well controlled one. It was easier to create one in 3D, of course.

TIP

To succeed in the 3D movie business, you'd best study art and animation first and filmmaking second. The best 3D artists in this business are artists and animators first and computer hackers second.

The place of 3D in the movies is assured. It lets moviemakers do things that were never possible before and take "cameras" where they could never before go. The key to good 3D in the movies and on TV is that it should be used as a means to enhance the story, not as an end in itself.

Reese's Rule of Movie Effects

While there will always be a place for movies with little plot but lots of special effects—they sell lots of popcorn—special effects should enhance and support the story, not be the story themselves.

The Rule: Special effects should not receive more attention than the story. If they do, you need a new script or fewer effects.

There's also a place for 3D behind the camera; in fact, before the cameras have ever begun to roll. It is now commonplace to use 3D to *previsualize* a movie. Previsualization involves building 3D computer models of all of the sets and locations and simulating all of the camera setups and moves. This lets the director, cinematographer, art director, and other creative personnel test out the look and feel of the movie before going onto the set. Previsualization can save a great deal of time and money during the production of a movie, as most of the kinks have been worked out before the expensive stars and crew are on the clock.

Another side benefit to previsualization is that it prevents avoidable disasters such as when the camera crane or major props won't fit into the set. A recurrent story in the industry, which may be apocryphal, insists that if previsualization had been used on *Hook*, the production company would have avoided the cost of having to rebuild a major set because the crane wouldn't fit.

Previsualization also has come to the stage. Now that many stage designers are making use of CADD to produce their sets, they can quickly visualize them in 3D to see how they look. Figure 8-17 depicts a previsualization of a stage production of the opera *Carmen*. By moving the 3D camera around the set, it lets the designers see how—and if—it all fits together.

Figure 8-17: A previsualization for the opera Carmen, courtesy of Artewisdom. (© 1996 Artewisdom, Ltd.)

I've talked about video gaming many times in this book, and it will continue to be a focus of the 3D business for the foreseeable future. Gamemakers like 3D because, first, players like its look. Second, it's quicker to produce multiple images for games using 3D than by hand-drawing. Third, again, you can do many things in 3D that are difficult if not impossible to do in any other way. Fourth, with 3D, you can use the first person perspective and enhance the game-playing experience. In Figure 8-18, another Artewisdom image, a castle awaits a gamer.

Figure 8-18: By using 3D, game designers can create wonderful, involving environments that let the player enter in first-person perspective. This castle invites the player to start the battle. (© 1996 Artewisdom, Ltd.)

Moving On

In this chapter, we examined how 3D is used in different applications to inform, persuade, and entertain. In the next—and last—chapter, I'll give you some tips and tricks that will let you solve special problems and create special effects in 3D. It'll be the chapter you probably will come back to the most after you finish reading this book.

9

Tips & Tricks

In this chapter, you'll find a potpourri of ideas that you can use in your next—or first—3D production. It'll cover tips and tricks that relate to composition, lighting, specific media, special effects, and so on. These techniques are by no means limited to the examples I've shown here, but should give you some valuable ideas on how to make your 3D images both better looking and more efficient. The next time you have a problem with a 3D scene, think in terms of some of the techniques shown here and perhaps you'll find a solution.

I've tried to make sure that the tips here are not platform- or product-specific. In general, you should be able to apply the tips and tricks in this chapter in almost any capable 3D program. By the way, it's no accident that many of these tips focus on the use of mapping to simulate objects and create effects. Mapping is one of the cross-platform techniques that can be applied in whatever program you use.

Simulating Particle Systems Effects

It's great to have all of the wonderful tools of high-end software available. You can reach into your 3D toolbox and pull out just what you need for a particular look or effect. But what if you don't have unlimited funds or your company just won't spend the additional money for the tools you feel you need? Well, in 3D, there's usually more than one way to skin a cat—or add a fiery explosion!

As I discussed in Chapter 6, particle systems are used in high-end systems to simulate fog, clouds, smoke, fire, explosions, water, rain, snow, and so on. Some of these effects, such as flowing water, cannot be simulated realistically using anything but a particle system, but others can be created using other techniques quite easily—and at a substantial savings in processing time and geometry complexity to boot.

Let's say that we want to add rocket exhaust flares to the two engines of a space fighter *without* particles. It's simple: we use mapping and a special set of image bitmaps designed just for this effect. First, I created special geometry to receive the maps, as in Figure 9-1.

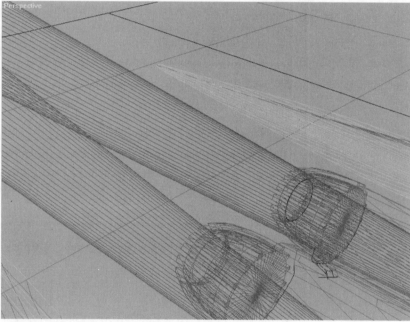

Figure 9-1: The two cones extending diagonally up to the left were added to the scene just to receive the exhaust textures.

The textures I used were from Pyromania[2] PC, a digital effects library from Visual Concept Entertainment. Together with its predecessor, Pyromania, it's a great tool to have tucked away on your shelf for when a special fire effect is required. All of the fire and flames on these CD-ROMs were filmed and then scanned at very high resolutions to make them useful in almost any situation.

I used a six-frame animation called ROCKET.AVI as my texture map and applied it to the diffuse, opacity, and self-illumination components of two different two-sided materials (shaders). The six frames are shown in Figure 9-2.

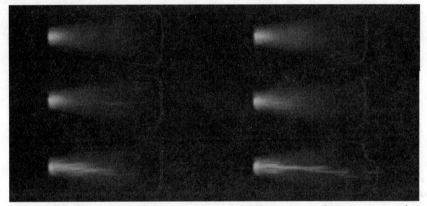

Figure 9-2: A simple six-frame sequence of a rocket exhaust from Pyromania[2] PC, a stunningly effective tool for cheap fire effects.

I created two different materials because I didn't want the two rocket exhausts to be synchronized. Nothing gives an effect away faster than overusing an effect or using a cyclical effect in synch at different points in a scene. I started one material at frame 1 and the other at frame 4, producing a realistic flame sequence, as shown in Figure 9-3.

Figure 9-3: The Pyromania rocket maps of Figure 9-2 produce this nice image when wrapped around the cones from Figure 9-1.

Do's and don'ts:

- When using mapping to simulate particle systems, use high-quality maps. While you can create animated fire bitmaps, unless you are a stunningly realistic artist, your rocket exhaust will look like it's animated.

- Match the style of the maps to the use. The Pyromania textures meld better with realistic geometry than with, say, Japanese-style anime.

- You may need to "fudge" the location and parameters of the shaders and geometry to get them to look right. And this brings me to the last of Reese's Rules; see the sidebar, "Reese's Rule of Graphics Expediency."

Reese's Rule of Graphics Expediency

If it looks good in the frame, go for it.

We're at the artistic and digital frontier here, trying to create imagery that is both effective and attractive. This 3D stuff is not quite an exact science yet, and you often need to apply unusual techniques to achieve the look or effect you want. That's OK, as long as no one gets hurt by it.

By the last comment, I only mean that it's not a good idea to retouch medical diagnostic imaging because you don't like the shape of a tumor. Retouching X rays never cured anyone, and I don't think that digital image manipulation will be much better.

But don't be afraid to try things in 3D. It's almost impossible to do permanent damage to your hardware or yourself while working in a 3D program (other than perhaps falling asleep during one of those overnight modeling sessions and knocking the monitor to the floor).

Try it, try something else, and try a third thing. Just remember to save often!

Imaging for Video

The video format was never designed for the bright colors of typical computer images. Creating images that work well on video requires care. These tips will help you create the best images for video.

Resolution

Remember when I discussed video and interlaced scanning way back in Chapter 1? Well, now that you're ready to put it all together, here are some tips on choosing the best output resolution:

- Use a final vertical resolution of 486 pixels for U.S. standard NTSC (National Television Standards Committee) video. This works well with its 525-line interlaced format; a higher vertical or horizontal resolution could result in the loss of image information. See Table 9-1 for a summary of the highest resolutions in each of the three major TV standards.

- If you must work in a higher resolution than 486 vertical pixels, be sure to maintain a 4:3 aspect ratio to match the video format and convert your final images to 640 X 486 for output.

- If your work is destined for other countries, check the TV standard they follow, as most don't follow our NTSC standard. The European PAL (Phase Alternation Line rate) and the French/former Soviet Union SECAM (Sequential Couleur avec Memoire) both use 625 vertical lines. Table 9-1 summarizes the differences between these systems.

System	Vertical Lines	Active Lines	Horizontal Resolution	Vertical Resolution	Frame Rate (fps)
NTSC	525	484	427	242	29.97
PAL	625	575	425	290	25
SECAM	625	575	465	290	25

Table 9-1: This table summarizes the differences between the three major TV standards used in the world today. Vertical and horizontal resolution refer to the maximum number of distinguishable bits of information in each direction.

Object Placement & Size

Only 484 of the 525 lines in the NTSC signal are available to display signal information. The rest are used for synchronization—they make up the black bar that you see when the picture rolls vertically on your television.

To prevent this synch, or *blanking* area from appearing on the screen, the industry uses *overscan*, which enlarges the 525-line picture in all directions so that the synch area is hidden. It's called the blanking area because the video signal is blanked out during this time to allow the electron beam time to move from the bottom of the screen to the top in preparation for the next scan without drawing a line on the screen.

Here are some tips for keeping your work on the screen where it belongs and not lost behind the bezel that surrounds the picture tube or in a scan converter, the device that translates your imagery to video:

- Make sure that you keep action and titles within the "safe" areas, or safe frames. Typical safe areas are 90 percent of the screen for action and 80 percent for titles, as shown in Figure 9-4.

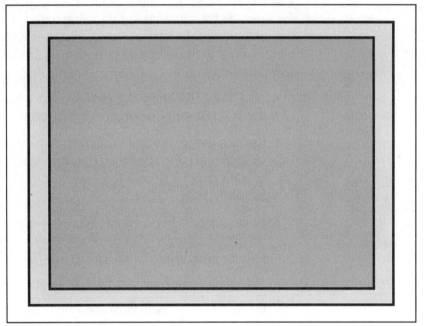

Figure 9-4: The video safe areas: 80 percent for titles and 90 percent for action. These are also called "safe frames."

- Don't use single-pixel horizontal or vertical lines. Horizontal lines will flicker badly because they will usually lie on only one scanline. Vertical lines will blur or lose their color.

- Objects should occupy at least five scanlines in order to display their own color if situated between areas of different colors.

- Avoid fonts with serifs where possible, such as the font in which this book is printed. Try to use sans serif fonts, such as Arial (**this is Arial**).

- Make all text at least 30 pixels tall. Smaller text may result in flickering, single-pixel horizontal lines that can make text almost unreadable.

Color for Video

Video color reproduction was never designed to accommodate the saturated colors that are typical in computer animation. It was instead designed to optimize the skin color of pink-skinned people. Follow these tips to optimize the appearance of your animation on video:

- Avoid red like the plague! Video has a hard time reproducing red without buzzing or shimmering.

- Reduce the saturation of all colors to 80 percent of fully saturated. Using the HLS (hue, luminance, and saturation) system and a 0–255 range, keep saturation levels at 204 or below.

- Avoid black levels of 0,0,0. Some video systems treat this as an illegal color, while others use it as a keying color. (Remember keying in Chapter 7?)

- Try using dark blue as a background color.

- If you have a choice between two contrasting colors (say, blue and orange) and two intensity levels of the same color (such as light blue and dark blue), the latter looks better on video.

- Use smooth color ramps where possible rather than abrupt color transitions, and avoid color transitions that occur on a single scanline, especially transitions between complementary colors.

Animation for Video

Here are some tips that will help you optimize your 3D animations for video:

- All the way from Chapter 1, I've told you that NTSC frame rates are 30 fps. For our purposes here, I felt that this was sufficiently accurate. The NTSC frame rate is actually 29.97 frames per second, or 59.94 fields per second. This may not sound like much of a difference, but when you calculate the number of frames to render to fill an NTSC time slot exactly, you must take this into account. You'll be happy to know, however, that the PAL and SECAM systems both use a frame rate of exactly 25 fps.

- Although 30 fps (OK, more or less) is the standard frame rate for NTSC video, you can slow down the action by duplicating frames. But keep the apparent frame rate above 15 fps for reasonably smooth movement.

- Allow at least 10 frames for any repetitive or cyclic motion.

- For smooth rotation, don't rotate an object more than 4 degrees per frame, or 120 degrees per second.

Hitting the Mark

Sometimes you may be required to produce an image component for compositing that must occupy a specific number of pixels in height or width. If your software has a video safe frame feature (see the section on imaging for video), you can use it to create precise output image dimensions. Here's an example:

To produce a figure that is exactly 1120 pixels tall, for example, use an 80 percent text safe frame and a 1400-pixel high image; then adjust the view to fit the figure precisely in the safe frame, as shown in Figure 9-5.

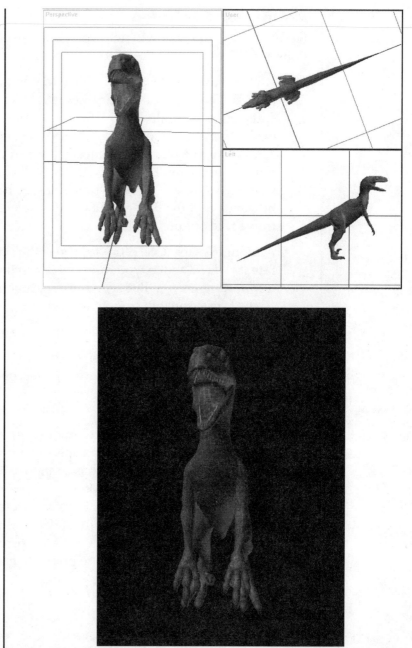

Figure 9-5: With the video text safe frame set at 80 percent, you can set the image size and zoom in or out on the subject to produce the exact size required. The viewport setup is on top, and the resultant image is below.

One caution: make sure that the window in which you set up the image has the same proportions as the output image.

Simplifying Text Geometry

Sometimes you may want to include text in a 3D scene. Most 3D programs let you create smooth outline text that you can use with the extrude function (remember Chapter 6?) to create nice, clean 3D text that can be viewed from any angle and still look great. There is one problem with this method: text, and especially the rounded letters, can produce extremely complex geometry which slows down rendering.

One solution is to use a *plate*, a simple geometric shape like a rectangle, and map your text onto it. (Refer back to Chapter 6 for a discussion of mapping.) From a distance, it can look almost as good as 3D text, as in Figure 9-6.

Figure 9-6: The text on the left was created as 3D text, while that on the right is bitmapped text on a simple plate. Note that both cast shadows.

In Figure 9-7, you can see the bitmap of the word **Text**. It's a very small file (725 bytes), low resolution (122-X 47-pixel) TIF black-and-white image.

Text

Figure 9-7: The simple word Text *in 72 point Arial text.*

I then used the *Text* bitmap as both diffuse and opacity texture maps. One minor problem arose because most 3D programs, mine included, use the luminance (brightness) value of the bitmap as the means to determine opacity; white is opaque and black is transparent. Here, the text image was black on white, so I had to invert the map colors of the opacity map. (It only required a simple mouse click on a check box to do this.)

I applied the texture maps as a material, or shader, to a simple plate I created for the purpose and then arranged it next to a 3D version of the same word. I added a shadow-casting spotlight and a floor to catch the shadow and the result was the image in Figure 9-6.

Advantages of this technique include:

- The 3D text required 816 faces to define the geometry compared to only 12 for the mapped rectangle.

- Simple geometry like the plate is easier to manipulate in the 3D program interface; you can easily bend it, twist it, move it, deform it—whatever you want to do.

- Changing the text involves nothing more than changing the map. You may need to readjust the mapping or the shape of the plate to fit the new bitmap, but it's less cumbersome than creating new 3D geometry.

- You can control the quality of the text by changing the resolution of the bitmap. Higher resolution text has smoother diagonals, but at the cost of slightly slower rendering and increased RAM requirements.

There are two disadvantages to this technique:

- The text is slightly fuzzier overall—note particularly the ragged, aliased diagonals on the X. This is particularly true when the text is viewed from a close vantage point, as in Figure 9-8.

Figure 9-8: The downside of mapped text. It's really ragged-looking when viewed this closely. One solution is to keep it away from the camera; another is discussed in the section on motion blur.

- You can't use mapped shadows—you must use ray-traced shadows, which can significantly increase the time required for rendering. In the image in Figure 9-9, I switched to mapped shadows for rendering speed—not a pretty result, I'm afraid.

Figure 9-9: Mapped shadows in some programs aren't designed to handle opacity-mapped objects. Look at the rectangular shadow of the object to the right—sure makes the nice, clean text outline look like a liar!

On balance, the increase in rendering time from ray-traced shadows is usually less than the cost of rendering complex 3D text. Of course, if your 3D software doesn't offer ray-traced shadows, then you must arrange your scene so that shadows from the text are not an issue. Or use 3D text!

Motion Blur, the Great Smoother

When rendering speed is an issue and you can sacrifice a bit of quality to achieve it, motion blur can cover a multitude of sins. Look at Figure 9-10. The two words *Text* have been captured while moving upward through the frame. The motion blur nicely captures the feeling of motion *and* masks the imperfections in the mapped text of the object on the right.

Figure 9-10: The motion blur masks the imperfections of the mapped text of the right-hand object. Both are now equally blurry.

Well, we've covered up one imperfection by adding motion blur, but introduced another. The shadows are just not right. The shadow of the 3D text is too crisp and clean, while that of the mapped text has started to fall apart. Neither would probably be noticed if this frame is a part of an animation; the viewer's eye would be drawn to the moving text and the shadows would just add pizzazz, particularly where, as here, the shadows will be changing dramatically as the text rises from the floor and shoots vertically out of sight.

Contour Lines

It can be difficult sometimes to determine the exact contours of an object in 3D. None of the methods for defining complex surfaces really make it easy to visualize the exact contours of a surface when viewed in two-dimensional views. One solution is to use a lined texture map, as in Figure 9-11.

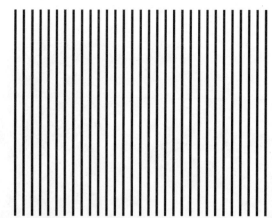

*Figure 9-11: This simple map can be used to
demonstrate the contour lines that describe an object.*

In Figure 9-12, I contoured a duck to show the effect of this
technique. I simply used a planar map projected from above onto
the duck's back. The effect is to "slice" Ducky-Wucky visually
and show evenly spaced contour lines.

*Figure 9-12: Sliced duck, anyone? When the map in Figure 9-11 is mapped onto
the duck from above using a planar map orientation, the result is as shown here.*

Backdrops & Surrounds

Most 3D software lets you composite the 3D scene over a background bitmap image. It's a quick and effective method of producing the appearance of distant scenery. It fails, however, when we introduce motion or must integrate 3D geometry into the bitmap environment.

We spent some time learning how to combine 3D geometry with bitmap imagery in Chapter 7 by compositing a 3D elephant with cast shadows onto an image of the Taj Mahal. Sometimes, however, we want to keep the background at a visual distance from the geometry—not put the elephant *in* the pool, but in front of distant mountains—and still have the viewpoint of the background change with camera movement. To do this, we must use a *backdrop* or *surround*.

In movies, television, or the stage, a backdrop is a simple two-dimensional image that's displayed behind the action. Our 3D software lets us do this automatically.

In the old days, backdrops were painted on canvas and unrolled, or dropped, down behind the set. Later, the technique of matte painting on glass was perfected to allow foreground and background compositing with live action using multiple exposures.

But motion in the foreground relative to the backdrop has always been a problem. For the classic view out the rear window of a car, the movies used a technique called *rear projection*, in which a changing road scene is projected onto a screen behind the actors. We've all seen the B movies where the actor "driving" the car doesn't follow the movements of the road behind him; there's a classic spoof of this in *Airplane*. The same problem, however, can arise in 3D work.

The solution is to use a curved plate that's far behind the foreground geometry and "paint" or map (Chapter 6 again) the background onto it. This surrounds the scene and lets us move the camera (within limits) to produce a changing background.

In Figure 9-13, you can see the basic geometry required to produce this illusion. I've simplified the scene to make the technique clear. To create the surround, I first created a circle just within the perimeter of the floor, and then deleted the half I didn't want. I then extruded it up from the floor to produce the surround; I did have to flip the normals so that the map would be visible from "inside" the object.

Figure 9-13: Here's a basic surround setup. It's a cylindrical segment that surrounds the foreground geometry. By using a cylinder, we avoid the distortion that could result from the use of a flat plate.

I then mapped a bitmap of the lake scene onto the surround and added a light and a camera. The results can be seen in Figure 9-14.

Figure 9-14: With our cylindrical surround, we can move the camera and see how the foreground geometry "moves" against the background.

Several things to watch out for when using surrounds to add a quick background are:

- Make sure that the relative scale and perspective of the foreground geometry matches the surround scene.

- Match the lighting and shadows of the foreground to the surround scene.

- Keep the surround far enough back from the foreground geometry that camera movements don't reveal the distortion introduced by wrapping a flat image around a cylindrical object.

- Match the proportions of the surround to the image. This may mean searching for or commissioning an image that fits the scene.

- Choose a background bitmap of a high enough resolution and color depth so that it does not "fall apart."

- Use ground fog or other atmospheric effect to hide the horizon if it's appropriate to the scene.

You can also modify this technique to add a blue sky with puffy white clouds or a starfield that surrounds a space ship. Let's look at the clouds first.

Figure 9-15 illustrates the geometry used for a skydome. It's a simple hemisphere with the normals pointed inward.

Because it's a dome, I can move the camera *almost* anywhere and keep the nice blue sky and puffy white clouds, as in Figure 9-16.

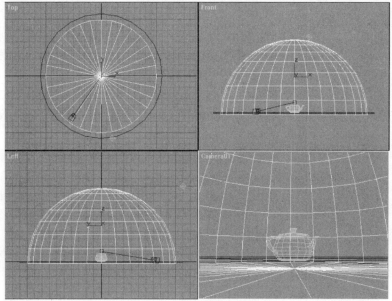

Figure 9-15: A skydome lets me move the camera almost anywhere within and keep a sky behind the foreground geometry.

Figure 9-16: Ah, summer and the soft white clouds dot the soft blue sky. Inside our skydome…

And now for the cautions:

- If your sky image is not tileable, that is, repeatable without showing a seam, make sure that you keep the seam behind the camera.

- Choose a sky bitmap of a high enough resolution and color depth so that it does not "fall apart" or produce clouds that are out of scale to the rest of the scene.

- Try to simulate a real cloudy sky. Usually, clouds lie in layers or have some horizontal component. Splattering a bitmap of clouds across a hemisphere, as I did in our example, does not produce the most realistic sky. The best solution is to use panoramic sky photos created with this use in mind. The second best solution is to carefully adjust the map angle and mirroring and limit the camera movement to produce an appropriately cloudy sky.

- For night scenes, replace the cloudy sky with a starfield bump map.

- Finally, if all else fails, camouflage the problems to distract the viewer from them. In Figure 9-17, I added a brick wall in the background to hide the fact that the clouds continue right down to the ground. You can also use atmospheric effects if appropriate to the scene.

Figure 9-17: I added a brick wall to hide the boundary between the clouds and the ground plane. The clouds look a little more plausible now.

For outer space scenes, you may need to move the camera more than the 180-degree hemisphere allows. Use a sphere mapped with a starfield in place of the hemisphere. If your 3D software lets you create starfields during rendering based upon camera position, so much the better. For a detailed look at how to create great space scenes, see the Ventana book by Jon A. Bell, *3D Studio MAX f/x*. You'll be amazed to see how you can create some great space effects.

Use Shadows to Break Up Surfaces

Sometimes, you can't avoid large flat surfaces—they're economical in the use of geometry and maximize rendering speed. But they can be boring! Try using shadows to add interest and break up the flat surface. (This technique uses a gobo, as discussed in Chapter 4.) Notice the difference between Figures 9-18 and 9-19.

Figure 9-18: A ball on a plane surface. Boring!

Figure 9-19: The same ball on the same plane surface with an intriguing shadow added. Exciting! Well, OK, interesting!

Use Maps to Define Surfaces

Look at the ellipses on the right side of Figure 9-20. They are not only boring, but you can't tell that they're actually disks, or if so, which side is which. Compare them to the disks on the left, which are mapped. (You can review mapping in Chapter 6.) You can immediately conclude both that they're disks and what their orientation is. The context in which we see objects helps us to determine their true shape and size.

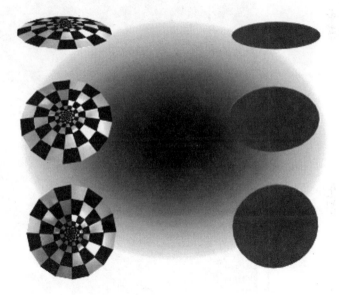

Figure 9-20: The ellipses at the right are actually identical in shape to those at the left, but you can't tell because there's no mapping to identify their orientation.

Avoid Tiling Maps

To make a material look more realistic, avoid the "wallpaper" look caused by repeating a material on a surface without introducing some irregularity. Natural materials like brick, stone, and rock have inherent irregularities; tiling them over and over will destroy the realistic look of even the best map, as in Figure 9-21. (Refer back to Chapter 6 if you want a quick refresher on mapping.)

Figure 9-21: The finest Benedetti marble map looks like wallpaper rather than marble when it's tiled too many times. Compare this to Figure 9-22.

To avoid the wallpaper look, either make the original bitmap large enough to encompass a large section of random surfaces, or create a complex material with added irregularities or map offsets, rotations, or scaling.

Figure 9-22: Now, this looks like marble. No tiling, no wallpaper.

Getting Down & Dirty

Making materials seem real to the scene is another problem often faced by the 3D artist. A spaceship that's supposed to be battle scarred looks wrong with a showroom-fresh "paint job." Realism, even for objects that never existed, comes when we add wear, stains, dents, and other signs we recognize as coming from "real life." There are solutions to this problem:

- Overlay your shaders with additional layers of "dirt." These maps can be simple random and subtle maps with spots and blobs. Figure 9-23 is an appropriately dirty spaceship skin map created by Jon A. Bell. (You can find it and the other textures shown in this section on the CD-ROM that accompanies Bell's book, *3D Studio MAX f/x*.

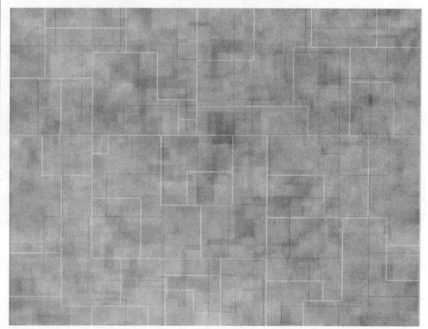

Figure 9-23: A spaceship panel map with a nice, subtle dirty overlay. (© 1996 Jon A. Bell.)

- Second, use maps that have their origins in real life. Look at the map in Figure 9-24; recognize it? It's a trash bin. Bell has made it a practice to roam the streets of San Francisco with a camera, taking pictures of anything he finds that might make a good texture map. This is one of his efforts.

Figure 9-24: What is it? A trash bin. But in the right industrial or space scene, it adds a nice touch with its aged and battered look. (© 1996 Jon A. Bell.)

Selective Opacity

Sometimes it's useful to vary the opacity in a scene to direct attention to the portions you want to highlight. We saw an excellent example of this in Chapter 8, shown again in Figure 9-25.

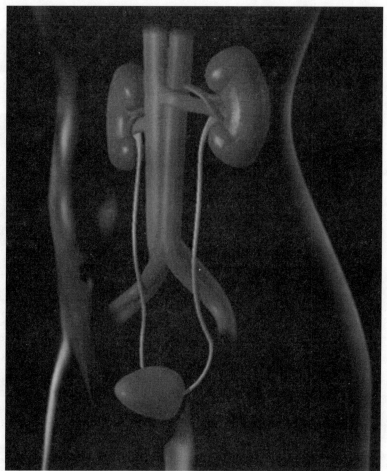

Figure 9-25: Note how the opacity of the body surface was carefully adjusted so that the location of the opaque organs is easily determined, but not so opaque as to interfere with seeing them. (© 1995 UTHHSC.)

The End

Well, we have come to the end of a long, three-dimensional road. There's no place to move on to from here, except to your own career in 3D. I hope that you have gained an understanding of 3D, some insights into its uses and peculiarities, and how it might fit into your future. And I hope you had some fun along the way. Thanks for sticking with me.

Appendix A

About the Companion CD-ROM

The CD-ROM included with your copy of *Looking Good in 3D* contains valuable software.

Navigating the CD-ROM

Your choices for navigating the CD-ROM appear on the opening screen. You can quit the CD, view the software, browse the Hot Picks, or learn more about Ventana.

The software is listed in the Install folder on the CD. You can install the items one at a time to your hard drive by dragging them from the folder onto your desktop.

To view the CD-ROM:

- **WINDOWS**—Double click on the LAUNCHME.EXE file from your Window Explorer or File Manager.

  You'll see a menu screen offering several choices. See "Navigating the CD-ROM" below for your option choices.

- **MACINTOSH**—Double click on the CD-ROM icon on your desktop.

  If the viewer does not run properly on your machine, follow the below instructions for optimum performance.

For optimum WINDOWS performance:

1. Copy the LAUNCHME.EXE and LAUNCHME.INI files to the same directory on your hard drive.

2. Open the LAUNCHME.INI file in a text editor such as Notepad. Find the section in the INI file that reads:

    ```
    [Memory]
    ;ExtraMemory=400
    ;Amount of kBytes over and above physical memory for
    use by a projector.
    ```

3. If your computer has enough memory to do so, delete the semicolon from the ExtraMemory line, and change the ExtraMemory setting to a higher number.

4. Save the changes to the LAUNCHME.INI File, and close the text editor.

5. With the CD-ROM still inserted, launch the viewer from the hard drive.

If the viewer still does not run properly on your machine, you can access the material on the CD-ROM directly through Windows Explorer.

For optimum MACINTOSH performance:

If the viewer does not rum properly on your machine, follow the below instructions for optimum performance:

1. Copy the Launch Me file to your hard drive.

2. Click once on the Launch Me file.

3. Select Get Info from the File menu.

4. If your computer has enough memory to do so, change the amount in the Preferred size field to a higher number.

5. Close the info box.

6. With the CD-ROM still inserted, launch the viewer from the hard drive.

If the viewer still does not run properly on your machine, you can access the files on the CD-ROM directly by double-clicking on the CD icon on your desktop.

Software on the CD-ROM

Software	Description
Caligari Pioneer v 1.1 Demo	Pioneer lets you easily create a unique VRML Web world. For more information about Caligari, visit their home page at http://www.caligari.com on the World Wide Web.
Virtus 3-D Website Builder 1.0 Demo	VRML world builders for the Internet. For more information visit http://www.virtus.com on the World Wide Web.
KPT Convolver Demo	Convolver is the first software program to unlock the incredible power of the Custom Convolution Kernel, that area of imaging mathematics that provides the empirical structures which generate well-known effects like Blur, Sharpen, Emboss, Edge Detection, Unsharp Masking and more, within a single advanced user interface designed by Kai. You can now generate directional sharpening, blurring and actually use kernel-based Tint and Hue controls. A powerful extension to Photoshop and Painter, KPT Convolver was designed to be your visual development lab for new filter effects. For more information visit MetaTools Web site at http://www.metatools.com on the World Wide Web.
Kai's Power Tools 3.0 Demo	Kai's Power Tools is a set of powerful extension and filter plug-ins for Adobe Photoshop, Fractal Design Painter, Color-It, and other programs that use Adobe's plug-in technology. KPT significantly expands the ability to create computer-generated artwork and manipulate scanned images. For more information visit MetaTools Web site at http://www.metatools.com on the World Wide Web.

Software	Description
Fractal Design Ray Dream Gallery 94 Demo	A demo of Ray Dream created 3D images. For more information on Fractal Design, visit http://www.fractal.com on the World Wide Web.
VRLI Vistapro	Vistapro allows you to create, animate, and explore stunningly beautiful landscapes. Professional users are astounded by Vistapro's ability to quickly produce high quality 3D landscape art. With the option of outputting your creations in a variety of formats, Vistapro is a powerful artistic tool which has swung the door wide open for commercial use. For more information, visit http://www.vrli.com on the World Wide Web.
The MECN Tree Factory demo	The MECN Tree Factory is a modeling tool, designed for quick generation of "realistic" 3D-based tree models. Once generated, these models can be exported in DXF, RAW, or LWO for use in your favorite 3D software for rendering and animation. The MECN Tree Factory Demo is fully functional except the file export function has been disabled. For more information, visit http://www.telepath.com/mecngr on the World Wide Web.
ARCHITECH.PC v 2.03	International award-winning ARCHITECH.PC is an integrated design program dedicated to architecture. It includes 2D, 3D, estimation, textures, rendering, animation, stereo imaging, and terrain/landscape features.

Technical Support

Technical support is available for installation-related problems only. The technical support office is open from 8:00 A.M. to 6:00 P.M. Monday through Friday and can be reached via the following methods:

Phone: (919) 544-9404 extension 81
Faxback Answer System: (919) 544-9404 extension 85
E-mail: help@vmedia.com
FAX: (919) 544-9472
World Wide Web: http://www.vmedia.com/support
America Online: keyword **Ventana**

Limits of Liability & Disclaimer of Warranty

The authors and publisher of this book have used their best efforts in preparing the CD-ROM and the programs contained in it. These efforts include the development, research, and testing of the theories and programs to determine their effectiveness. The authors and publisher make no warranty of any kind expressed or implied, with regard to these programs or the documentation contained in this book.

The authors and publisher shall not be liable in the event of incidental or consequential damages in connection with, or arising out of, the furnishing, performance, or use of the programs, associated instructions, and/or claims of productivity gains.

Some of the software on this CD-ROM is shareware; there may be additional charges (owed to the software authors/makers) incurred for their registration and continued use. See individual program's README or VREADME.TXT files for more information.

Appendix B
Resources

In a book that touches on so many subjects, the resources should be at least as broad. I've gathered together a list of resources that I found useful in researching this book. Some may seem a bit off-the-wall to you, but I guarantee that you'll find most of them worthwhile.

We've made every effort to ensure that there are no errors in this appendix, but I'm also sure that by the time you buy this book, one or more will be out of date. If you find any errors, please contact Ventana at http://www.vmedia.com, and we'll get them right—for one brief shining moment—before the next edition goes to press.

Books

Arijon, Daniel, *The Grammar of the Film Language, Reprint Edition*
Paperback
$24.95
Samuel French Trade, 1991
ISBN: 187950507X

Bain, Steve with Daniel Gray, *Looking Good Online*
Softcover
$39.99
Ventana, 1996
ISBN: 1566044693

Bammes, Gottfried, *The Artist's Guide to Animal Anatomy*
Hardcover
$14.98
Transedition Books, 1994
ISBN: 07858000557

Beck, Jerry, Editor, *The 50 Greatest Cartoons: As Selected by 1,000 Animation Professionals*
Hardcover
N/A
Turner Pub, 1994
ISBN: 187868549X

Bell, Jon A., *3D Studio MAX f/x*
Softcover
$49.99
Ventana, 1996
ISBN: 1566044278

Bendazzi, Giannalberto, *One Hundred Years of Cinema Animation*
Paperback
$39.95
Indiana University Press, 1996
ISBN: 0253209374

Blair, Preston, *Cartoon Animation*
Softcover
$24.95
Walter Foster Publishing, 1994
ISBN: 1560100842

Brenner, Alfred, *The T.V. Scriptwriter's Handbook*
Softcover
$9.95
Writer's Digest Books, 1980
ISBN: 0898791782

Champlin, Charles, *The Creative Impulse: Lucasfilm's First Twenty Years*
Hardcover
$39.95
Harry N. Arbams, 1992
ISBN: 0810935643

Culhane, Shamus, *Animation: From Script to Screen, Reprint Edition*
Paperback
$14.95
St. Martin's Press, 1990
ISBN: 0312050526

Ebert, Roger, *Ebert's Little Movie Glossary*
Hardcover
$12.95
Andrews and McMeel, 1994
ISBN: 0836280717

Fahey, Mary Jo and Jeffrey W. Brown, *Web Publisher's Design Guide*
Softcover
$34.99
The Coriolis Group, 1995
ISBN: 1883577616

Faigin, Gary, *The Artist's Complete Guide to Facial Expression*
Hardcover
$35.00
Watson-Guptill, 1990
ISBN: 0823016285

Goodnow, David, *How Birds Fly*
Softcover
$15.95
Periwinkle Books, Inc., 1992
ISBN: 0963424408

Halas, John, *Contemporary Animator*
Hardcover
$54.95
Focal Press, 1991
ISBN: 0240512804

Hamm, Jack, *Drawing the Head and Figure*
Softcover
$7.95
Perigee Books, 1982
ISBN: 0399507914

Hince, Peter, *Figures: The Concise Illustrator's Reference Manual*
Hardcover
$24.98
Quatro Books, 1995
ISBN: 078580515X

Hince, Peter, *Nudes: The Concise Illustrator's Reference Manual*
Hardcover
$24.98
Quatro Books, 1995
ISBN: 078580514X

Hoffer, Thomas, *Animation: A Reference Guide*
Hardcover
$59.95
Greenwood Press, 1982
ISBN: 0313210950

Johnston, Ollie and Frank Thomas, *The Disney Villain*
Hardcover
$45.00
Hyperion, 1993
ISBN: 1526827928

Kent, Sarah, *Composition*
Hardcover
$16.95
Dorling Kindersley, 1995
ISBN: 156458612X

Laybourne, Kit, *The Animation Book*
Softcover
$15.95
Crown, 1979
ISBN: 0517529467

Lenburg, Jeff, *The Encyclopedia of Animated Cartoons*
Hardcover
$40.00
Facts on File, 1991
ISBN: 0816022526

Lenburg, Jeff, *The Great Cartoon Directors*
Hardcover
$28.50
McFarland & Co., 1983
ISBN: 0899500366

Morrison, Mike, *Becoming a Computer Animator*
Softcover
$39.99
Sams Publishing, 1994
ISBN: 0672304635

Murray, James D. and William Van Ryper, *Encyclopedia of Graphics File Formats, Book & CD Edition*
Paperback
$79.95
O'Reilly & Associates, 1994
ISBN: 1565920589

Muybridge, Eadweard, *The Human Figure in Motion*
Hardcover
$24.95
Dover Press, 1989
ISBN: 0486202046

Muybridge, Eadweard, *The Male and Female Figure in Motion*
Softcover
$10.95
Dover Press, 1984
ISBN: 0486247457

Muybridge, Eadweard, *Animals in Motion*
Hardcover
$29.95
Dover Press, 1989
ISBN: 0486202038

Muybridge, Eadweard, *Horses and Other Animals in Motion*
Softcover
$9.95
Dover Press, 1985
ISBN: 0486249115

Nash, Constance and Virginia Oakey, *The Screenwriter's Handbook*
Softcover
$5.95
Perennial, 1974
ISBN: 006463454X

Noake, Roger, *Animation Techniques*
Hardcover
$22.98
Chartwell Books, 1988
ISBN: 1555213316

O'Rourke, Michael, *Principles of Three-Dimensional Computer Animation : Modeling, Rendering, and Animating With 3D Computer Graphics*
Hardcover
$48.00
WW Norton & Company, 1995
ISBN: 0393702022

Parker, Roger C., *Looking Good in Print, Deluxe CD-ROM Edition*
Softcover
$34.99
Ventana, 1996
ISBN: 1566044715

Peck, Stephen Rogers, *Atlas of Human Anatomy for the Artist*
Softcover
$12.95
Oxford University Press, 1951
ISBN: 0195030958

Pintoff, Ernest, with Candace Raney and Stacey Guttman (Editors), *The Complete Guide to Animation and Computer Graphics Schools*
Paperback
$16.95
Watson-Guptill, 1995
ISBN: 0823021777

Potts, Anthony, David H. Friedel, Jr., Anthony Stock, *3D Studio MAX Design Guide*
Softcover
$39.99
The Coriolis Group, 1996
ISBN: 1883577837

Reese, Stephanie, *Character Animation with 3D Studio MAX*
Softcover
$39.99
Coriolis Group Books, 1996
ISBN: 1576100545

Russet, Robert and Cecile Starr, *Experimental Animation: Origins of an Art, Reprint Edition*
Hardcover
$14.95
Da Capo Press, 1988
ISBN: 0306803143

Smith, Thomas, *Industrial Light and Magic: The Art of Special Effects, Reprint Edition*
Hardcover
$80.00
Del Rey, 1988
ISBN: 0345322630

Smoodin, Eric, *Hollywood Cartoons from the Sound Era (Rutgers Series in Communications, Media, and Culture)*
Paperback
$15.95
Rutgers University Press, 1993
ISBN: 0813519497

Solomon, Charles, *The Disney That Never Was: The Stories and Art from Five Decades of Unproduced Animation*
Hardcover
$40.00
Hyperion, 1995
ISBN: 0786860375

Straczynski, J. Michael, *The Complete Book of Scriptwriting, Revised*
Hardcover
$19.99
Writer's Digest Books, 1996
ISBN: 0898795125

Thomas, Frank and Ollie Johnston, *Disney Animation: The Illusion of Life, Revised*
Hardcover
$60.00
Hyperion, 1995
ISBN: 0786860707

Vannini, Vanio and Giulano Pogliani, Editors, *The Color Atlas of Human Anatomy*
Softcover
$6.95
Harmony Books, 1979
ISBN: 05170545144

Various authors, *3D Studio Hollywood & Gaming Effects*
Softcover
$50.00
New Riders Publishing, 1996
ISBN: 1562054309

Various Authors, *3D Studio Special Effects*
Softcover
$50.00
New Riders Publishing, 1994
ISBN: 1562053035

Vaz, Mark Cotta and Patricia Rose Duigan, *Industrial Light & Magic: Into the Digital Realm*
Hardcover
$80.00
Del Rey, 1996
ISBN: 0345381521

Vince, John, *3-D Computer Animation*
Hardcover
$45.25
Addison-Wesley, 1992
ISBN: 0201627566

Watt, Alan, *3D Computer Graphics, 2nd Edition*
Hardcover
$49.50
Addison-Wesley Pub Co., 1993
ISBN: 0201631865

Watt, Alan H., Mark Watt, and Alan Watt, *Advanced Animation and Rendering Techniques : Theory and Practice*
Hardcover
$46.25
Addison-Wesley Pub Co., 1992
ISBN: 0201544121

Weston, Trevor, MD, *Atlas of Anatomy*
Hardcover
Publisher Out of Stock
Book Sales, 1993
ISBN: 1555219764

White, Tony, *The Animator's Workbook*
Softcover
$18.95
Watson-Guptill, 1988
ISBN: 0823002292

Whiting, Frank M., *An Introduction to the Theater, Third Edition*
Hardcover
Out of Print
Harper & Row, 1969
ISBN: None

Zettl, Herbert, *Sight, Sound, Motion: Applied Media Aesthetics, Second Edition*
Hardcover
$53.95
Wadsworth, 1990
ISBN: 0534079520

Zettl, Herbert, *Television Production Handbook*
Hardcover
$69.95
Wadsworth, 1996
ISBN: 0534260586

Zettl, Herbert, *Video Basics*
Paperback
$37.95
Wadsworth, 1994
ISBN: 0534247865

Magazines

3-D Artist
Columbine, Inc.
P.O. Box 4787, Santa Fe, New Mexico 87502
505-982-3532
$5.00/issue
Subscription price not given, Bimonthly

3D Design
Miller Freeman Inc.
600 Harrison St., San Francisco, CA 94107
415-905-2200
$3.95/issue
Subscriptions: $29.95/year, Monthly

Advanced Imaging
PTN Publishing Co.
445 Broad Hollow Road, Melville, NY 11747-4722
516-845-2700
No charge to qualified professionals
All others, $60/year, Monthly

American Cinematographer
ASC Holding Corporation
1782 N. Orange Dr., Hollywood, CA 90028
800-448-0145
$5.00/issue
Subscription: $35/year, Monthly

Animation
30101 Agoura Court, Suite 110, Agoura Hills, CA 91301
818-991-2884
$4.95/issue
Subscription: $45/year, Monthly

Animerica
Viz Communications, Inc.
P.O. Box 77010, San Francisco, CA 94107
415-546-7073
$4.95/issue
Subscription: $58/year, Monthly

Cinefantastique
7240 W. Roosevelt Rd., Forest Park, IL 60130
708-366-5566
$5.95/issue
Subscription: $48/year, Monthly

Cinefex
Box 20027, Riverside, CA 92516
$8.50/issue
Subscription: $26.00, Quarterly

Cinescape
Cinescape Group, Inc.
1920 Highland Ave, Suite 222, Lombard, IL 60148
708-268-2498
$4.99/issue
Subscription: $29.95/year, Monthly

Digital Imaging
Micro Publishing Press, Inc.
2340 Plaza del Amo, Suite 100, Torrance, CA 90501
310-212-5802
Free to qualified professionals
All others $24.95/year, Bi-monthly

Digital Video Magazine
IDG Worldwide
600 Townsend St., Suite 170 East, San Francisco, CA 94103
800-998-0806
$4.95/issue
Subscription: $29.97/year, Monthly

New Media
Hyper Media Communications
901 Mariner's Island Blvd, Suite 365, San Mateo, CA 94404
415-573-5170
Free to new media professionals, $4.95/issue for others
Subscription $52/year, Monthly

Wired Magazine
Wired Ventures Ltd.
PO Box 191826, San Francisco, CA 94119-9866
415-222-6200
$4.95/issue
Subscription $39.95/year, Monthly

Papers

Lasseter, John, "Principles of Traditional Animation Applied to 3D Computer Animation" *Computer Graphics*, July 1987, Proc. SIGGRAPH '87.

Course notes from "Animation Tricks" (course offered at SIGGRAPH '94). Lecturers were Chris Wedge, John Lasseter, Jim Blinn, and Ken Perlin.

Graphics & Animation Newsgroups

alt.3d
3d perception

alt.animation.warner-bros Warner Bros.
animation

alt.binaries.pictures.*
Images of all kinds

alt.graphics.pixutils
Image manipulation, conversion

alt.movies.visual-effects
Special Effects

comp.graphics.misc
Image generation and modeling

comp.graphics.algorithms
Graphics algorithms

comp.graphics.animation
Animation topics

comp.graphics.raytracing
Ray tracing

comp.graphics.visualization
Scientific & data visualization

comp.graphics.apps.wavefront
Wavefront Visualizer

comp.graphics.apps.alias
Alias Research Power Animator

comp.graphics.apps.lightwave
NewTek Lightwave

comp.graphics.apps.softimage
Softimage | 3D

comp.graphics.apps.photoshop
Adobe Photoshop

comp.graphics.packages.3dstudio
Autodesk 3D Studio

comp.graphics.rendering.raytracing
Raytracing software (POV, etc.)

comp.graphics.rendering.renderman
RenderMan

comp.graphics.rendering.misc
Miscellaneous rendering

comp.multimedia
Multimedia

rec.arts.animation
Traditional animation

rec.arts.disney.animation
Disney animation

rec.arts.anime*
Japanese animation

rec.video.desktop
Desktop video

rec.video.production
Desktop video

sci.image.processing
Heavy-duty image processing

sci.virtual-worlds*
Anything about VR

comp.compression
Image and animation compression

Web Sites

The World Wide Web is truly an amazing organism. Every time I
went out on the Web to do research for this book, I found a
dozen new sites that were fascinating, useful, entertaining, or all
three. I've included some of the best sites I found. I sorted these
in groups that I hope are meaningful.

This list is by no means exhaustive. You didn't buy an Internet Yellow Pages, but a book about 3D. I have included the sites I found, plus others to which I was directed, plus links, and so on. Because of the nature of the Internet, I surfed my way around the world and probably only touched down at 10 or 20% of the relevant sites. This list will get you started; from some of the more general sites, you should be able to find what you want.

3D & Computer Graphics—General

**ftp://avalon.viewpoint.com/pub/FAQs/
computer.animation.school.faq**
Computer Animation Schools FAQ

ftp://avalon.viewpoint.com/pub/FAQs/cga-faq/
Computer Graphics and Animation FAQ

**ftp://rtfm.mit.edu/pub/usenet/news.answers/graphics/
fileformats-faq**
Animation file formats

http://www.primenet.com/~grieggs/cg_faq.html
Comp.Graphics.Misc FAQ

http://arachnid.cs.cf.ac.uk/Ray.Tracing/
The Ray Tracing Home Page

http://lesowww.epfl.ch/radiance/radiance_long.html
RADIANCE detailed description

http://www.3dgraphics.com/
3Dgraphics

**http://www.bergen.org/AAST/ComputerAnimation/
CompAn_Applications.html**
Applications of Computer Animation

**http://www.cis.ohio-state.edu/hypertext/faq/usenet/graphics/
top.html**
Other Computer graphics FAQ's

http://www.cs.unc.edu/~manocha/collide.html
Collision detection

http://www.pixelfreak.com/
Pixelfreak

http://www.realsoftint.com/book.htm
Spline Modelling Book

http://siggraph.org/
ACM SIGGRAPH Online!

http://www.3dsite.com/3dsite/
3DSite

http://www.dataspace.com/WWW/vlib/comp-graphics.html
The World-Wide Web Virtual Library: Computer Graphics and
Visualization

http://www.digitaldirectory.com/animation.html
The Digital Directory

http://www.gweb.org/
GWEB (Graphics Web) Home Page

http://wise.igd.fhg.de/
Computer Graphics in Darmstadt

http://www.isisnet.com/dayglo/anim.html
ANIMATION AND COMPUTER GRAPHICS RESOURCES
MPEG

**http://www.u-aizu.ac.jp/public/www/labs/sw-sm/FrepWWW/
F-rep.html**
F-rep Home Page: Function Representation in Geometric
Modeling & Computer Graphics

3D Model Sources

http://cedar.cic.net/~rtilmann/mm/
Mesh Mart Home page

http://www.cgw.com/cgw/Connections/models.html
CGW: Cool Connections: 3D Models

http://www.acuris.com/
Acuris Home Page

http://www.baraboo.com/3dcafe/
3D CAFE(tm) (3D Mesh Model Geometry and Graphical
Imaging)

http://www.ozemail.com.au/~grind/
Stephen Seefeld's 3D Studio and 3D MAX Archive

http://www.viewpoint.com/
Viewpoint DataLabs

http://www.viewpoint.com/avalon
Avalon Public Domain Page

http://www.zygote.com/
Zygote Home Page

Advertising

http://www.clioawards.com/
The Clio Awards

Animation and Art Reference

http://animation.filmtv.ucla.edu/animatrx.html
Animatrix, Journal of the UCLA Animation Workshop

http://animation.filmtv.ucla.edu/
UCLA Animation Workshop

http://www.awn.com/sas/index.html
Society for Animation Studies

http://found.cs.nyu.edu/fox/art/
Texas.net Museum of Art

http://warren-idea-exchange.com/
Warren Idea Exchange

http://www.cartoon-factory.com/wb_bc.html
Animation Art by Bob Clampett

http://www.cinesite.com/
CineWebSite:Animation

http://www.demon.co.uk/rushes/index.html
Upcoming Animated Features

http://www.digitaldirectory.com/animation.html
The Digital Directory

http://www.inwap.com/Reboot.html
Reboot

http://www.mpsc839.org/mpsc839/index.html
Local 839 IATSE's Home Page

Animators & Animation Houses

http://www.amblin.com/
Amblin Imaging

http://www.artewisdom.co.uk/
Artewisdom

http://www.colossal.com/
(Colossal) Pictures

http://www.disney.com
Disney

http://www.pdi.com/
Pacific Data Images

http://www.primenet.com/~jbirn/
Jeremy Birn's 3D Renderings

http://www.pixar.com/
Pixar's Home Page!

http://www.rga.com/index.html
R/GA Digital Studios

http://www.rhythm.com/
Rhythm & Hues Studios

http://www.rhythm.com/~goodman/Library/library.html
J. Goodman Library

http://www.spe.sony.com/Pictures/index.html
Sony Pictures Entertainment Home Page

Bookstore

http://www.amazon.com
Amazon.com Books!

Forensic Animation

http://ash.lab.r1.fws.gov/
Forensic Science Reference List

http://www.cnet.com/Content/Features/Techno/Digital/digital2.html
Features - techno - guilty! digital animations

http://toltecs.lab.r1.fws.gov/forensic/refs.htm
References

http://www.shadow.net/~noslow/forensic.html
Forensic and Law Enforcement Web Sites

http://www.texlaw.com/tech/produp1.htm
Law Tech Product Update

http://www.visuallaw.com/
Visual Law

Government

http://lcweb.loc.gov/copyright/
U.S. Copyright Office Home Page

http://lcweb.loc.gov/
Library of Congress World Wide Web Home Page

http://www.gsfc.nasa.gov/NASA_homepage.html
NASA Information Services

http://www.nsf.gov/
National Science Foundation World Wide Web Server

http://www.si.edu/
Smithsonian Institute

Media

http://www.3dartist.com
3D Artist

http://www.cgw.com/
Computer Graphics World

http://www.cinefx.com/
CineFX

ftp://ftp.coriolis.com/
Coriolis Group FTP

http://www.enews.com/magazines/avv/
Entertainment News

http://www.livedv.com
Live Digital Video

http://www.livedv.com/PlanetStudio/
PlanetStudio

http://www.vmedia.com/
Ventana: Home Page

Motion Capture

http://www.bio-vision.com/
Bio-Vision Home Page

Movies

http://cruciform.cid.com/~werdna/sttng
Star Trek: The Next Generation

http://members.aol.com/widenews/index.html
Wide Gauge Film and Video

http://www.afionline.org/
AFI OnLine

http://www.ampas.org/ampas/
Academy of Motion Picture Arts and Sciences

http://www.cyberfilmschool.com/cfs.htm
Cyber Film School - Main Home Page

http://www.demon.co.uk/rushes/motion.html
Motion Control Studio

http://www.filmmaker.e-domain.com/
FilmMaker Magazine

http://www.imdr.com
Internet Movie Database

http://www.movieweb.com/
MOVIEWEB: Home Page

http://www.ugcs.caltech.edu/st-tng/
Star Trek: The Next Generation

Museums

http://eagle.online.discovery.com/DCO/doc/1012/world/science/muybridge/navpage.html
Eadweard Muybridge

http://www.king.ac.uk/kingston/museum/muytext0.htm
EADWEARD MUYBRIDGE of Kingston Upon Thames

http://www.linder.com/newmedia.html
Pacific Interactive Media presents New Media Pioneers

Research/Education

ftp://ftp.cis.upenn.edu/pub/graphics/public_html/pelachaud/workshop_face/workshop_face.html"
FINAL REPORT TO NSF OF THE STANDARDS FOR FACIAL ANIMATION WORKSHOP

http://www.bergen.gov/AAST/ComputerAnimation/CompAn_TopPage.html#MainMenu
Computer Graphics and Animation Home Page

http://mambo.ucsc.edu/psl/cg.html
Computer Graphics at University of California at Santa Cruz

http://mambo.ucsc.edu/psl/fan.html
Facial Animation

http://www.cc.gatech.edu/gvu/
Graphics, Visualization and Usability Center, Georgia Tech University

http://www.cc.gatech.edu/gvu/animation/index.html
GVU: Animation Lab

http://www.cc.gatech.edu/gvu/animation/Areas/secondary/secondary.html
Animation Lab: Simulating Secondary Motion

http://www.cs.ubc.ca/nest/imager/contributions/forsey/dragon/top.html
The Dragon Wing

http://www.cs.ubc.ca/nest/imager/contributions/bobl/imagergallery/top.html
The Imager Gallery Foyer

http://www.cs.unc.edu/graphics/
Graphics groups, UNC-Chapel Hill CS Department

http://www.cis.upenn.edu/~hms/
Center for Human Modeling and Simulation

http://www-graphics.stanford.edu/
Graphics at Stanford University

http://www.uchsc.edu/sm/chs/
Center for Human Simulation

http://zeppo.cs.ubc.ca:5656/
Welcome to FaceMaker

Scientific & Medical Imaging

http://expasy.hcuge.ch/pub/Graphics/
Index of /pub/Graphics/

http://expasy.hcuge.ch/www/expasy-top.html
Welcome to ExPASy

http://www.afit.af.mil/Schools/EN/ENG/LABS/GRAPHICS/GRAPHICS.html
Virtual Environments, 3D Medical Imaging, and Computer Graphics Lab

http://www-bmb.med.uth.tmc.edu/MAMI/Mike/Delaflor.html
Mike DeLaFlor Medical Illustration

http://www.scar.rad.washington.edu/SCAR/JDI.html
Journal of Digital Imaging

http://www-sci.lib.uci.edu/HSG/MedicalImage.html
Medical Imaging Center - Martindale's Health Science Guide

http://www.sdsc.edu/
SDSC:A National Center for Computational Science and Engineering

Software & Hardware

http://ns1.win.net/~real3d/
RealSoft Real 3D

http://www.3dgraphics.com/meshpaint.html
MeshPaint 3D by Positron

http://www.4dvision.com
4DVISION Home Page

http://www.adobe.com/
Adobe Systems Inc. Home Page

http://www.aw.sgi.com
Alias I Wavefront Home Page

http://www.bytebybyte.com/softfx.htm
SoftF/X Page

http://www.cadonline.com/MAX/animindex.html
Complete Support for 3D Studio MAX

http://www.complete-support.com/
Complete Support for 3D Studio MAX

http://www.eai.com/
EAI Vislab

http://www.electricimg.com/
Electric Image Inc.

http://www.eye.com/
3D/EYE TriSpectives

http://www.gig.nl/1/Online/
ElectroGIG 3DGO

http://www.hash.com/~hashinc/
Hash Animation Master

http://www.hsc.com/
MetaTools Inc. Web Site

http://www.intergraph.com
Intergraph Corp.

http://www.ktx.com/
Kinetix Home Page

http://www.netnet.net/users/truespace/
Caligari TrueSpace

http://www.newtek.com/
NewTeK Lightwave 3D

http://www.photomodeler.com/
Eos Systems Inc - PhotoModeler Information

http://www.spadion.com/anicom/
3D Choreographer

http://www1.heathcomm.no./max/
The MAXimum resource page!

http://www.3dchor.com/
3D Choreographer - 3d Animation Software

http://www.povray.org/
Persistence of Vision Ray Tracer

http://www.prism.uvsq.fr/public/wos/multimedia/
Conversion utilities

http://www.rem-infografica.es/
REM INFOGRÁFICA. Home Page

http://www.seas.gwu.edu/student/gritz/bmrt.html#what
Blue Moon Rendering Tools Home Page (BMRT RenderMan-like)

http://www.rhino3d.com/
Rhino-NURBS modeling in Microsoft Windows

http://www.sidefx.com
Side Effects

http://www.sisyphus.com/
Sisyphus Software

http://198.105.232.5:80/Products/Softimage/
SOFTIMAGE FrontPage

http://www.strata3d.com/Main.html
Strata's Home Page

http://www.sun.com/sunworldonline/swol-11-1995/swol-11-pixar.html
SunWorld Online - November - News (About Toy Story and Pixar)

http://www.threedee.com/
Syndesis Corporation Home Page

http://www.truevision.com/
Truevision

http://vexcel.com/prod_srv/fotog.html
FotoG-FMS

http://www.vce.com
Visual Concept Entertainment (Pyromania)

http://www.virtus.com/demosoft.html
Virtus Corporation: 3-D Website Builder Demo

http://www.vissoft.com
Renderize Live & Visual Reality

http://www9.informatik.uni-erlangen.de/Research.english/Vision/RenderMan/RMan.html
RenderMan

http://www.vrli.com/
Virtual Reality Labs, Inc.

http://www.work-of-art.com/science.d.visions/
Matchmoving System 3D-Equalizer

Texture Maps

ftp://wuarchive.wustl.edu/multimedia/images
Images

http://www.meat.com/textures/
Textures

Video & Photography

http://isdl.ee.washington.edu/CE/ConsElectHome.html
Consumer Electronics Education Project, Univ. of Washington

http://www.americanet.com/Fvesco/dollie.htm
Fvesco - Dollies & Stabilizers

http://www.curtin.edu.au/curtin/dept/design/STOCKPHOTO/
The STOCKPHOTO Stock Photography Discussion Group Web Site

http://www.io.org/~proeser/#Manufacture
The Film and Broadcast Page

http://www.lucamera.com/home.html
Lee Utterbach Cameras

http://www.nab.org/
National Association of Broadcasters Home Page

http://www-scf.usc.edu/~hunziker/cim/cim.htm
Cinematographers Online Bible

http://www.timelapse.com/tvlink.html
TVLINK - Huge links page for the Film & Television Industry

http://www.ultimatte.com/
Ultimatte Website

Animation Schools

This list is as current as I could make it in mid-November, 1996. I checked and correlated several lists, but alas, I fear I didn't get a chance to call each of these schools! (With thanks to Dave DeBry.)

Academy of Art College
79 New Montgomery, San Francisco, CA 94105
Undergrad. Admissions: (415) 274-2200
CEC: Dennis DiSantis (415) 274-2245
Motion Picture: Patrick Kriwanek (415) 274-2257
Career Services: Susan Pelosi (415) 274-8675

Allan Hancock College
800 S. College Dr., Santa Maria, CA 93454
(805) 922-6966 Ext 410
(805) 928-7905 FAX
Contact: Edward Harvey

American Animation Institute
4729 Lankershim Blvd., N. Hollywood, CA 91602
(818) 766-0521
(818) 506-4805 FAX
Contact: Lyn Manta

Animation Lab at TNLC
800-3rd Street NE, Washington, D.C. 20002
(202) 546-0769
(202) 675-4182 FAX
Contact: Christopher Grotke

Animators Training Project-Unit
318201 Yorba Linda Blvd., Yorba Linda, CA 92686
(714) 528-4264
Contact: Tris Mast

Art Center College of Design
1700 Lida St., Pasadena, CA 91103
Undergrad. Admissions:(818) 396-2314
Computer Graphics: (818) 396-2359
Illustration Chair: (818) 396-2355
Fine Arts: (818) 396-2348
Career Resources Dept.: (818) 396-2320

California Institute of the Arts (CalArts)
24700 McBean Parkway, Valencia, CA 91355
Undergrad. Admissions: (805) 255-1050
Dept. of Film & Video: (805) 253-7825
Character Animation: (805) 253-7818
Career Services: Frank Terry (805) 222-2761

California Institute of Technology Graphics Group
MS 256-80, Computer Science Dept., Pasadena, CA 91125
(818) 356-6430
(818) 795-1547 FAX
Contact: Al Barr

California Institute of Technology/Project Mathematics
305 S. Hill St., Pasadena, CA 91106
(818) 356-3750
(818) 356-3758
(818) 356-3763 FAX
Contact: Don Delson or Jim Blinn

California State University, Chico
Normal Avenue, Chico, CA 95929-0005
(916) 898-4421
(916) 898-5369 FAX
Contact: Rick Vertolli

California State University, Long Beach
Advanced Media Production Center
(310) 985-4352

Central State University
Computer Center for the Arts
1 Welsey Dr., Wilder Force, OH 45384
(513) 376-6610
Contact: Bing Davis

Chapman College
Communications Dept.
333 N. Glassel, Orange, CA 92666
Contact: Greg Hobson

Cogswell Polytechnical College
175 Bordeaux Drive, Sunnyvale, CA 94089
(408) 541-0100
(408) 747-0764 FAX

Columbia College Chicago
600 S. Michigan Ave., Chicago, IL 60605
(312) 663-1600 Ext. 367
Contact: Barry Young

Columbus College of Art and Design
107 North 9 St., Columbus, OH 43215
Main #: (614) 224-9101

Commercial Animation Program
2055 Purcell Way, North Vancouver, B.C. V7J 3H5 Canada
(604) 986-1911
(604) 984-4946 FAX
Contact: Don Perro

Computer Arts Institute
310 Townsend St., Suite 230, San Francisco, CA 94107-1607
(415) 546-5242
(415) 546-5237 FAX
Contact: Dick Howard

Concordia University
Dept. of Cinema
1455 De Maisoneuve, Montreal, Quebec, H3G 1M8 Canada
(514) 848-4668
Contact: Prof. Stefan Anastasiu

Connecticut College
Mohegan Avenue, New London, CT 06320
(203) 447-1911
Contact: David Smalley

Dancing Hand Ltd.
230 N. Kenwood Street, Suite 316, Burbank, CA 91505
(818) 567-1950
(818) 567-1950 FAX
Contact: Dan Haskett

De Anza College
Dept. of Cinema & Photography
21250 Stevens Creek Blvd., Cupertino, CA 95014
(408) 996-4519
Contact: Zaki Lisha

De Pauw/Art Dept.
110 Art Center, Greencastle, IN 46135
(317) 658-4800
Contact: David Herrold

Dun Laoghaire College of Art & Design
Carriglea Park, Kill Avenue, Dun Laoghaire County, Dublin,
Ireland
353-1-280-1138
353-1-280-3345 FAX
Contact: Larry Lauria

Ecole De L'Ordinateur
15 Rue De La Commune Quest, Montreal, Quebec H2Y 2C6
Canada
(514) 849-1612
(514) 982-0064 FAX
Contact: Herve Fischer

Edinboro University of Penn.
Art Dept. Hamilton Hall, Edinboro, PA16444
(814) 732-2406
Contact: George Shoemaker

Emily Carr Institute
1399 Johnston St., Vancouver, BC, CANADA V6H 3R9
Main #: (604) 844-3800

Fashion Institute of Technology
7th Ave. & 27th St., New York, NY 10001
Main #: (212) 760-7665
Computer Graphics: (212) 760-7938

Films for Kids, Films by Kids
22 W. 90th Street, Suite 3R, New York City, NY 10024
(212) 595-1549
Contact: David Lasday

M.D. Ford Vocational-Technical Center
17212 Lenore, Detroit, MI 48219
(313) 533-9363
Contact: Vic Spicer

WM. D. Ford Vocational-Technical Center
36455 Marquette, Westland, MI 48185
(313) 595-2135
Contact: John Prusak

Freed-Hardeman University
158 E. Main Street, Henderson, TN 38340
(901) 989-6000
(901) 989-6065 FAX
Contact: J.D. Thomas

Grand Valley State University
268 LSH, Allendale, MI 49401-9403
(616) 895-3101
Contact: Deanna Morse

Harper College
Algonquin & Roselle Roads, Palatine, IL 60067
(312) 397-3000
Contact: Ken Dahlberg

Harvard University
VES Dept., 24 Quincy Street, Cambridge, MA 02138
(617) 495-3254
Contact: Derrick Lamb, Susan Pitt

Henderson State University
HSU Box 7521, Arkadelphia, AR 71923
(501) 246-5511
Contact: Edwin Martin

Hollywood Hands On
4729 Lankershim Blvd, 2nd Floor, North Hollywood, CA 91602
(818) 762-0060
(818) 762-2341 FAX

Films by Huey
103 Montrose Ave., Portland, ME 04103
(207) 773-1130
Contact: Huey

Kansas City Art Institute
4415 Warwick Boulevard, Kansas City, MO 64111
Main #: (816) 561-4852

Joe Kubert School of Cartoon & Graphic Art
37 Myrtle Ave., Dover, NJ 07801
(201) 361-1327
(201) 361-1844 FAX
Contact: Mike Chen

Kutztown University
Art Education & Crafts
Kutztown, PA 19530
(215) 683-4000
Contact: Dr. Thomas Schantz

L.A. City College
Radio -Film -TV Dept.
855 N. Vermont Avenue, Los Angeles, CA 90029
(213) 669-4267
Contact: John Acken

Universite Laval
Ecole des Arts Visuels
Pavillion Casault, Ste-Foy, Quebec, Canada
(418) 656-3412
(418) 656-7807 FAX
Contact: Gerard Desbiens

Lycoming College
Box 14, Dept. of Art, Williamsport, PA 17701
(717) 321-4000
Contact: Jon Bogle

MacCurdy Animation Workshop
Metro School for the Arts
320 Montgomery Street, Syracuse, NY 13202
(315) 475-5414
Contact: Johnny Robinson

Memphis College of Art
Overton Park, Memphis, TN 38112
(901) 726-4085
(901) 726-9371 FAX
Contact: Gordon Dover

Mercer County Community College
1200 Old Trenton Road, Trenton, NJ 08690
(609) 586-4800
Contact: Frank Rivera

Mission College
Great America Parkway, Santa Clara, CA 95054
(408) 988-2200
Contact: Hal Rucher

MIT Media Laboratory
20 Ames Street, Cambridge, MA 02139
(617) 253-5114
Contact: Linda Peterson

Universite de Montreal
Etudes Cinematographiques
3150 Jean Brillant, Montreal, Quebec H3C 3J7 Canada
(514) 343-6182
Contact: Daniel Thaimann

New York University
Institute of Film & TV
721 Broadway, 8th Floor, New York City, NY 10003
(212) 998-1778
Contact: John Canemaker, Greg Pair

New York Workshops
1501 Broadway, Suite 2907, New York City, NY 10036
(212) 840-1234
Contact: Judi Fogleman

Northwestern University
1905 N. Sheridan Road, Evanston, IL 60208
(312) 489-4191
Contact: Annette Barbier

Nova Scotia College of Art & Design
Microcomputer Center
5163 Duke Street, Halifax, Nova Scotia B3J 3J6 Canada
(902) 422-7381
(902) 425-2420 FAX
Contact: Daniel Potvin

New York Institute of Technology Computer Graphics Lab
Box 170, Old Westbury, NY 11568
(516) 686-7644
(516) 626-0716 FAX
Contact: Susan L. Van Baerie

Ohio State University / ACCAD
1224 Kinnear Road, Columbus, OH 43212
(614) 292-3416
Contact: Susan Amkraut

Orange Coast College
Computer Graphics & Fine Arts
2701 Fairview Road, Costa Mesa, CA 92628-5005
(714) 432-5629
(714) 432-0202 FAX

Oregon Art Institute
Northwest Film & Video Center
1219 SW Park Avenue, Portland, OR 97205
(503) 221-1156
(503) 226-4842 FAX
Contact: Ellen Thomas

Pratt Institute
200 Willoughby Ave.
Brooklyn, NY 11205
Main #: (800) 331-0834
Undergrad. Admissions: (718) 636-3600
Computer Graphics & Interactive Media: (718) 636-3411
Career Services: (718) 636-3506

Purdue University
2101 Coliseum Boulevard E., Fort Wayne, IN 46805
(219) 481 6100
Contact: S.P. Phipps

Griffith University: Queensland College of Art
PO Box 84, Morningside Q 4170 Australia
61-07-3875-3174
61-07-3875-3199
Contact: John Eyley

Regent University
Virginia Beach, VA 23464
(804) 424-7000 Ext. 4202
(804) 523-7205 FAX
Contact: John Lawing

Rhode Island School of Design
Two College St., Providence, RI 02903-2791
Main #: (401) 454-6100
Film/Video/Computer Animation: (401) 454-6233
Career Services: (401) 454-662

Ringling School of Art and Design
2700 N. Tamiami Trail, Sarasota, FL 34234
Main #: (941) 351-5100
Undergrad. Admissions: (941) 359-7523
Center for Career Services: (941) 359-7501
Film/Video: (941) 359-7574

Rochester Institute of Technology
One Lomb Memorial Drive, Rochester, NY 14623-0887
(716) 475-2754
(716) 475-5804 FAX
Contact: Erik Timmerman or Prof. Marla Schweppe-MFA Coordinator for Film/Video/Animation at marlak@cs.rit.edu; http://www.cs.rit.edu/~mks/CompAnim/index.html

Rocky Mountain College of Art & Design
6875 E. Evans Avenue, Denver, CO 80224-2359
(303) 753-6046
Contact: John Hein

Rowland Heights High School
Animation/L.P.V.-R.O.P.
2000 S. Otterbein Avenue, Rowland Heights, CA 91709
(818) 965-3448 Ext. 294
(818) 810-4859 FAX
Contact: Dave Master

Rutgers University
Art Dept.
Third & Linden, Camden, NJ 08102
(609) 757-6176
Contact: Maria Palazzi

San Fransisco Art Institute
800 Chestnut St., San Fransisco, CA 94133
(415) 771-7020
Contact: Larry Jordan

San Francisco State University
1600 Holloway Ave., San Francisco, CA 94132
3D Animation and Multimedia: (415) 338-1629
Multimedia/Film: (415) 338-1629
Career Services: (415) 338-1761
Multimedia Certificate Program: (415) 904-7700
Inter Arts: (415) 338-1478

Savannah College of Art and Design
548 E. Brounghton St., Savannah, GA 31401
Main #: (912) 238-2400
Computer Animation: (912) 238-2425
Director of Career Services: (912) 238-2401

School of Communication Arts
2526 27th Ave. South, Minneapolis, MN 55406
Main #: (612) 721-5357
Director of Placement: (612) 721-5357

School of the Art Institute of Chicago
Film-Making Dept.
Columbus Drive & Jackson Blvd., Chicago, IL 60603
(312) 443-7309
(312) 332-5859 FAX
Contact: Sharon Couzin

School of the Museum of Fine Arts
230 The Fenway, Boston, MA 02115
(617) 267-1218
(617) 424-6271 FAX
Contact: Alan H. Van Reed

School of Visual Arts
209 East. 23rd St., New York, NY 10010
Undergrad. Admissions: (212) 592-2000
Film/Video/Animation: (212) 592-2180
Career Planning & Placement Ctr.: (212) 592-2373

Senior College
Ballyfermot Road, Dublin 10, Ireland
01-626-9421
01-626-6754 FAX
Contact: Jerome Morrissey

Sheridan College
Schools of Communication Design
1430 Trafalgar Rd., Oakville, Ontario CANADA L6H 2L1
Undergrad. Admissions: (905) 845-9430
Career Services: (905) 815-4046
Animation: (905) 845-9430 ext. 2579

Southern Illinois University
Dept. of Cinema & Photography
Carbondale, IL 62901
(618) 453-2365

St. Olaf College
Art Dept.
Northfield, MN 55057
(507) 663-2222

Syracuse University
College of Visual & Performing Arts
Room 222, Smith Hall, Syracuse, NY 13210
(315) 443-1033
Contact: David Hickock

Texas State Technical College
PGCC 24-14 CAA, Waco, TX 76705
(817) 799-3611 Ext. 3314
Contact: Anthony Taylor

The Troll Animation Workshop
713 Ashman, P.O. Box 2031, Midland, MI 48640
(517) 839-0810
Contact: Bonnie Larson

University of the Arts
333 S. Broad St., Philadelphia, PA 19102
(215) 875-1022
Contact: Sky David

Kuskokwim Campus-UAF
P.O. Box 368, Bethel, AK 99559
(907) 543-4500
Contact: Barry Sponder

UCLA Film and Television Dept.
405 Hilgard Ave., Los Angeles, CA 90095
Main #: (310) 825-4321
Animation Workshop: (310) 825-5829

University of Central Florida
4000 Central Florida Blvd., Orlando, FL 32816
(407) 823-3456
(407) 823-5156 FAX
Contact: James Welke

University of Illinois at Chicago
Dept. of Art & Design
Box 4348, Chicago, IL 60680
(312) 996-3337
Contact: Martin Hurtig

University of Illinois
NCSA CSO/DCL
1304 W. Springfield, Urbana, IL 61801
(217) 333-8931
Contact: Brian Evans

University of Louisville
Dept. of Electrical Engineering
Louisville, KY 40292
(502) 588-5555
Contact: Dr. Thomas Cleaver

University of North Carolina at Greensboro
Broadcasting Cinema
Dept. of Communications & Theater
Taylor Bldg., Greensboro, NC 27412-5001
Contact: Emily Edwards

University of Oregon
Fine Arts Dept.
Eugene, OR 97403
(503) 686-3610
Contact: Ken O'Connel

University of South Carolina
Dept. of Media Arts
Columbia, SC 29208
Contact: Reg Brasington

University of Southern California
School of CNTV
University Park, Los Angeles, CA 90089-2211
Main #: (213) 740-2311
Computer Animation: (213) 740-3985
Film: (213) 740-7679
Career Services: (213) 740-5627

School of Computing and Math
University of Teesside
Middlesbrough, TS1 3BA UK
44-1642-342639
44-1642-342067 FAX

University of Utah
3190 MEB
Salt Lake City, UT 84112
(801) 581-5642
Contact: Rod G. Bogart

Vancouver Film School
1168 Hamilton St. #400, Vancouver, BC CANADA V6B 2S2
Main #: (604) 685-6331

University of Wisconsin
SSEC Rm. 631, 1225 W. Dayton Street, Madison, WI 53706
(608) 263-4427
Contact: William L. Hibbard

Wesleyan College
Communication & Dramatic Arts
Buckhannon, WV 26201
(304) 473-8000

Yale University
316 WLH, New Haven, CT 06520
(203) 432-2600
Contact: Faith Hubley

Index

discover the award-winning online magazine for Netscape users!

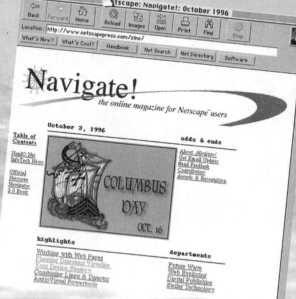

stellar technology (digital publishing future wave web exploring

Navigate!™

for Netscape Navigator users at all levels:

- interviews with industry experts
- easy tutorials for the latest Netscape software
- in-depth articles on timely topics
- exciting site reviews
- software treasures

Navigate!
the online magazine for Netscape™ users

http://www.netscapepress.com/zine

Follow the leader!

Hot on the heels of the runaway

international ***bestseller*** comes the

complete Netscape Press line:

easy-to-follow tutorials;

savvy, results-oriented ***guidelines***;

and **targeted** titles that zero in on

your ***special interests***.

All with the **official**

Netscape seal of approval!

http://www.netscapepress.com

Netscape Press is an imprint of **VENTANA**.

$39.99
1-56604-468-5

$34.99
1-56604-453-7

$39.95
Win 1-56604-420-0
Mac 1-56604-421-9

International Bestseller **250,000+** in its first edition!

NETSCAPE PRESS

OFFICIAL

"Destined to become the bible to the world's most popular browser."
—*PC Magazine*

$39.99
Windows 1-56604-500-2
Macintosh 1-56604-512-6

Netscape Navigator 3.0
BOOK

NETSCAPE

The definitive guide to the world's most popular Internet navigator

By Phil James
Foreword by Marc Andreessen

International Bestseller!
More than 250,000 in print!

OFFICIAL
Multimedia Publishing
FOR Netscape

Make your Web pages come alive!

$49.95
1-56604-381-6

OFFICIAL
Netscape Guide to Online Investments

The Complete Reference for Online Banking and Financial Management

$24.99
1-56604-452-9

OFFICIAL
Netscape
Beginner's Guide
TO THE Internet

Your First Book on the Net & Navigator

$24.99
1-56604-522-3

OFFICIAL
Netscape Guide
TO Internet Research

$29.99
1-56604-604-1

OFFICIAL
HTML Publishing
FOR Netscape

Your complete guide to Web design and production

$39.95
Win 1-56604-288-7
Mac 1-56604-417-0

Design Online!

Interactive Web Publishing With Microsoft Tools

$49.99, 818 pages, illustrated, part #: 462-6

Take advantage of Microsoft's broad range of development tools to produce powerful web pages; program with VBScript; create virtual 3D worlds; and incorporate the functionality of Office applications with OLE. The CD-ROM features demos/lite versions of third party software, sample code.

Looking Good Online

$39.99, 450 pages, illustrated, part #: 469-3

Create well-designed, organized web sites—incorporating text, graphics, digital photos, backgrounds and forms. Features studies of successful sites and design tips from pros. The companion CD-ROM includes samples from online professionals; buttons, backgrounds, templates and graphics.

Internet Business 500

$39.95, 450 pages, illustrated, part #: 287-9

This authoritative list of the most useful, most valuable online resources for business is also the most current list, linked to a regularly updated *Online Companion* on the Internet. The companion CD-ROM features a hyperlinked version of the entire text of the book.

The Comprehensive Guide to VBScript

$39.99, 864 pages, illustrated, part #: 470-7

The only encyclopedic reference to VBScript and HTML commands and features. Complete with practical examples for plugging directly into programs. The companion CD-ROM features a hypertext version of the book, along with shareware, templates, utilities and more.

 Books marked with this logo include *Online Udates*™, which include free additional online resources, chapter updates and regularly updated links to related resources from Ventana.

Web Publishing With Adobe PageMill 2
$34.99, 450 pages, illustrated, part #: 458-2

Here's the ultimate guide to designing professional web pages. Now, creating and designing pages on the Web is a simple, drag-and-drop function. Learn to pump up PageMill with tips, tricks and troubleshooting strategies in this step-by-step tutorial for designing professional pages. The CD-ROM features Netscape plug-ins, original textures, graphical and text-editing tools, sample backgrounds, icons, buttons, bars, GIF and JPEG images, Shockwave animations.

Web Publishing With Macromedia Backstage 2
$49.99, 500 pages, illustrated, part #: 598-3

Farewell to HTML! This overview of all four tiers of Backstage lets users jump in at their own level. With the focus on processes as well as techniques, readers learn everything they need to create center-stage pages. The CD-ROM includes plug-ins, applets, animations, audio files, Director xTras and demos.

Web Publishing With QuarkImmedia
$39.99, 450 pages, illustrated, part #: 525-8

Use multimedia to learn multimedia, building on the power of QuarkXPress. Step-by-step instructions introduce basic features and techniques, moving quickly to delivering dynamic documents for the Web and other electronic media. The CD-ROM features an interactive manual and sample movie gallery with displays showing settings and steps. Both are written in QuarkImmedia.

Web Publishing With Microsoft FrontPage 97
$34.99, 500 pages, illustrated, part #: 478-2

Web page publishing for everyone! Streamline web-site creation and automate maintenance, all without programming! Covers introductory-to-advanced techniques, with hands-on examples. For Internet and intranet developers. The CD-ROM includes all web-site examples from the book, FrontPage add-ons, shareware, clip art and more.

Make it Multimedia

Microsoft SoftImage|3D Professional Techniques 🌐

$69.99, 524 pages, illustrated, part #: 499-5

Here's your comprehensive guide to modeling, animation & rendering. Create intuitive, visually rich 3D images with this award-winning technology. Follow the structured tutorial to master modeling, animation and rendering, and to increase your 3D productivity. The CD-ROM features tutorials, sample scenes, textures, scripts, shaders, images and animations.

LightWave 3D 5 Character Animation f/x 🌐

$69.99, 700 pages, illustrated, part #: 532-0

Master the fine—and lucrative—art of 3D character animation. Traditional animators and computer graphic artists alike will discover everything they need to know: lighting, motion, caricature, composition, rendering ... right down to work-flow strategies. The CD-ROM features a collection of the most popular LightWave plug-ins, scripts, storyboards, finished animations, models and much more.

3D Studio MAX f/x 🌐

$49.99, 552 pages, illustrated, part #: 427-8

Create Hollywood-style special effects! Plunge into 3D animation with step-by-step instructions for lighting, camera movements, optical effects, texture maps, storyboarding, cinematography, editing and much more. The companion CD-ROM features free plug-ins, all the tutorials from the book, 300+ original texture maps and animations.

Looking Good in 3D 🌐

$39.99, 400 pages, illustrated, part #: 434-4

A guide to thinking, planning and designing in 3D. Become the da Vinci of the 3D world! Learn the artistic elements involved in 3D design—light, motion, perspective, animation and more—to create effective interactive projects. The CD-ROM includes samples from the book, templates, fonts and graphics.

To order any Ventana title, complete this order form and mail or fax it to us, with payment, for quick shipment.

TITLE	PART #	QTY	PRICE	TOTAL

SHIPPING

For all standard orders, please ADD $4.50/first book, $1.35/each additional.
For "two-day air," ADD $8.25/first book, $2.25/each additional.
For orders to Canada, ADD $6.50/book.
For orders sent C.O.D., ADD $4.50 to your shipping rate.
North Carolina residents must ADD 6% sales tax.
International orders require additional shipping charges.

SUBTOTAL = $ _____

SHIPPING = $ _____

TAX   = $ _____

TOTAL   = $ _____

**Or, save 15%–order online.
http://www.vmedia.com**

Mail to: Ventana • PO Box 13964 • Research Triangle Park, NC 27709-3964 ☎ 800/743-5369 • Fax 919/544-9472

Name _____

E-mail_____ Daytime phone _____

Company _____

Address (No PO Box) _____

City_____ State_____ Zip_____

Payment enclosed ___VISA ___MC ___ Acc't # _____ Exp. date_____

Signature _____ Exact name on card _____

Check your local bookstore or software retailer for these and other bestselling titles, or call toll free:

800/743-5369